To Move a Mountain

To Move a Mountain

Fighting the Global Economy in Appalachia

EVE S. WEINBAUM

THE NEW PRESS

NEW YORK
LONDON

Published in the United States by The New Press, New York, 2004
Distributed by W. W. Norton & Company, Inc., New York

LIBRARY OF CONGRESS CATALOGING–IN–PUBLICATION DATA

Weinbaum, Eve S.
    To move a mountain : fighting the global economy in Appalachia / Eve S. Weinbaum.
        p.   cm.
    Includes bibliographical references and index.
    ISBN 1-56584-784-9 (hc.)
    1. Plant shutdowns—Appalachian Region—Case studies.   2. Globalization—
Social aspects—Appalachian Region—Case studies.   3. Appalachian Region—
Social conditions—Case studies.   4. Social movements—Appalachian Region—
Case studies.   I. Title.

HD5708.55.U62A558   2004
338.7'1'09768—dc21
                                                                                2003046399

The New Press was established in 1990 as a not-for-profit alternative to the large,
commercial publishing houses currently dominating the book publishing industry.
The New Press operates in the public interest rather than for private gain, and is committed
to publishing, in innovative ways, works of educational, cultural, and community value
that are often deemed insufficiently profitable.

The New Press, 38 Greene Street, 4th floor, New York, NY 10013
www.thenewpress.com

In the United Kingdom: 6 Salem Road, London W2 4BU

Composition by dix!

Printed in the United States of America

2   4   6   8   10   9   7   5   3   1

Contents

לא עלך המלאכה לגמור
ולא אתה בן חורין להבטל ממנה

"It is not up to you to finish the work, and yet you are
not free to abandon it."
—Pirke Avot 2:21

To Move a Mountain

1

The Organizing Moment

For a week in November 1999, the eyes of the world were focused on Seattle, Washington. As the World Trade Organization (WTO) began its "Millennium Round" negotiations, the streets erupted in protest. Steelworkers from Pennsylvania marched alongside human-rights activists from Indonesia, farmers from France, nuns in their habits, and college students in their sneakers. While the mainstream media highlighted the disruption, the militance, and the broken windows, other observers realized that a major social movement had been born: the movement against corporate globalization. But where had it come from? Who had started it? No one had predicted the explosion of this movement, and no one was sure who was leading it.

As the mass demonstrations continued and spread to Genoa, Washington, D.C., Quebec City, and beyond, journalists, scholars, and activists all struggled to understand the phenomenon. Large, traditional institutions including the national AFL-CIO and the Sierra Club marched beside anarchists and radical student groups, challenging the most basic elements of American foreign policy. Middle-class, middle-American men carried signs proclaiming "Teamsters Love Turtles"; children wore banners with "Kids Say NO to WTO." Only weeks before, most Americans had never heard of the WTO and thought of globalization as a vaguely menacing natural development they could neither predict nor control. Suddenly people were in the streets behaving as if their actions could change the course of world capitalism.

Even more remarkable was how rapidly change began to come. The WTO, its proceedings in Seattle temporarily disrupted by 100,000 people in the streets, postponed its next meetings and promised greater "transparency." Some of the most notorious corporate violators of human rights standards, including Nike and the Gap, scrambled to strengthen their codes of conduct and improve factory monitoring in order to demonstrate their commitment to global justice. The World Bank defined poverty reduction as a central focus. The IMF began to reevaluate its priorities. Debt relief emerged at the top of the G-8 agenda for international development. The World Economic Forum made public statements on debt slavery and the AIDS pandemic. The United Nations invited transnational companies to join a Global Compact to raise standards, and urged nations to enforce labor standards and human rights. The AFL-CIO, which had equivocated on the WTO before Seattle, launched a Campaign for Global Fairness, reaching out to workers across the globe and joining with almost one hundred trade union federations to demand equitable and progressive growth as well as workers' rights standards. Nobel Prize–winning economists Joseph Stiglitz and Amartya Sen broke with the mainstream economic establishment, using decades of research to support the protesters' claim that corporate globalization was undermining equality, democracy, progress, poverty relief, world health, and sustainability. As John Sweeney, president of the AFL-CIO, pointed out, "The 'Washington Consensus' isn't even consensus in Washington anymore."[1]

Within months the national and international debate had changed dramatically. Most observers said that it happened "overnight."[2] The movement seemed spontaneous, unorganized, springing fully formed from the heads of a few impassioned individuals.[3] But these journalists missed what is arguably most important about social movements like this one: the years of painstaking education, networking, activism, and mobilization—often in secret, or without media attention, or in remote areas—that took place before protest could emerge on a larger stage.

Some economists and intellectuals argued that Seattle was a direct result of economic changes, especially the severe decades-long downturn in core manufacturing industries, which cost hundreds of thousands of jobs, mainly to foreign competitors. According to this analysis, the protests were no different from trade union protests or Luddite actions of earlier generations. American workers, fearing dislocation because of increasing international trade, immigration, or technology, were marching out of pure self-interest, to protect their jobs and incomes. But this simple economistic argument was directly contradicted by the events. The labor movement strongly supported the protests, and continued to organize demonstrations against capital mobility—but its members were a small minority of the activists in Seattle, Genoa, or Quebec. Environmentalists, students, religious communities, and working people from nations in the global South as well as the North filled the streets. Most marchers were not demanding improvements in their own wages or working conditions, but a global system based on justice and equity rather than profits and greed.

Moreover, the American economy had been "global" for many years, if not centuries. While the pace of transnational capital mobility had intensified during the 1980s and 1990s, no major depression or sudden economic shift catapulted workers into action in November 1999. This movement was political rather than economic in nature, and it had a political history. As one leader said, "What we witness is not a backlash, but birth pangs. And it is not *against* globalization, but *for* a new internationalism. This movement is building from the bottom up, not the top down."[4] The global justice movement had deep roots long before the Seattle protests surprised the international community.

This book investigates what would seem an unlikely setting for the international social movement that exploded onto the world scene in Seattle: Appalachian Tennessee, during the 1980s and 1990s. For most of this period, we were told, American prosperity was on the rise and working people—on the surface—were quiescent. But in fact, all across the country, people were struggling with issues of economic justice in their own communities. In the three Appalachian communities I profile here, as in many other towns across the United States, the battles were often short-lived, and most were unsuccessful. Nobody outside their community paid any attention. The activists didn't start out knowing many details about international trade, economic development policy, or global capitalism. But they fought against plant closings, deindustrialization, and other injustices in their own backyards. In the process many of them learned about the global economy and its impact on their lives. And these small struggles, unbeknownst to the participants at the time, connected years later with a much larger movement that would take them to Seattle and beyond. In the hills of Tennessee, as in communities across the country, activists were fighting for their own survival and challenging the nature of the global economy.

Mobilization and Failure

In 1988 the General Electric electronics factory in Morristown, Tennessee, was "a wonderful place to work."[5] Wages were high for the area—up to $12 an hour—and workers considered their jobs with the huge international company stable and prestigious. Nonetheless, when management instituted unpopular new policies, employees decided they wanted a union to represent their collective interests. After a majority of workers had signed membership cards and a union election was scheduled, the company began an energetic anti-union campaign. GE supervisors and managers warned workers not to vote for the "outsider" union, and held meetings where captive audiences were forced to listen to horror stories about the union's Mafia connections, union leaders' million-dollar summer houses, strikes and plant closings at unionized factories. Finally, GE produced a video, with an original country-music song called "The GE Family" and footage of the Morristown workers and their families, promising that GE would take care of its "associates." GE's campaign was successful, and the union was defeated. One week later the workers were shocked to learn that the warehouse had closed. Their jobs at GE were gone. State agencies told them that only temporary jobs were now available in Morristown.

At first glance, this is a familiar story of deindustrialization in small-town America. A low-skill, labor-intensive factory closes its doors, to the dismay of its workers and others in the community. But this is not simply another account of a firm's ineluctable pursuit of efficient production in the global marketplace—and it is not simply another story of a depressed community in economic crisis. For the Morristown workers did not move on quietly. Instead, working together as they had during their union campaign, the workers created a new organization called Citizens Against Temporary Services (CATS). They learned that GE's decisions were not predestined, and the workers were not willing to accept the company's rationale. During several years of activity CATS fought GE, the town of Morristown, Hamblen County, the state of Tennessee, and the United States government. The group demonstrated, picketed, rallied, held public hearings, wrote legislation, held conferences, formed alliances, and confronted policymakers. They failed to win back their jobs. But the activists of CATS transformed local institutions and slowly became aware of the national and even global dimensions of their situation and their struggle for economic justice. They created the first statewide campaign in the country proposing to regulate contingent work, joined the national struggle against NAFTA and free-trade policies, talked about the global trend toward sweatshop labor, and traveled to Mexico in solidarity with low-wage workers across the border. Some members of their coalition made the trip to Seattle, and those who stayed home cheered on the activists and supported the campaigns that emerged.

Looking back on CATS and other community efforts a full decade after the plant closings that sparked their organizing campaigns allows us to examine in close detail the effects and outcomes of their activism. This perspective is rarely allowed to scholars of social movements, most of whom focus on the emergence and causes of social movements. Many writers have lamented the fact that so few researchers have studied the consequences of activism, whether large-scale or small-scale.[6] This book begins to remedy that shortcoming by studying in detail the process and impact of community-based activism. We see that given the appropriate leadership, resources, and support, the most unsuspecting women and men can become leaders in an evolving social movement. In this case, workers in Tennessee became part of not only the global economic justice movement but also the living-wage movement and the anti-sweatshop movement. To their surprise, they ultimately became involved in some of the most vibrant and promising progressive movements of the early twenty-first century.

The effects of the global economy can be observed in every corner of the United States, even in communities that think of themselves as insulated, marginal, or irrelevant. In most cities and towns across the country, working people feel powerless to change the trajectory of the economy or public policy. But sometimes people are not willing to watch passively the economic destruction of their hometowns, and they devise ways to struggle against the new regime's harshest effects.

This book examines the response of three Appalachian communities to recent plant closings. In each case the plant closing created a crisis in the community, inaugurating a period of hardship. All of the factories had provided stable work in small towns in poor rural areas, where most other manufacturing jobs had either moved abroad or become part-time or seasonal. The workers knew that, once laid off, they would not easily find work again, except at fast-food restaurants or malls, as domestic workers, or through temporary agencies. The crises accompanying these closings provoked political mobilization in each community, either before the closing (with the goal of preventing it), afterward, or both. Each group of workers, sometimes together with other organizations, mounted a community-wide campaign with various goals: to convince the company to stay, to induce local government action, to get their back pay and benefits due, and/or to influence state legislation and economic development policy.

Mobilization in the wake of a plant closing is extraordinary. Most American citizens believe that decisions about "downsizing," "restructuring," and "outsourcing" are private rather than public decisions, economic rather than political activities, appropriately left in the hands of the firms themselves. Workers, who may or may not accept this argument, usually believe themselves to be powerless in the face of such corporate strategies—and they are often correct. Accordingly, in most shutdowns workers do not actively resist.[7] In these three cases, however, they did. Understanding why and how they mobilized and sustained a campaign over time provides crucial insights into the nature of organizing, and its consequences for the participants and for the state.

The mobilizations took very different forms in each of the three communities. Most observers would consider each to be a story of failure, and therefore a story not worth much attention. After all, no employer was successfully pressured to provide more local opportunities for meaningful work. None of the groups was able to improve the economic circumstances of the community. Although they may have won minor victories along the way, every campaign failed to retain the plant and its jobs. Similarly, every effort to pass state legislation addressing issues of economic justice was defeated.

And yet some of these initiatives had a tremendous long-term impact. Organizing campaigns that scholars and journalists alike would have labeled as failures, in fact led to institution-building, activist networks, and long-term coalitions to protest economic injustice and develop alternative public policies. These failures were the early battlegrounds in which men and women developed the strategies, arguments, and methods for the larger struggles to come. Failures, in retrospect, were actually critical turning points that created the conditions for later success. By closely studying these nascent grassroots social movements, this research points toward new avenues for labor and community activism around the global economy.

The State of American Communities

Recent scholarship in American politics and democratic theory has focused on the contemporary American community. Robert Putnam has argued that there is a crisis of more "social capital"—Americans are no longer forming communities, joining organizations, and supporting their neighbors, but rather "bowling alone." Civic engagement, in his analysis, has declined precipitously since the 1960s.[8] Similarly, Theda Skocpol has lamented the decline of political participation and participatory organizations, from the Grange to the PTA. She argues that as a result, American social policy no longer addresses the needs and values of the great majority of citizens. What we urgently need, according to Skocpol, is a new movement "rooted in actual relationships among ordinary citizens."[9] And William Greider writes about the lack of "mediating institutions" in contemporary American politics—the essential organizations that interpret political issues and policies to a lay constituency, educating and mobilizing the public. Greider argues that the overwhelming influence of money in politics and policy making precludes involvement by average citizens, and makes collective action either impossible or largely ineffective. "Self-centered and cynical" behavior, he says, "demonstrates a practical response to the political reality of impotent citizens." [10] All of these authors argue that, for various reasons, Americans have become apathetic, individualistic, or at least completely apolitical.

Scholarship on social movements similarly depicts communities—especially in low-income areas—as apathetic and quiescent, that is, disengaged from social and political events and unlikely to protest their fate. John Gaventa, for example, argues that the past failures of marginalized groups—failures to achieve political victories, to mobilize for their rights, or simply to make economic gains—teach them powerlessness. Powerlessness, in turn, leads to inaction "through the shaping of beliefs about the order's legitimacy or immutability." [11] Similarly, Lawrence Goodwyn argues that agrarian rebellion in the late nineteenth century was a failure, and one that destroyed possibilities for progressive political movements in subsequent decades. He quotes a "prophetic" leader of the populist movement, who predicted, "If the Alliance is destroyed, it will be some time before the people have confidence in themselves, and one another, to revive it, or organize anything new." [12]

None of these writers would ever have predicted the stories in this book. Instead, according to their framework, they would expect plant closings in rural areas of Tennessee to be met with quiet resignation. And the groups' failures should have destroyed workers' confidence and activism. All three communities were marginalized by geography, opportunity, and socioeconomic status, and in each case the plant closing served to further disperse and depress local residents. The communities were not extraordinary by tradition or demographics; they were very similar to other factory towns across the southern and midwestern United States. And yet in some of these places extraordinary things happened. Organizations formed around economic justice at the community level, challenging the status quo, the corporate agenda, and local leaders—and these organizations persisted after failure. They went on to win victories large and small. The evidence refutes Putnam's and other scholars' conclusion that quiescence and apathy are determined by past failure, technology, values, the "awesome machine"[13] of the global market, or quantifiable factors in the external environment.

The efforts of community-based activists argue against three main premises of recent scholarship on civil society and social capital. First, contrary to the claims of pessimists, civil society not only exists, it is vital and flourishing. People in all sorts of communities are connecting with one another when the need arises, forming organizations and acting collectively. Second, it has potential to be not localist but internationalist in outlook. In order to preserve their communities and fight for better opportunities for themselves and their children, the citizens in the following chapters found that they would have to become involved in struggles and networks way beyond the tiny towns of Appalachian Tennessee. Far from absorbing themselves in bowling leagues, they became involved in anti-NAFTA coalitions and union organizing in other states. Third, civil society in these communities is not quiet, neighborly, and charity-minded. Instead it is organized, aggressive, confrontational, and visionary. Pursuing their own vision of civil society, people in communities from Seattle to the economically depressed areas of Appalachian Tennessee want to rewrite the rules of the global economy.

Local political mobilization around economic crises, therefore, has the potential to change the way we think about politics in the global economy. These three small communities challenge many of the assumptions and theoretical methods social scientists have held dear. Besides contributing to an alternative approach to the study of social movements, this research challenges mainstream evaluations of democracy and power in American politics.

This book is a local study of what has become a national social movement: the movement for economic justice in the global economy. Economic justice is not an easy concept to define, and the events of

September 11 dealt a heavy blow to movements for global solidarity. And yet the activists in the chapters that follow present a clear vision. They conceive of democratic participation in determining which economic decisions and policies best promote the community's interests, and they advocate an active role for the government in securing this framework. Insofar as political decisions and public policies influence the economy, they argue, the goal of economic policy should be to promote the welfare of the community. Although the labor movement has been one voice for economic justice, the protomovement discussed here is quite different from traditional forms of organized labor, as it is based in local communities and driven by community and class interests. New local groups are increasingly forming alliances with existing organizations and coalitions, and in the process growing steadily in numbers and importance. The process that started in remote corners of Tennessee, and gained momentum and influence in events from Seattle to Genoa to Porto Alegre, has only begun.

The Power and Potential of Grassroots Organizing

Chapter 2 examines arguably the most important public policies in determining the welfare of a region: policies of economic development. In particular I analyze the formulation and implementation of economic development policy in Appalachian Tennessee. Interviews with political officials in Tennessee suggest the profound barriers to mobilization around issues of economic justice. In the very same towns where poverty seems entrenched and plant closings have wreaked havoc on entire communities, elected and appointed officials freely declare their determination to continue the policies that have led to these circumstances. They actively recruit businesses from more prosperous areas by advertising Tennessee's low wages, low union membership, racial homogeneity, and high rates of unemployment. States and localities compete against one another for business investment on the basis of depressed economies, government incentives, ethnic background, and whiteness of the workforce—not on the basis of the "human capital," advanced technology, and "symbolic analyst" skills that economists have predicted—thereby encouraging capital flight and an endless race to the bottom.

Chapter 3 presents a community that organized to protest one instance of capital flight, the closing of Greenbrier Industries. An apparel factory where 700 workers produced body bags, parkas, and tents for the United States military, Greenbrier had been one of the largest employers in Clinton, Tennessee, for decades. One day in the middle of July 1993, without any warning, the company suddenly locked its gates. Not only were workers out of a job, they soon learned that their last paychecks had bounced, their health insurance had not been paid for at least six months, and the money they had been saving in company 401(k) accounts had disappeared. The parent company had shifted production to a number of subsidiaries, from Tennessee to Israel, and then declared bankruptcy. The workers were out of luck. After months of meetings, protests, picket lines, press conferences, and lobbying, workers knew that the plant had closed for good and that their health insurance and retirement money was gone. Angry and depressed, the workers eventually determined that further activity was futile, and the group disbanded.

The second case study, in chapter 4, shows that this ending to the Greenbrier story was not inevitable. This chapter analyzes the struggle around a plant closing at Acme Boot Company. Once the largest Western boot producer in the world, Acme had been an important employer in many Tennessee towns for generations. In 1992 the company moved its production to Puerto Rico and closed its last manufacturing operation in Tennessee. Acme workers had been represented by the United Rubber Workers Union for decades, and the union mounted an impressive campaign to stop the plant from closing, rally public support for the workers' cause, and challenge the public policies that made the move possible and profitable. The story of the workers who mobilized against a seemingly inevitable sequence of events exposes the barriers to—but also the possibilities for—democracy and collective action in the context of this political economy. Their story exposes both the strengths and the political limitations of an organized union and community collaboration, and in many ways it should be considered a "successful failure"—an effort that led to both individual transformations and the potential for future victories in Tennessee and beyond.

Chapter 5 tells the story of workers at General Electric in Morristown, Tennessee, described above. The group that formed after that plant closed is perhaps the best example of a "successful failure." Although CATS did not win back workers' jobs, or prevent GE from moving, it took on issues of contingent work, job-training policy, economic development policy in the county and state, free-trade policies, and economic justice in the global economy. The failure to prevent a plant closing in Tennessee was only the beginning of a political effort that continues to challenge the course of the "awesome machine" of transnational capitalist growth. CATS is a story of a grassroots organization developing the ability to address a range of issues and take its struggle from local to global.

Many differences distinguish the three case studies. In some instances workers interpreted the plant closing narrowly, as a personal betrayal or as a single plant's failure to compete; in other situations, they saw it in broader terms, as part of the changing structure of the American economy. Some groups were more interested in punishing the corporate criminals, and some were more concerned with broader social change. Collective action also focused on a variety of targets: the supervisors, the plant manager, the corporation, or the local, state, or federal government. As this analysis shows, the way the plant closing was framed and the corresponding campaign were never determined by the material circumstances themselves, but represented choices made by participants and leaders in the early stages of a campaign. In each case, organizers formed a coalition, and drew in others who provided resources, models, and support. Their ability to do so depended on many factors, including the degree of previous organization in the workplace and the community, their history and traditions, and the leadership and organizing skills of those involved in the drive.

These cases show that organized and sustained struggle requires enormous resources and support. Groups mobilizing must rely on pre-existing institutions that help to provide education and organizing skills, sources of publicity and information, support networks, and formal and informal local leadership. The differences in the way groups defined issues, waged campaigns, and formed coalitions, as well as the changes in participants' understandings and their material conditions are directly related to the type of leadership and organizing that characterized each effort.

Sustained political struggle also requires a willingness to fail along the way. In each of the three communities, concerted action failed to recover a single job. This is not surprising, for when small, rural, economically and politically marginalized groups confront national and international institutions over the direction of the global economy, they will seldom get their way. But the success or failure of any mobilizing effort by a marginalized group must not be judged by immediate outcomes alone. The experience of political mobilization itself effected changes in individual participants and in their communities. Through this process a new collective consciousness was shaped, which in turn influenced political behavior and the development of local and regional institutions. Individuals came to understand many things in an entirely different way: their own power and potential for collective action; power relations in their communities; their individual relationships to various types of authority; the "economy" and public policy issues debated nationally; politics and the role of elected officials; and their commonality with working people across the country and the world. Their stories illustrate how these understandings were translated into actions and activities that formed the basis of a potential social movement around economic justice.

My ethnographic research and in-depth interviews with participants from all three communities demonstrate striking differences among their understandings of their experiences and of politics. Where people sustained grassroots mobilization—in two of the three case studies—they developed a much stronger comprehension of fundamental political issues and, as important, a revised understanding of themselves in relation to those issues. Organizing was likely to increase conventional forms of political participation and thus strengthen local democracy, educate citizens on local and national issues, nourish leadership, and foster solidarity and collective responsibility, demonstrating the power and potential of grassroots organizing. In a region usually known for its poverty, anti-unionism, and insularity, workers took on entrenched business interests and governments and became part of a growing national movement for economic justice. Participants and leaders from local community and union efforts went on to work with national and international alliances and campaigns, building a movement whose potential we have only begun to observe. Given the appropriate political opportunities, community-based organizations resisting plant closings and other local crises have the potential to influence American politics in the twenty-first century. Indeed, they already have.

2

Selling Poverty: The Politics of Economic Development in the South

Practical men, who believe themselves to be quite exempt from any intellectual influences, are usually the slaves of some defunct economist.

—John Maynard Keynes
The General Theory of Employment, Interest, and Money

Introduction

In 1990, two weeks after a unionization vote among its employees, with no warning to anyone, General Electric closed its distribution center in Morristown, Tennessee. GE moved thirty miles down Highway 11E, to the next county, where an independent contracting company took over hiring. The new jobs, which were exactly the same as the old jobs, paid $6 an hour—as opposed to previous wages of $10 to $12—and provided almost no benefits. GE was generously rewarded with economic incentives from Knox County, warehouse space in an industrial park, and state job-training money to train new employees. The company refused to hire back any Morristown workers. The county's economic development package was based on the assumption that new jobs were being created, and hiring back old employees would have meant relinquishing the job-training funds.[1]

The story of GE, typical in many ways, challenges our assumptions about deindustrialization in America. Daily media reports of plant closings presume the process to be the inevitable result of autonomous market forces, chiefly globalization, which causes fierce competition for jobs. But while the global economy is purportedly a recent phenomenon, plant closings have been around for over a century. Capital mobility is not just a function of international trade agreements—firms are much more likely to relocate within national borders than to move overseas.[2] In most cases, as with GE, plant closings and relocations are driven primarily by decisions by corporations in conjunction with local political elites, who broker the deals and determine their outcomes. Corporate leaders are not making efficient calculations of profit and loss. Public officials instead decide what kinds of firms are established, how they are regulated, what the taxpayers provide, and whether they hold companies accountable. In the process, whether a plant moves down the road or to a new continent, the workers at the original site lose their relatively well-paying jobs, and the "lucky" workers at the new site receive jobs that are inevitably substandard, largely because of the state's role in marketing a region's poverty and desperation. Both locations lose out. And yet the competition continues.

Like most states, Tennessee has a record of bending over backward to persuade companies to locate within its borders. As Dennis R. Judd and Todd Swanstrom argue, an enduring tension counterposes business recruitment against political legitimacy.[3] Local governments' overriding emphasis on attracting new private investment is frequently and dramatically at odds with the exigencies of a democratic polity and community. In this light, our economic crisis is not global at all, but rooted firmly in American political structure and ideology.

The Idea of Economic Development

"Economic development" has always been a problematic concept. While nearly everybody agrees that some version of it is desirable and we need more of it, no one seems to know what exactly it is or how to do it. In the academic literature the term refers to a wide variety of policies and phenomena, from corporate tax incentives to public-works programs to sustainable cooperatives and self-help housing. But practice seems to lag far behind scholarship. Although political scientists, urban planners, and public policy experts have documented the serious difficulties and drawbacks inherent in traditional approaches to economic development, very few localities have dared to reject the traditional methods. Despite the availability of a plethora of innovative "alternative" and "progressive" models, most state and local governments continue to practice economic development in ways that have not changed very much for a hundred years. While the economy has continued to metamorphose rapidly and in unforeseen directions, the policies designed to mediate its impact on citizens have not kept pace.[4]

This chapter examines the dominant "business incentive" approach, as it actually works in Appalachian Tennessee. In the communities examined in the following chapters' case studies, political leaders are involved, either directly or indirectly, in the effort to recruit and sustain private enterprise in a region—as one political scientist characterizes it, emphasizing "the public provision of financial incentives to attract investment."[5] This practice defines the most widespread approach to economic development in most of the southeastern United States: "The alternative (or progressive) approach remains conspicuously less developed."[6]

In the academic literature and in practice, the dominant model considers economic development to be a universal good. Expenditures of public resources on attracting private investment are considered efficient, because the benefits of economic development are in the interests of the community as a whole. As John F. Kennedy stated in 1961, "This country cannot prosper unless business prospers. The country cannot meet its obligations and tax obligations and all the rest unless business is doing well. Business will not do well . . . unless there is a chance to make a profit. So there is no long-run hostility between business and government. There cannot be. We cannot succeed unless they succeed."[7]

Economic development policy is assumed to be a purely technical problem, one that relies on expert predictions, efficient strategies, and economic modeling of costs and benefits—absolutely separate from political processes. In 1981, Paul Peterson revitalized the field of urban political science when he argued that the decentralized federalist political structure in the United States compelled cities to pursue economic development before all other goals. Because each city, county, and state is responsible for the creation of wealth within its own borders, it must constantly vie for new sources of investment and employment. According to Peterson, unlike the clearly controversial *redistributive* policies, which were designed to alleviate poverty and promote fair distribution of resources, economic development was universally desirable. "*Developmental* policies are those local programs which enhance the economic position of a community in its competition with others. They strengthen the local economy, enhance the local tax base, and generate additional resources that can be used for the community's welfare."[8] Although business elites and local officials crafted the economic development strategies, according to Peterson, city residents joined in a "unitary interest" in pro-development policies. Following economist Charles Tiebout, Peterson argued that there was an identifiable "city interest" that consisted of more than merely the summation of individual interests, but could be ascribed to the entity taken as a whole.[9] Economic development politics that benefited business were seen as noncontentious and universally beneficial. "Good government" was defined as "government that gave precedence that strengthened economic productivity," and the most qualified practitioners were "wealthy socialites; prominent professional people; politicians, especially those

with links to state and national governments." Democratic deliberation
is seen as inappropriate and even deleterious in this domain, because the
determination of optimal economic development initiatives is considered to be beyond the abilities of even the best intentioned citizens. Officials and business elites should be granted the leeway they require:
"Developmental policies . . . are often promulgated through highly
centralized decision-making processes involving prestigious business-
men and professionals. Conflict within the city tends to be minimal, decision-making processes tend to be closed until the project is about to
be consummated."[10] Since the city as a whole benefits from economic
development, a democratic process would be inappropriate. As Edward
Banfield and James Q. Wilson pointed out in their pivotal study of
urban politics, "city government is usually treated more as a matter of
'administration' than of 'politics.' "[11] While academic studies have
moved well beyond the narrow type of analysis Banfield and Wilson deplored, local elites remain convinced that "administration" is preferable
to "politics." Economic policy decisions are treated as technical matters
understood only by experts.

Behind this technocratic impulse is a faith that the free market is an
autonomous force, guided by natural laws of economics. The market is
seen as existing prior to politics, and is considered to be a separate realm
with its own internal dynamics. Within the market sphere, equilibrium
and efficiency are the goals. Government can hinder these purposes by
imposing regulations that impede firms' ability to maximize profits, or
local governments can accept the laws of competition, supply and demand, and work within them. Since politics cannot transform market
laws in any fundamental way, the optimal role of the state is therefore to
facilitate market goals by lowering barriers to enterprise, such as information costs and transaction costs. Competition, trade, efficiency, productivity, and profit are all seen as nonnegotiable imperatives for firms.
The best government is one that does not interfere with private profit
maximization.

But the community and labor coalitions discussed in the next few chapters were not willing to accept this understanding of economic development. Against the advice of economists and political scientists, they confronted and challenged the experts, demanding both a more democratic process and economic development outcomes more favorable to average citizens. They learned, through personal experience, that traditional approaches to economic development were not working; the community as a whole did not benefit when industries were recruited into a locality.[12] Rather than a happy consensus, economic development policy became a source of intense community-level conflict, and led activists to examine wider issues of economic justice—proof of the "enduring tension" between democratic legitimacy and accumulation of wealth.[13]

Despite a strong consensus for "self-help" and "participatory community development" in low-income communities, policymakers in fact exclude local residents thoroughly and intentionally from economic development decisions. As Banfield and Wilson showed, while participatory democracy was a central feature of American political culture, political structures in the postwar era had actually tended to limit popular involvement in the political process. "Citizen participation, which as we have shown has always been characteristic of the highly decentralized governmental institutions of American cities, has in recent years come to be regarded in many quarters as a normative principle inseparable from the idea of democracy itself. Indeed, the spread of the doctrine that there *ought* to be 'grass roots' participation in local affairs has largely coincided with a reduction in real opportunities for ordinary citizens to exercise influence in the matters of importance to them."[14]

In East Tennessee, the dominant model of economic development is not premised on creating new opportunities for the majority of citizens. Rather, public officials have come to understand business recruitment as a goal unto itself. An examination of recruitment materials reveals that officials believe business to be motivated primarily by two concerns, influenced by the market's competitive pressures: reducing labor costs, and keeping the workforce busy and docile. Guided by this knowledge, local governments see their main task as a marketing function. They offer their localities to any bidder that will take them. The system is not driven by the democratic goal of furthering the interests of local residents; instead it is premised on the idea that local residents must stay exactly where they are—poor and desperate—in order to make the system work. East Tennessee officials reveal that they are active participants in economic processes, creating market incentives where none existed and conspicuously shaping the choices available to firms. They are not mere technocrats. They have significant political power—concentrated in their hands because of the lack of democratic participation in the economic sphere—and their actions are guided by a set of political assumptions about the people they represent and about business itself. Guided by a different set of assumptions, these officials would shape a very different type of policy and create very different outcomes for their constituents. Interviews with government officials and authorities responsible for economic development show that some very old and deeply rooted assumptions—racism, sexism, and a disdain for poor and uneducated people—are very influential in the formation and implementation of policy. Far from a purely "rational," technical enterprise, the dominant model of economic development rests on highly ideological premises. Economic development policy provides a lens through which to better understand the crisis of democracy in the global economy of the 1990s.

The Disappointing History of Southern Strategies

Politicians and economic development officials in Appalachia, as in most of the South, have concentrated on one economic development strategy: recruiting industry from the North. Rather than becoming "laboratories of democracy,"[15] Southern states—and poorer regions generally—have relied solely on tax incentives, industrial development bonds, and other business recruitment programs. These strategies have assumed that any increase in economic activity is beneficial, and they have rarely differentiated between one industry and another, or one community and another. The programs have also reflected the theory that the benefits of economic development "trickle down" to the people who need them most. A century of history challenges these assumptions.

At least as early as the 1880s, a pattern of economic development was established in the South that would shape its industrial structure for the next century. A primarily agricultural economy, the South had much less indigenous manufacturing, commerce, and investment capital than the North. But the South was rich in both natural resources and an abundant supply of workers. So state officials, promoters of a "New South," set out to attract labor-intensive industries that would utilize the agricultural products and raw materials of the region. Advocates of the New South envisioned a region less dependent on Northern manufactured goods and truly part of the modern industrial age.[16] But from the beginning the manufacturing operations recruited by Southern states generally employed very few skilled workers. Rather, they located in towns in rural areas in order to draw on the surplus agricultural labor pool. Thus the New South did produce many new jobs, but without the predicted accumulation of capital, or industrial and commercial independence for the South. The new employers were most concerned with obtaining the maximum possible productivity for low wages. They hired former sharecroppers, women, children—the employees least likely to protest substandard wages or working conditions. Plants located in these areas attracted a virtually untapped labor pool from the surrounding hinterland. Small cities in the region grew rapidly around the turn of the century, as rural whites and blacks moved off the farms in search of employment.

Knoxville, the major city in East Tennessee, was a perfect example of the New South movement. Its ambitious civic and commercial elite seized growth opportunities after the Civil War, using excellent railroad connections, natural resources, and a large pool of available workers to attract industry. Knoxville attracted workers from rural areas of Tennessee, Virginia, and North Carolina, experiencing impressive growth for consecutive decades and becoming the region's major commercial and industrial center.[17] This economic growth brought tremendous social costs. Rural whites and blacks who moved to the city resented the demands of industrialization, which cut them off from their traditional institutions. Depressions of the 1890s and 1930s threatened progress, and political tensions arose between economic elites and those who spoke for the working class.[18]

Industries moved south in order to escape increasing taxation and restriction elsewhere. In the late nineteenth century, Southern officials and policymakers worked with business leaders to hold down taxes and regulation. In the name of a better "business climate"—necessary to attract industry—they shortchanged education and human services in order to allow more freedom for corporations. Tennessee recruited iron mills, coal companies, furniture factories, textile mills, and apparel factories. Skilled labor to run the plants was imported with the companies, while unskilled jobs went to local residents and migrants from rural areas. Although the newcomers found work, they mostly lived on the edge of starvation and homelessness. Knoxville could not afford paved roads, a sewer system, or clean water. As historians of the South have observed, the industrial recruitment strategy of New South boosters resulted in severely underdeveloped infrastructure, institutions, and human capital.[19]

Thus the wave of industrialization that swept the region around the turn of the century, intended to build a New South and wipe away the poverty and backward history of Appalachia and the Southern states, never fulfilled its promise. Then the Great Depression interfered, hindering state governments' efforts to recruit new industry. By the mid-1930s the dream of a revitalized region seemed a failure. President Franklin D. Roosevelt called the South "the nation's number one economic problem." [20] New Deal–era state and federal government officials, including Roosevelt, placed great faith in the ability of a modernized industrial economy to eliminate race discrimination, reactionary politics, and other undesirable aspects of the Southern heritage. [21] But in the states and counties of the South, the actual processes of economic development were carefully designed not to jeopardize the social and political hierarchies that had characterized the region for decades.

In 1936 Mississippi became the first state to legalize what had been going on for many years: government's active promotion of business expansion. Its legislature passed the Balance Agriculture With Industry (BAWI) Act, ushering in an era of industrial subsidization that would spread quickly throughout the South in the post–World War II era. [22] The first state-sanctioned and supervised use of tax dollars and government-backed guarantees, BAWI issued municipal bonds to finance plant construction. Other states followed Mississippi's lead, competing with one another to subsidize business development. In Tennessee, "smaller industry-hungry communities engaged in extreme forms of industrial subsidization . . . [with] a desperate hunger for new industry at practically any cost." Local leaders "decided that propaganda and hard sell were not enough. . . . [They] accelerated their efforts to buy and steal them as well." [23] An industrial-subsidy frenzy defied the state constitution's specific prohibition of such activity. A 1937 survey of forty-one towns showed that fifty-six plants built in the previous seven years had gotten some subsidy from the state. Many had been financed by bonds and authorized by the state legislature, although all were unconstitutional.[24]

As one of the poorer Appalachian states in the 1930s, Tennessee was notorious for its desperation and its susceptibility to "fly-by-night" entrepreneurs. Descriptions of its economic development strategies from that time sound remarkably similar to current practices. James Cobb provides examples from the 1930s. A necktie manufacturer occupied a city-funded building rent-free. Using the labor of city-paid "trainees" for thirty days, the company produced enough ties for the Christmas buying season, at no cost to the firm. When the busy period was over, it closed up the shop and moved on. The town of Dickson, Tennessee, lured a garment plant away from Pennsylvania by offering a free building, a tax exemption for five years, and free electric power and water. Dickson then financed the building with a 6 percent mandatory employee salary deduction, particularly painful to the 62 percent of the company's employees who earned less than $5.55 per week. Lewisburg, Tennessee, used a municipal bond issue to build a town hall, held one meeting in it (as required by law), and turned it over to the General Shoe Corporation, whose employees were then required to pay half the cost of the building out of their salaries. General Shoe received the town hall building for free.[25]

Local subsidies to industry were sold to taxpayers as an emergency plan, to end as soon as the South's recovery was well under way. BAWI was passed, overriding constitutional prohibitions, when the governor declared an acute economic emergency. This rhetoric was similar to that used to defend national New Deal programs: spending money to save in the long term, investing in jobs in an emergency to protect the "general welfare" and the "public interest." With federal programs, this language was used to justify aid to dispossessed people. In the South, it was used to justify aid to corporations.

In East Tennessee during and after World War II, federal government money created a new thriving manufacturing industry. Government contracts supported Rohm and Haas, which made Plexiglas for airplanes; the huge Aluminum Company of America (Alcoa); Oak Ridge labs, home of the Manhattan Project; and the Tennessee Valley Authority (TVA).[26] And yet there were huge problems. Growth in employment began to slow drastically throughout the region, never reaching its earlier highs. Cities were in debt, and residential areas and infrastructure were deteriorating. The only solution was to recruit new industries in the hope of revitalizing a stalling economy.[27] So a pattern was established that continues to this day.[28]

Factories moved south for several reasons. Union avoidance was primary. Plants fled Indiana, Illinois, and Pennsylvania after wage disputes and labor unrest. Towns in the South worked to avoid those undesirable situations, preserving the non-union climate that kept wages low and workers under control. Some incoming companies persuaded municipalities to sign agreements to this effect. When Real Silk Hosiery Company relocated to Grenada, Mississippi, the city signed a union-avoidance agreement: "The [company] pledges itself to be fair in all of their dealings with employees and to pay fair and reasonable wages, and the [city] agrees that it will so far as possible prevent any interference from outside sources which may cause or result in labor disputes or trouble, and the payroll guarantee hereunder by the [company] shall be canceled during the period of any labor disturbance caused by outside interference."[29]

Race was also an issue in industrial recruitment. Each area boasted, in more or less veiled terms, a white workforce. Mississippi governor Hugh White advertised not only the low production costs possible because of an abundance of labor but also the high percentage of "native Anglo Saxons" in his state's population. Mississippi, he said, could offer manufacturers a labor pool free from the "disturbing elements so common in larger industrial centers."[30]

Subsidy programs were always politically controversial. Initially, resistance came from farmers, who resented the state supporting industries that would lure low-income workers away from agriculture. But the programs increasingly came under attack from local businesses as well. Industrial commissions' caution and protectiveness led to favoring Northern companies with strong reputations and long histories in manufacturing. The commissions were charged repeatedly with discrimination against local projects. Local businesspeople demanded greater support for locally owned plants to process local mineral and agricultural resources. They argued that inviting "foreign" companies encouraged the flow of raw materials out of the region, for processing elsewhere. The profits from those resources were siphoned away from the South, to be invested in companies based elsewhere.

The critics of subsidy programs also argued, as they continue to argue today, that industrial recruitment policies facilitated the exploitation of Southern workers. The programs did absolutely nothing to increase local pay scales, or to improve labor standards—for the companies were attracted precisely by the lack of such standards. Precursors to the contemporary living-wage movement mobilized in the 1930s, calling for guarantees that subsidized plants pay wages commensurate with the national average. If the state was going to use public funds to support industries, they argued, it should demand accountability. The firms should be required to adhere to a set of standards—labor practices, wages, and good citizenship—otherwise there was no justification for government aid to corporations. But despite the public outcry, requirements were never attached to recruitment programs. Desperate communities competing for jobs were afraid to make demands of companies and lose the jobs altogether. The evidence shows the results. Local wages did not increase. States that embraced aggressive strategies did not show higher gains in employment or production. More than anything else, a poor, unorganized, and relatively desperate working class lured industries to the South. The companies that moved did not want these conditions to change. And the companies attracted by these qualities were not stable or lucrative enough to form the basis of a New South economy.

How the State Recruits Business

In the twenty-first century, as in the past, by far the most prominent strategy for "development" involves attracting industry from other areas. Policies convince corporations to move work from plants in other states to Tennessee, rather than stimulating internal economic development or regional creation of wealth and opportunity. The state attracts these companies with a message that focuses heavily on the poverty of the region—by advertising low wages, a lack of unionization, and a large rural unemployed population. This strategy may bring jobs to Tennessee, but it produces profits for nonindigenous corporations, to be invested outside the region. It creates jobs very similar to those that exist already—low-wage and unskilled—rather than moving toward a vision of a better economic future. It capitalizes on the poverty and disadvantage of the region, and in doing so, preserves it.

Images of the "Sun Belt Boom" evoke the glittering corporate towers of metropolitan Atlanta or Houston, full of well-educated white-collar employees skilled in high-technology and international enterprises. The Sun Belt—the region that has lured away corporate giants from the Rust Belt and the Snow Belt—is the new land of plenty. Old smokestack-chasing tactics would seem to be unnecessary and certainly undesirable in a region so full of potential and abundant job opportunities. But the reality in most of the South is very different. While great wealth exists in pockets of some cities, the vast areas of rural tracts and small towns that comprise most of the region remain dependent on archaic manufacturing plants and mired in severe poverty. Public policy has not changed much in the past hundred years; efforts to attract foreign investment have only intensified. Recruitment programs are built around low-wage, labor-intensive industries, just as in the New South at the turn of the century.

In the 1990s, when the plant closings in the following chapters took place, the regional competition for industry was especially fierce. A special advertising section created in 1994 for business magazines by a group of public and private economic development agencies in East Tennessee includes over twelve pages of glossy ads and text inviting companies to locate in the area. The section begins, "If you are seeking the best place to live and work; with the ultimate in high technology, . . . a strong work ethic and a business climate that favors free enterprise, then East Tennessee must be high on your list. . . . You've found your location to make a profit."[31] The advertisement, published in magazines such as *Financial World,* contains comments from many business executives extolling the virtues of East Tennessee as a place of business. Considering the region's history, the quotes sound surprisingly familiar. "Being located in the Northeast Tennessee area is advantageous for a manufacturing company because of the excellent work ethic and aptitude of the people," says the CEO of Exide Corporation. "This region has created one of North America's most fertile business climates," says the general manager of Holston Electric Company. "It's location and people. You put good people in a good environment and marvelous things can happen," says the founder of mobile-homes manufacturer Clayton Homes. "You always get full measure from East Tennesseans," says the CEO of petroleum retailer Pilot Corporation. "What we have to sell is a quality of life and a terrific work force with a great work ethic," says the chairman of the Greater Tri-Cities Business Alliance in Johnson City, Tennessee. Besides the quality of the "work ethic" and the availability of labor, the advertisements mention the region's transportation and easy access, quality of life, outdoor recreational opportunities, and natural beauty. More prominently they highlight tax advantages and incentives, government-subsidized training programs, inexpensive energy sources, and "pro-business government." [32]

At the state level, the Department of Economic and Community Development is responsible for industrial recruitment. The materials they produce sound the same themes as private advertisements, sometimes even more blatantly. The first theme—according to officials, by far the most important—is the availability of a cheap, docile, abundant labor force. In a one-page flier promoting Tennessee as a business location, the first four points are spelled out in bold type:

Tennessee's 1992 average hourly wage for production is **lower** than the national average.

      Tennessee......$10.12   United States......$11.45

Tennessee's 1992 union membership for all industries/*manufacturing* is **lower** than the national average.

      Tennessee......10.4%/*17.5% mfg.* United States......15.8%/*21.0% mfg.*

Tennessee is a right-to-work state.

Tennessee has strong management/labor relations in both union and nonunion endeavors.

After labor environment, the next most emphasized feature of the Tennessee business climate is the tax incentives. The flier mentions the fact that Tennessee has no personal income tax, wage tax, property tax, or sales tax on industrial machinery and equipment. [33] It lists the investment tax credit on machinery, the new jobs tax credit, the tax exemption for distributors' inventories, the availability of subsidized training assistance, and the availability of four Foreign Trade Zones within the state, where imports and exports are facilitated and deregulated. Finally, the ad lists the state's other attractions, including easy transportation access, mild climate, high grades for livability, and well-managed state budgets. [34]

The emphasis in advertising materials on "high technology," the "global marketplace," and other features of "the 21st Century" is particularly striking. Despite the futuristic rhetoric, the substantive policies—and all the selling points used to lure industry—are quite reminiscent of the past. The emphasis on moving into the future is ironic and often contradictory. Tennessee's Resource Valley, for instance, uses interactive CD-ROM devices to advertise a high-technology industrial revolution in the mountains of East Tennessee. Yet TRV waxes poetic about the traditional values of the region. In a brochure called "Mountains of Business Opportunity," it describes an area "where people greet each new dawn . . . with yesterday's values still intact—hard work, loyalty, and quality."[35] This is not mere rhetoric; the ad emphasizes the point that these "values" embrace hard work for low wages:

> People here in Tennessee's Resource Valley are as exceptional as the mountains around them. They take pride in a job well done. Pride that springs from a heritage of quality mountain craftsmanship and an honest day's work for an honest day's pay. Pride that transcends into one of the highest productivity rates in America . . . Over 400,000 highly intelligent, trainable men and women who still take the traditional approach to their work and lives.
>
> - One of the lowest worker turnover and absenteeism rates in the U.S.
> - One of the lowest unionized **urban** areas in America—only 13.7%
> - Proud of the **Right-to-Work**—and work hard—at wages 17% below U.S. average

A side panel notes that the unionization rate in East Tennessee, the "resource valley," is well below the statewide rate, and less than half of the national rate.[36]

Contradictions between progressive and regressive impulses are apparent in most of the materials. On one hand, polished brochures tout Tennessee's commitment to education, "state-of-the-art public school classrooms," the community colleges and large state university prepared for the new, high-tech workplace. On the other hand, the economic development agencies' advertisement campaigns focus on one theme: low wages and a large pool of unemployed, unskilled, rural laborers. Citing statistics touting the availability of inexpensive, unorganized labor, the state calls into question its commitment to promoting higher education—which would raise wage rates and eliminate the ready workforce so appealing to business.

In the areas with the most aggressive marketing campaigns, such as Hamblen County in East Tennessee, most new manufacturing jobs in the 1990s and 2000s hired all their employees through temporary agencies. They receive minimum wage and no benefits, a below-poverty living standard although most work full-time and year-round. The companies are not part of the high-technology revolution; on the contrary, many are the same industries historically found in the area: furniture, apparel, and distribution warehouses. The major new additions are in the service sector: maintenance, food service, security, clerical, and other categories also requiring few technical skills and often operating on a temporary or part-time basis. The state and county now provide these companies with tax-free financing, construction of infrastructure, "training" for workers, and low-cost or even free land in industrial parks. Hamblen County's chamber of commerce, for example, boasts that most of the hourly occupations surveyed have "a mean wage less than the statewide average for each particular job. Of the occupations paid weekly, eight out of ten reported a mean wage less than the statewide average for that job title."[37] And unionization is almost non-existent, below 5 percent.

Government Incentives

Besides the focus on an available, inexpensive, quiescent labor force, the other major attraction to Tennessee is the generous incentive packages the government provides to business. Again, Tennessee is not alone—cities and states are increasingly in the news for offering huge economic bonuses in order to attract stadium developers, baseball teams, or just to induce firms to remain within the city limits. These packages may contain many components, from actual gifts of land or buildings, to complicated financing schemes advantageous to employers. The incentives demonstrate the state's active role in facilitating capital mobility and growth. Despite a nationwide revolt against governmental involvement in local affairs—especially prominent in Southern states—incentive-based economic development policies are far from "free-market." The trend toward "corporate welfare" programs contradicts the conservative conviction that government should stay out of the private sector.

The most common program is probably tax incentives. States, localities, and even the federal government negotiate cut rates, give rebates, or simply waive corporate responsibility for taxes. The Tennessee Department of Economic and Community Development's promotional packet contains a document entitled "Tennessee Tax Incentives," listing ways businesses can avoid paying corporate excise taxes, franchise taxes, sales taxes, property taxes, and income taxes—as well as other tax credits and reimbursements available. Approximately twenty different ways to evade taxes are advertised.[38] The flier accompanies a longer, nine-page list of available reductions in fees and taxes. A chart including all the states in the Southeast region shows that Tennessee's overall tax burden is lowest. It ranks lowest in state taxes as a percentage of personal income and state taxes per capita. The governor refers to these as "our innovative tax policies."[39]

One of the glossiest brochures created by the state is called "Tennessee: The Ticket to Tomorrow." In the introduction, Democratic governor Ned McWherter welcomes businesses to the state, promising "we have created a pro-business environment unlike anywhere else in America." The brochure goes on to list even more tax incentives, and workers' compensation and unemployment insurance rates "among the sunbelt's lowest." [40] Other state publications contain detailed descriptions of federal and state programs. These include the Tennessee Industrial Infrastructure Program, which provides infrastructure needed by new businesses; private activity bonds; revolving loan funds available through local development corporations; the Tennessee Valley Authority's Special Opportunities Counties Program, designed to promote business development in the state's poorest rural areas; the rural economic development revolving loan program for rural electric and telephone cooperatives, providing zero-interest loans to companies; the U.S. Small Business Administration's 7A and 504 Direct Loan Programs, which can be utilized by a wide range of manufacturing and other industries.

These programs are now standard throughout the country. But many studies are suggesting that incentives do not make enough of an impact on industrial decisions to warrant the expenditures. A 1993 study by Deloitte & Touche consulting firm, for example, showed that corporate executives ranked incentives fourteenth out of seventeen criteria when they made relocation or expansion decisions. Much more important were "labor force issues," real estate costs, transportation, availability of facilities, and access to markets. Economic developers, however, had different views: 42 percent of them said incentives and subsidies were "very important." Whatever their relative importance in actually attracting business investment, incentives are on the rise. Despite executives' dismissal of their importance, most economic developers surveyed agreed that there had been a marked increase since 1990 in the level of incentives companies were seeking from them as a condition of locating in their communities. [41]

A few particularly egregious examples have received national attention, and although they have been widely criticized by economists and politicians alike, they indicate a national trend. When BMW was considering locating an assembly plant in the United States, for instance, South Carolina won the highly publicized location competition. The state offered aid worth more than $150 million for the Spartanburg facility. If the plant eventually employs its estimated 1,900 workers, the state will have spent at least $79,000 per job. The plant is BMW's first non-union plant in the world, and pays wages and benefits considerably lower than those of its German counterparts. Kentucky enticed a Canadian steel mill to move south, providing an incentive package worth $140 million for just 400 promised jobs—$350,000 per job. These "smokestack chasing" deals are not unique to Southern states. In 1992, Minnesota granted Northwest Airlines a package valued at $838 million for two repair facilities, or $558,000 for each of 1,500 jobs. Offering millions of dollars in incentives, Ohio won a Honda plant, Michigan a Mazda plant, Illinois a Nissan plant—all in competition with other states. And increasingly, companies need only threaten a move in order to win huge incentive packages. By threatening to leave New York City, Prudential Securities, CBS, Chemical Bank, and five commodity exchanges have received hundreds of millions of dollars in tax and regulatory concessions from the city. When Sears threatened to leave Chicago and its famous Tower, Illinois gave the company a huge suburban land package worth $240 million, no strings attached.[42] In 1994 Exxon won long-term tax abatements from Baton Rouge, Louisiana, totaling $14,372,600. Exxon had projected that it would create only one new job.[43]

Incentives may not be sufficient to induce a business to uproot itself and move to another area, all else being equal. But these examples demonstrate what both executives and economic development officials know: incentives and subsidies are most important in the role of "tie-breaker," when companies are considering a number of different locations.[44] When several sites provide essentially similar business opportunities, large firms can simply announce a number of "finalists" in the site competition and watch cities and states outbid each other.

One of the most publicized incentive packages was the $253 million Alabama provided for a Mercedes-Benz plant in 1993. When Mercedes announced its intention to build a manufacturing facility in the U.S., more than thirty states prepared and submitted site proposals to the company. Eventually Mercedes narrowed its choice to six states: North and South Carolina, Georgia, Tennessee, Mississippi, and Alabama. A fierce competition began. Officials from all the states visited Mercedes headquarters in Germany to lobby for themselves. Rumors spread in the media as each state's representatives claimed they were on the short list, until finally the Associated Press noted that "confirming details about meetings with Mercedes officials can be like trying to prove an Elvis siting [sic]."[45] The bidding war ensued; state legislatures and city councils passed voluminous bills authorizing innovative packages to entice Mercedes. The North Carolina legislature approved new construction of a $35 million Advanced Automotive Technology Center, dubbed "Mercedes University," just to train workers—at government expense—for jobs at the Mercedes plant. The state also offered $20 million in land, $8 million in training programs, and $15 million in infrastructure improvements around the site. Georgia then offered to provide free land, a low-interest loan, a brand-new training center that would train workers to Mercedes' specifications, improved highways adjacent to the industrial site, and a taxpayer-funded "Learning Center" inside the plant.[46]

Alabama's governor called a special session of the state legislature, winning a nearly unanimous vote for a new tax-break law to lure companies to Alabama. The company could use the money it would normally owe the state in corporate income taxes for debt service on its own manufacturing facility. Furthermore, in a move hearkening back to the 1930s, the company was permitted to withhold 5 percent of the wages and salaries of its employees, and to use wages for debt service as well. The state and local governments agreed to pay the automaker's total capital costs. State officials and journalists calculated the tax incentive package alone at a value of more than $300 million.[47] The economic development official responsible for putting together Tennessee's offer says, "It was an incredible incentive package. . . . Compared to our incentive package that we provided to the company, and my understanding of North Carolina's and South Carolina's, Alabama's was a magnitude of probably three [times greater]."[48] When Mercedes announced its new site, Alabama governor Jim Folsom crowed, "This, my friends, is a new day for Alabama, a day when we move to the forefront of economic development."[49]

The details of the incentive package were concluded in private negotiations between the development office and the company, and were never revealed to the public. After winning, the Alabama Development Office urged state, city, county, and educational institutions to buy and lease Mercedes automobiles because "we need to express our support to this company, our gratitude, our appreciation."[50] The governor and others immediately began driving Mercedes. Eventually it was revealed that as part of the incentive package, the state had made a binding commitment that state institutions would purchase 2,500 Mercedes sport utility vehicles, at a cost to Alabama taxpayers of $75 million. When that part of the deal was leaked to the public, the governor had another problem: a state law passed in 1976 required state and local agencies to purchase vehicles exclusively from authorized dealers of Ford, Chrysler, General Motors, and American Motors. The deal with Mercedes was explicitly illegal. And the General Motors plant in Decatur, Alabama, which employed 3,500 people (many more than Mercedes, and with no subsidies), was outraged. The governor justified the deal by stating that without the commitment to buy the 2,500 vehicles, Alabama would have lost the plant. He also said his decision had been based on "very reliable information" that South and North Carolina had each agreed to purchase 2,000 Mercedes vehicles as part of their recruitment packages.[51]

The revelations continued. Alabama had committed to pay the salaries and wages of all 1,500 new Mercedes employees for at least a year. The company itself would pay no wages to its workers; the taxpayers would pay. At a cost of $45 million, payroll had been included as part of the subsidized "training" expenses the state would cover. No one expressed much surprise at this disclosure. As a Tennessee official said, "Employee training—that's a given in any project. . . . All the large projects that I'm familiar with have included a package in which the state underwrites the training of the new employees."[52] Moreover, the governor had assigned the National Guard to clear the land and prepare the thousand acre construction site for Mercedes, again at taxpayers' expense. The Guards were paid active-duty wages while doing the site work. The governor called this good training for the soldiers. Local residents pointed out that when their communities had tried to get the National Guard to help repair schools after natural disasters, the state had refused on the grounds that it would constitute "competition with private business."[53]

All of the officials involved in the later phases of the competition acknowledged that the dollar amounts offered to Mercedes would never be recovered from the plant itself. Instead the cost-benefit analysis that justified incentive packages relied on calculations of "externalities," secondary benefits that would accrue indirectly to the state. States used econometric models to estimate the effect of a Mercedes plant on economic activity in the area. They assumed that new businesses would spring up to supply the plant with materials and equipment, service it, and transport its products. Even more important, Mercedes would enhance Alabama's image as a business location. Officials conjectured that other automobile and related factories would see the state as a desirable business location if Mercedes was there. They estimated the dollar value of "trickle-down" benefits that would accrue to adjacent communities, as Mercedes managers and employees spent their wages in local neighborhoods. All of these externalities are extremely difficult to estimate, and some states quit the incentive war, convinced they would never see the return on such a large investment. But others intensified their pursuit.

Several state officials, in Alabama and elsewhere in the South, expressed disgust at the extent of the giveaways, dismayed at the taxpayers' underwriting of such blatant "corporate welfare." As the revelations about just what had been promised to Mercedes continued, the *Birmingham News* editorialized, "We can appreciate everyone's enthusiasm. . . . But this is pandering. This is groveling. This is downright pathetic. This is why people make fun of Alabama." [54] A leading political columnist in the state commented, "In the wake of recent disclosures, I wish I had been a little less exuberant. Only now are we learning the price. . . . I have seen a lot of taxpayer ripoffs in my time, and this surely ranks in the Top 10. Maybe No. 1." And an editor of the *Atlanta Journal* argued that, to its detriment, Alabama had demonstrated a willingness to sacrifice "anything—natural resources, clean air and water, their economic future—for something of value now." He argued that the "dramatic giveaway . . . has shocked public officials into a reassessment of the game of corporate tax giveaways." [55]

But in places such as East Tennessee, one of the very last finalists for the Mercedes site, the game continues. Although economic development officials declare that Alabama gave away too much, it is clear that Tennessee was prepared to go to similar lengths—the state had already promised "a museum and visitor center at the interstate exit, those types of things" [56]—and will in the future. Because the details of its negotiations with Mercedes remain secret, it is impossible to know exactly what

Tennessee offered. But it is clear that East Tennessee is eager to get back into the game. The Oak Ridge Chamber of Commerce immediately developed an attractive folder intended for new potential investors. "Mercedes wiggled off the hook . . . ," it says on the outside. On the inside, a colorful fish nearly three feet long dangles enticingly, and the Chamber announces, "We're casting about for another **BIG FISH.**" The poster inside explains, "Mercedes looked at 169 potential sites for their new manufacturing facility. They chose Oak Ridge, Tennessee as one of four for serious consideration. But Mercedes went elsewhere, and this exceptional site is now primed, ready and available. **Here's the Lure:** . . ." After listing Oak Ridge's outstanding features, the Chamber says, "If you're a big fish looking for a place to land, we've got what it takes to hook you. Oak Ridge has all the right characteristics for your major industrial operation. **We invite you to take the bait.**"[57]

The Politics of Economic Development

"Democracy? . . . Thought it was a cuss word!"

—Steve Queener
City Manager, Clinton, Tennessee

Despite the obvious problems with traditional economic development strategies, public officials have not wavered in their reliance on the old approaches. In Tennessee communities that had recently suffered major plant closings, I interviewed mayors, county executives, and a range of public officials responsible for economic development in their towns or regions.[58] Public officials consistently emphasized several themes. First, although low labor costs are of great importance to firms, in their analysis a compliant workforce is at least as important. "Flexibility" and a lack of organization are great selling points. Public officials not only advertise these features, they support policies to ensure that the region remains low-wage and anti-union. This is the truth behind the ideology of the new, "high-tech" economy. Second, racism and other biases motivate economic development practices. Whether the public officials are simply reflecting prejudices they find in the business community or intensifying those preferences, they are clearly complicit in a regime of discrimination. This evidence contradicts the argument that rational principles of efficiency govern economic policy making. Racism is neither rational nor efficient—and yet it shapes the political environment in which business decisions are made. Third, business has assumed a dominant role in local politics in East Tennessee. The public officials described the community, its land and natural resources, and the workers as commodities to be offered up at the auction block. Their primary goal is to keep the business community happy, in what one official calls a "marriage." They are much less concerned about the needs of the people, suggesting that firms have supplanted citizens as their constituency. Fourth, these officials invest great confidence in the self-governing market. They do not make demands of industry because they believe this would be impossible. They accept competitiveness and international trade as justifications for exploitation and impoverishment. Finally, the public officials expressed startling opinions about politics. An important theme throughout the interviews was the subordination of political concerns to economic enterprises. Although they hold positions with great responsibility for promoting public welfare, these officials do not see their roles as political. They trust experts, economists, and corporate leaders above the citizens. Accordingly, they are dismissive of the people they represent. The idea of democracy is an anathema. Public participation in government is seen as a hindrance.

Just as they did in the 1930s, states and municipalities are finding ways of getting around the state constitution, which still prohibits using public lands for exclusively private enterprise. As Dwight Kessell, county executive of Knox County, puts it, "There are some little hickeys in the law that cause some problems."[59] For example, it is illegal for the government—cities and counties—to do certain kinds of economic development. Just as the state cannot simply give away tax dollars to a private entity, authorities entrusted with the public welfare cannot give away public property for commercial enterprise. They can sell it at market value, of course, but that would not contribute much as an industrial recruitment strategy. As a result, it is illegal for public agencies to buy tracts of land and designate them as industrial parks or commercial real estate—but Knox County has found ways of getting around the legal limits. The county executive believes "there's a little bit of leeway in there in the law." For instance, if the county provides public land to a private company but maintains some partial share of the real estate, it can claim some legitimate interest in the property over time, and the deal is legal.[60] Kessell continues, "You can't *purposely* make a cold-turkey deal with anybody, but you can do it on the basis of the people are gonna buy it over a period of time, so the county's still got an interest in it—something like that." Kessell believes, however, that he is still within the spirit of the law: "The county will get its money back from property tax, eventually. . . . We don't do things illegally. We don't need to."[61]

The most important strategy for circumventing constitutional restrictions is to transfer economic development responsibilities to an "independent" nonprofit organization, in this case the Knox County Development Corporation (KCDC).[62] While the chamber of commerce is responsible for going out and recruiting businesses to move into the Knoxville area, KCDC sees itself as a business that markets city resources to interested companies. As Bill Niemeyer says, "Just like Proctor & Gamble sells laundry detergent, we have a specific product: the five business parks. . . . The Development Corporation has a mission, just like in most businesses. Our mission is simple—it's three words: To Create Wealth."[63] In the industrial parks, KCDC installs utilities, roads, site drainage, sewers, water, and other infrastructure. On behalf of the county, they take care of all necessary environmental, geo-physical, and archaeological testing, engineering, and site preparation. They grade the land and sometimes even install rail lines. They arrange financing, zoning and environmental permits. If the companies prefer, KCDC builds the buildings necessary for production. They even put in green space, fountains, recreational facilities, and jogging trails.

Set up as a private 501(c)(3) nonprofit company, KCDC is able to buy land from the city or the country and then use it for private devel-opment, for example in an industrial park. This would be illegal if a gov-ernment agency did it. The law requires that when a public agency spends money on private enterprise—by buying the land, building roads, installing sewers, providing water and power—that agency must prove it will recover the money it puts in. Government is not allowed to expend public assets for private profit—but KCDC is allowed. "We de-veloped [KCDC] in order to do a kind of horse trading with people. The county can't do that as a county. The city can't do that as a city."[64] So the county executive and three county commissioners sit on the KCDC board—along with several bankers, real estate developers, and financial analysts—to help make decisions about economic develop-ment. "The county still sort of controls that board—sort of."[65] KCDC allows economic development to become a process of public adminis-tration and management, rather than a political issue. "With the Devel-opment Corporation, we don't have to go through that whole political process in doing our economic development."[66] KCDC, with its public funding, can administer the programs without regard to their impact on the county as a whole.

Another common practice in East Tennessee is for cities and coun-ties, along with private corporations, to pay a private organization to do the external industrial recruitment. One example is Tennessee's Re-source Valley (TRV), an organization headed by Jim Henry. Henry ex-plains that TRV does not officially recruit companies, but rather markets the region nationally and internationally. Local governments

pay to be included in its efforts, and TRV then passes on hot prospects
to those localities. In Oak Ridge, as another example, it is the chamber
of commerce that primarily handles economic development. Under a
contract with the city government, the chamber receives $160,000 each
year from the city and in turn it is responsible for recruiting companies
and negotiating incentive packages. Lawrence Young, who directs the
chamber's economic development efforts, explains that this came about
largely in order to insulate economic policy from the demands of democratic politics. "I worked for the city of Oak Ridge in economic development," and he and the mayor "came to the mutual conclusion that
I personally was better suited for a job in the chamber. It was a little less
constraining than the one I had—less binding, I guess, if you will . . .
particularly with the sunshine laws that we have in Tennessee."[67] When
the city was in charge of economic development activities, it was required to provide public access to its files. Lodged within the chamber,
those files and activities could remain private and not subject to public
scrutiny.

Moreover, taking the city's economic development function techni-
cally outside of the public sector allowed greater freedom for the officials involved. When the city was responsible for the program, for
example, Young had been frustrated. "It would look askew if one, let's
say, leased a yacht to take the governor and Mercedes-Benz officials out
on the river, which we did last year, when Mercedes-Benz was active in
pursuit of our site . . . As a city official, I just couldn't have done that . . .
There would have been too many questions associated with that. So
there is a lot more latitude available in a quasi-private organization like
the chamber of commerce."[68] It was easier to get results with the chamber, because no one asked questions during the process. After a deal was
settled, no one would question the methods used to bring it in. "Once
you have a bird in hand, it's a little tough for a public official to say, 'No,
we don't want 300 jobs.'"[69]

Marc Sudheimer explained the factors that make his town attractive to business recruits. Morristown, he says, is "geographically blessed to be right in the middle of the eastern U.S." and has a good transportation network to provide easy access. But then he says, "we provide all the services of a metro area, but we don't have all the problems of a metro." Those problems? "Generally, higher labor [union] rates. Generally, more of a leaning toward organized labor."[70] These labor "problems," Sudheimer says, have made it possible for him to recruit businesses away from big cities. "We've actually made an attempt to recruit from California, but have been unable to convince them there's life east of the Mississippi. But—Chicago's been very good to us. New York has been pretty good to us."[71] All of these places have lost jobs to Morristown, Tennessee.

Although their region has clearly lured companies from other regions and other countries, the economic development officials do not accept any responsibility for encouraging industries to move and thus destroying jobs elsewhere. Jim Henry admits he has encountered some resentment at trade shows—"people yelling at us, blaming us for taking their jobs away from the North." But he rejects their logic. "Companies are going to leave. They've already decided to move. We just want to convince them to move here . . . They *have* to move, to keep their costs down, to make a profit. So why should they move to South Carolina, or Mexico? We think they should move *here*."[72]

Henry, who recruits industry to fifteen counties in East Tennessee, says without hesitation that the number-one reason for businesses to relocate to the area is the fact that it is a right-to-work state. "Most of these industries are moving from the North, or from places where they have had to deal with labor. They know they won't have to here. . . . Ninety-nine percent of businesses come here because they want an environment where they will not have to have a union. They do not want to have a union. Our environment here is pretty well labor-free."[73] Kessell agrees that companies move to Tennessee to flee unionized workforces. "A lot of it's wage rates . . . St. Louis, Chicago, all those bigger centers, the cost of doing business has gone up so much—they're heavily unionized, and then even if you aren't unionized, you have to be competitive to get workers, and so those wage rates are so high, that there's no way you can compete in the world market—you're just out of it!"[74]

But Henry disputes this analysis. "It has *nothing* to do with money!" he says. Financial considerations play little part in businesses' decision to escape unions. "This is not about dollars at all. They do not want to deal with a third party . . . Versatility is the most important thing in a worker, and unions destroy that. If you have a union, they're constantly looking to create problems, because that's how they survive."[75] Sudheimer and others corroborate this; companies that move south to escape labor unions are escaping not only high wages but "work rules, especially . . . What they want is the flexibility to develop a team without somebody saying no, you can't do it that way."[76] Sudheimer chuckles about the failure of unions to organize in his area. "All the industrial developers in the state had a pool when Nissan was having a union vote. I got the percentages right, I got the numbers wrong. It got defeated like three to one. It was absurd . . . they were like 60 percent above the prevailing wages in the area, the best benefits they'd ever heard of. And the work that they were doing was so much easier than what they were used to doing anyway—be it farming or furniture."[77]

This comment raises another point. The public officials interviewed for this chapter believe that the workers in East Tennessee are willing to do any kind of work for any wages—and that they will be better off than they were before.[78] Sudheimer, who is from Michigan himself, believes that any industry is a step up for the Appalachian workers he represents. For himself, of course, these jobs are unthinkable. "I did a three-month sentence in a General Motors plant when I was growing up. Yup, it convinced me to go on to school."[79] Exactly as developing countries do, public officials in East Tennessee use the workers' desperation and the unsatisfactory nature of existing opportunities extensively when marketing their counties as industrial locations. Henry says of his constituency: "These people have been poor. They have worked on farms or in factories. They are used to hard work, and they don't mind it. They will work harder than other people."[80]

"Flexibility" is therefore one of the most important concepts for economic developers. Henry says, above all, "Companies need workers with flexibility. They need workers with an ability to move around a lot, to do a lot of different jobs if they're needed to."[81] Kessell reports that the president of the Panasonic Corporation from Japan visited that company's plant in Knox County and praised the people of East Tennessee. "He said, 'This is the best labor force in the land we've got anywhere in the United States . . . If they were all like yours, we'd be happy.'" Kessell boasts that Appalachian workers "are very trainable people, and they're not great troublemakers. They believe in working . . . They generally have a great work ethic."[82]

Along with flexibility, this question of "work ethic" comes up repeatedly in interviews with economic development officials. When pressed, it seems to represent one thing: workers will accept whatever the employer requires. Docility seems to be even more important than the willingness to work for low wages. Compliance and the improbability of unionization or protest make a workforce desirable. This is a different image from the ones usually associated with the contemporary "high-tech" workforce. Yet this is the workplace of the future. New industries—whether service-sector or manufacturing, high-tech or low-tech—are still seeking the characteristics they sought a hundred years ago. And political leaders are still assisting their demands.

Even more disturbing is the attitude toward the workforce the interviews revealed. The politicians in East Tennessee almost unanimously assert that "work ethic" has a racial component. "Part of it is the way you're raised. Part of it is inherent to certain types of ethnic groups," says

Kessell. "This is Scotch, Irish, Swiss, German, basically. . . . We have less ethnic problems here than in other areas."[83] Jim Henry believes that immigration and ethnic diversity are dangerous to the economy. "The *biggest* problem in this country . . . [is] all the Mexicans who are just walking across the border. It's absolutely *destroying* our economy."[84]

Jack Hammontree, head of the Knoxville Chamber of Commerce, is most blunt. Looking at a map of the United States, he argues that there is a single factor that makes his region competitive in the struggle to attract industry: "We have the lowest minority population in the hundred-mile radius around Knoxville, than any other place east of the Mississippi. This part of the mountain region of Appalachia . . . we were out of the Black Belt—and there's never been a high concentration of minority population anywhere in this Appalachian region. . . . That is still one of our major selling points. Now, you're really going to think I'm a racist—but it's a fact!"[85] The low number of African Americans and other ethnic minorities makes for a desirable workforce and a good "work ethic." Hammontree explains that this is cultural. "The German people—any of those European tribes—I think they have a higher drive to be successful, more of a responsibility about doing a good job and trying to have self-satisfaction. If they agree to do something for somebody, they'll do a good job doing it and they're proud of what they've done. I think that this part of the country being settled by a lot of those people, most of it German and British and Scotch-Irish, they're hard-drinking, fun-loving people in some respects, but yet they had initiative, and you don't get that with a lot of other ethnic backgrounds. And because we have remained that way—we've had not too many infusions of other people coming in—those values have been passed down."[86] He reminisces about his own mother and grandmother instilling a work ethic in him, and speculates that this explains the attraction of East Tennessee to major industries. Because of the region's ethnicity, he says, economic development is booming.

Flexibility and a good work ethic seem much more important than the more "rational" need for "human capital" as traditionally understood by economists. Education and skill levels are all but irrelevant in the actual recruitment of industry to this area. Despite the national consensus that high-skilled, high-tech jobs are the wave of the future, this new economy has not come to most of East Tennessee. Although the public officials asserted that companies do "want a quality workforce," in practice this meant: "Can you get people? Will they work hard?"[87] These two questions were foremost on everyone's list. Quality seemed indistinguishable from poverty and desperation. None of the economic development officials found low skill levels to be an important barrier to recruiting new industries. Instead, they discovered, "the main thing they'd like to see in an employee is the ability to read, write, and think. And if they can do that, they can learn to do anything."[88] Henry agreed: "You have to read and write . . . but not specific skills. They want someone to work hard and learn the job. A good versatile workforce." Indeed, "CETA and JTPA were major disasters. They didn't work at all. They just take people's time, and train them in useless skills."[89]

Again, versatility was associated with racial or ethnic characteristics. Kessell reported that companies come to the East Tennessee region because of the Appalachian people's "innate ability to be trained. They are basically shade-tree mechanics—they are very easily trained in the ways of production." He believes this too has a genetic component: "They are more mechanically inclined in some areas. I think Tennesseans have a heavy mechanical bent because there are a lot of Irish Catholics." Kessell's explanations rivaled the most atavistic understandings of racial difference: "The farther south you get, the dexterity begins to fade. . . . Southerners, by nature, the more you approach the hotter climate, on the average, they tend to work at a different pace than people who are raised in colder climates. . . . We [in East Tennessee] are halfway between, so I think we get a little bit of the best of both worlds."[90]

Jim Henry argues that incentives are only a symbol, part of a package that convinces firms that they will be well treated. Incentives alone don't work; on this fact Henry agrees with most economists. "No one will come here because of industrial revenue bonds anymore—everyone in the country has those! And they won't come here because of tax exemptions or other incentives. But you have to have those things because business is only going to locate here if they know the community is going to be a partner. They don't want to be the only one taking a gamble. The community needs to have something to risk. If they're willing to put in power lines, water, sewer systems, rail lines, visitors centers—then the business knows they're serious about making this work." [91] Henry's comment is very revealing. He expresses well the attitude of corporations. The old idea that a firm's stockholders share the risk—and therefore deserve to share the profits—has been expanded to argue that the entire community should share the risk. There is an important difference, however. Unlike shareholders, the members of the community are unlikely—except in very unusual circumstances—to share the company's profits in any significant way. This certainly is not part of the contract. Nonetheless, businesses are able to demand that the risk be shared among all the citizens.

Officials locate recruitment prospects in several ways. Some companies are referred to the locality by the state's economic development agency, the Tennessee Department of Economic and Community Development. Others are recruited by the local agencies, or by regional outfits like Tennessee's Resource Valley. Sudheimer explains that the Hamblen County Chamber of Commerce spends about $200,000 annually on "recruitment, advertisement, equipment, travel, and so forth. We've been all over the world. . . . We develop our own [targets] through recruiting trips, through cold calls on the phone, through referrals of existing industry . . . through our contacts with foreign consulate offices in Atlanta, New Orleans, New York, through a network of consultants that we keep in touch with. . . . We'll make cold calls to a geographic area—hit a broad range of industrial groups, just whoever's in the area. And try to get appointments and have volunteer recruiters call on them." This aggressive recruitment strategy has paid off. "Morristown's got like the third largest presence of international investments in the state on a per capita basis. Got nine foreign flags represented by fourteen different companies, I believe it is. The international presence here has been a lot of fun. You get to go to Germany and Japan and say you're working." [92] Once the prospects are recruited, the Chamber works on situating them in Morristown. With the help of federal, state, and city funds, Sudheimer and others have developed huge industrial parks and other properties, which the Chamber then leases or donates to companies willing to locate in the area.

All of the officials interviewed spend a high percentage of their time catering to the needs of corporations in their communities. This is facilitated by the nominally private organizations responsible for economic development programs. High priority is placed on business's comfort. As Niemeyer explains, "[Knox] County decided to get out of the economic development business . . . since, in essence, business traditionally looks at government as a regulator. So to be able to best offer economic development, . . . [KCDC is] in other words, a business interacting with a business." [93] Privatization of economic development puts industry at ease.

Even when city or county officials are directly responsible, helping business is at the top of their agenda. Queener says, "I try to stay in relationship with all the industry that are here today. . . . We meet quarterly with the plant managers throughout our city . . . just to talk about their situation, what can the city do better . . . [for instance] to pave an industrial parkway, to put a turn lane here, to do this where eighteen wheelers are having a problem entering and exiting. . . . It just helps their operation a little better and we hope by helping them it helps the growth of the company, which also will help fund their personnel. . . .

We got a real good relationship with our industry people. I try to stay in touch with the plant managers quite often, and it's good for them to know what we're doing as well as it is for us to know what they're doing."[94] Sudheimer puts it most poetically: "When folks land here, we tell them that we're getting married, we're not just going out. You can't get rid of us! . . . We don't leave them alone. If they have a need, we'll continue to work with them as a community."[95]

The public officials interviewed seemed much more concerned about the needs of businesses within their community than about the needs of citizens. Queener, who managed the city of Clinton, expressed regret about the closing of Greenbrier Industries, one of the town's largest employers. As chapter 3 explains in detail, the plant closed without any warning, and the company had deprived the workers of money and benefits to which they were legally entitled. And yet Queener's response was, "I think it was just one of those things. . . . I guess that's the cruel world today, make a dollar today and forget you tomorrow." When asked if the city could help the workers recover the pay owed them, Queener looked surprised: "To be honest with you, I haven't even checked into that. . . . I hadn't thought of it, but that's very possible."[96] In Queener's town, over 500 people had just lost their jobs with no notice. Queener himself admitted, "I knew hundreds personally that worked there." He knew that the loss of jobs had been devastating to these workers, many of whom were left stranded without their last paychecks and without coverage for thousands of dollars in hospital bills. When asked to enumerate the biggest problems facing the town of Clinton, however, Queener thought for a while and said, "One thing that's at the top of my mind is to improve our sewers—sewer and water system."[97] The problems facing low-income residents without work were not seen as the concern of the city manager. In fact, a plant's decision to close seemed unrelated to his job of fostering economic development.

Henry, who recruits business for an area covering several counties, was more explicit. He blamed the workers themselves for the plant closings: if they had performed better, they would not have lost their jobs. "People are not as willing to work as hard as they used to. It is the affluent society. There are easier ways to make a buck." He believes the companies that leave are forced to do so because "the labor force is not available." And he rejects the notion that higher wages and better conditions would make it easier to find a willing workforce. "It is *not* the money! People won't do these jobs at any price. . . . Some of these cut-and-sew operations pay $15 an hour, and they still can't find the people they need. The jobs will be here long after the people to do them are gone. That's why these shops have to move to Taiwan, or India, or Mexico. They have to find people who will do the work."[98] Again, his explanations are directly contradicted by interviews with the workers themselves.

When justifying businesses' locational decisions, as well as other decisions, the public officials sounded like neoclassical economists. They explained that the market dictated firms' decisions. The economy was changing in ways that were beyond their control, and they saw their job as accepting these changes and working within the constraints of the market. Moreover, the officials ridicule workers who protest the loss of good jobs in the community. They believe that deindustrialization is a process of nature. As Sudheimer says, the traditional job base is disappearing in Morristown, and the new jobs are "not at the level of pay and benefits they've been enjoying out there." He understands plant closings and downsizing as a good correction to an inflated market. "You got people twenty-five years in a union environment in a textile mill, and they're going to be in for a rude awakening when they hit the marketplace. It's unfortunate—first they're going to have to go to work!" The work in textile mills, he explains, was too easy. "There's nothing to it. They sit there and watch this thing spin fiber out of a machine. If it breaks, you tie a chicken-head knot, and go back to reading your book.

They're gonna have to learn that production means production. And that seniority doesn't mean a whole lot anymore." He laughs. "*I* have to be elected yearly, so, *what* job security?"[99]

Even in terms of economic development, public officials often seem more interested in generating a new enterprise—any enterprise—than in ascertaining exactly what that enterprise would bring to the region. No industry is truly off-limits, no matter how few jobs are expected, how low the wages expected, or how unpleasant the work. As Young says, "I would love to recruit companies that only benefit the greater good of the U.S. or community, or whatever, but . . . you deal with the micro-scale that you have control over."[100] Even as they are offering incentives with taxpayers' money, economic development officials do not ask potential employers what wages they intend to pay citizens who get jobs there. "That's almost a gift-horse-in-the-mouth type of thing!"[101] On the contrary, the employers ask *them*. "They'll ask what the prevailing wage is. . . . And they'll try and come in and hit right in that general area. Most of the time, a new plant coming in wants to be a good neighbor with the other industries and the town, and so they aren't going to come in and inflate wages."[102] Henry echoes this. "They ask *us* what the wages are. They look at the average wages in the area and they try to meet that." Public officials do not attempt to raise the standards in the area, and do not encourage businesses to pay a living wage. Public funds are spent on any industry willing to locate in these towns. Similarly, no one asks if potential recruits are planning to stay for a while. If they did, Young says, "They'd say yeah. I don't ask, because that's exactly what happens: they would say, 'Well of course, what do you think?! Our mission is to put deep roots down!' And if they do, that's wonderful. Ultimately, my job is to make sure that there's an environment that they do put deep roots down. But if they don't, what are you going to do?"[103]

No one would turn away a target because they gave unconvincing answers—or for almost any other reason. "It's rare that we say, 'Nah, we'd just as soon not talk to you . . . ' We have some companies that, by covenant, are not allowed into our industrial parks [because of hazardous waste or other public dangers]."[104] If it's not illegal, and if there is land that suits its needs somewhere in the county, Sudheimer will recruit it. Similarly, when asked if he would ever refuse government assistance to any firm interested in locating within Knoxville, Niemeyer says, "No."[105]

Local officials are not apologetic that most industry recruited to small towns in the South is low-wage and low-skill manufacturing or service work. In fact, most of them believe it is a virtue. They do what they can to make sure it stays this way. Sudheimer explains that the West Coast, for example, is having problems because wages are too high. "Their workforce hasn't figured out that cost the component has something to do with competitiveness in this global market. And that a company doesn't owe them a job once they're out there."[106] Lawrence Young complains that one of the greatest obstacles to recruitment in Oak Ridge is the high wages paid to government employees in the city. Relative affluence—and the presence of unions at Martin Marietta—is a big problem. "It's just as easy to locate, let's say, twenty miles from here, and if all you need to do is attract semiskilled laborers, it's probably easier there. . . . It's a no-brainer."[107] The only thing that makes recruitment possible, Young says, is that "while Oak Ridge is relatively affluent, we're still in Appalachia. One needs to only go over that hill to see some abject poverty. I don't go over that hill very often, but I know it's there!"[108] Poverty is not only an incentive for companies to locate in East Tennessee, but also a threat that keeps the workforce in check: any worker who misbehaves is going back to the other side of that hill.

Jim Henry says the companies he recruits pay close attention to the unemployment rates in an area they are considering. In the area of Oak Ridge, Tennessee, which is within TRV's jurisdiction, he says, the unemployment rate is just too low. "Right now that's hurting us, because we don't have much unemployment. They don't want to come here. They would have to steal workers from other companies. They don't want to do that—that's not right, that's not the way things are done." [109] Rather than compete for employees in an open labor market, companies prefer to find areas with high levels of poverty and unemployment, where workers will be thankful for even a low-wage job. The state facilitates this process.

Some of the public officials acknowledge that they are participating in the "race to the bottom" that so many policy analysts and advocates have deplored. By advertising their region's poverty and even its good "work ethic," they are encouraging businesses to eliminate well-paid jobs (usually in the North, but sometimes literally down the road, as with GE in Morristown) and create worse opportunities in their place. Henry, for example, agrees this is happening, but argues it is the result of inevitable market forces. "We have to compete with all these countries now. Detroit doesn't just have to compete with Tennessee and Pennsylvania, it has to compete with Korea and Japan." The only possible response, he says, is for workers in the United States to lower their expectations. "The wages of the workers over there are not going to rise to the level of the UAW—the UAW is going to have to fall to meet their wages if we want to compete. Maybe Americans will have to make $4,000 a year. Maybe."

Like Sudheimer, he blames those who resist this logic; they have had it too easy all along. "You know, they have people in Detroit making $70,000 a year just for putting screws in a car. They don't deserve that! *No one* deserves that much. So their wages need to come down. People going to work now are *never* going to earn what their parents did. . . . No one pays like that anymore." Again, the workers themselves are to blame. "Maybe their services aren't really worth that much anymore. They're not *worth* what they used to be. That's the answer." [110]

Finally, the officials interviewed are surprisingly disparaging toward politics itself. They treat it as a nuisance and a barrier to the work they are trying to do. They prefer a citizenry that, like the workforce, is quiescent and accepts authority. Democracy, and the U.S. Constitution, are necessary evils that they must tolerate but whose restrictions they will always try to avoid.

Above all, public administrators like Steve Queener value peace in local politics. When Robert Dahl wrote about city government nearly forty years ago, he surmised that people who don't get involved in public affairs must be content with their lives and their government. As he said, "citizens are confronted with a variety of opportunities for gaining their primary goals without ever resorting to political action at all. Essentially, this is why the level of citizen participation is low." [111] Although scholars have since rejected this reasoning, having uncovered power relationships that enforce inactivity, Queener agrees with the early pluralists. When asked if he thinks most people in Clinton know the structure of their city government, or who their representative on the city council is, or what the job of the city manager is, Queener says, "Probably not. And I don't mean that negative. I just mean I think people in Clinton are pleased with the services they get and pleased with the tax rate they have. . . . So, when you're happy and satisfied, [why participate?]" [112] Queener boasts about the low levels of involvement: "Our council meets maybe once a month, and I bet all of twelve months we might have five people—five residents—attend. They just don't come . . . I think they're just satisfied." [113] As chapter 3 will demonstrate, interviews with citizens of his town reveal a decidedly different picture.

Queener is the perfect example of the technocratic public administrator. He sees his job as implementation rather than policy making. He eschews ideology and partisanship. He sees himself as a manager rather than a politician. He says about his job, "I don't look at it as political. I'm not elected. I look at whatever policy that they want us to do, it's my job to see that it's followed through. Basically I just look like a quarterback of a football team that runs the offense. . . . I'm not going to say that I'm not in the public's eye, because I am—I'd be crazy to say that!—because I work for all 10,000 [citizens of Clinton], because that's who pays my salary." Queener acknowledges that he often must respond to residents' requests and, in collaboration with his various department heads, designs the programs that make the city run. But he vehemently denies that he is a politician. "I don't play the politics scene. I just wish we could put all that to the side and forget that, and work together for whatever is best for the country, the state, the community. . . . I always feel you hire the person to do the best job, and that's probably the most qualified." When asked to define *democracy*, Queener is stumped. "I don't know what to say. It didn't cross my mind. Lord, I guess I've really never thought about it." He joked: "I haven't heard that word in so long, I thought you was cussing me or something! Thought it was a cuss word!"[114]

Although these officials themselves claim very little understanding of economic trends, they invest complete confidence in the technical advice of experts and the autonomy of the market sphere. For example, Knox County executive Dwight Kessell complains that the people do not understand why it is beneficial for the county (or its agents) to spend millions of dollars in public resources to recruit small or medium-size companies. Experts, he says, have proven that this is worthwhile. "If this creates say 200 or 250 new jobs, then they take the economic stream that that creates. The idea being, I think, it's seven to one. In other words, if you create 250 jobs, you will end up with a seven-to-one ratio of jobs here because of that. That's a multiplier effect that a lot of people don't understand."[115] Although Kessell himself cannot explain how this multiplier works, or provide any data suggesting that any business has provided seven times the number of jobs it created, he absolutely believes it to be true, and disparages the citizens he represents who do not understand its magic.

Similarly, Bill Niemeyer states with confidence, "Of course, all of these things are done on a cost-benefit basis. If the benefit's not there, we're not going to put the cost into doing it." When pressed, however, he admits that he has no idea how cost and benefit are evaluated. He himself is not involved, he says; the board of directors assesses each project. Yet, he assures the interviewer, "All of that's calculated! They look at it upwards and downwards. . . . It's all based on cost-benefit basis. They look at the whole picture."[116]

Many of the officials recognize that their information is very imperfect, and that economic development decisions are made at least as much on political as on economic grounds. No cost-benefit equation is used to evaluate contracts. Jack Hammontree says, "People try and tell you there is [a standard]. I think it depends on the community, it depends on how desperate you are and how desperate the state is. Alabama was apparently pretty desperate [to win Mercedes], for political reasons as well as economic reasons. I don't think there's really a rule of thumb."[117] Lawrence Young admits that all of his economic calculations are fallible: "I would like to say that most communities and states go through a rather rigorous cost-benefit analysis. But I don't think that they do. I think that you have some reasonably bright people in economic positions that can do some rudimentary cost-benefit, and it'll almost *always* turn up positive. . . . A lot of emotion gets into it. A lot of emotion. Particularly when you have the prestige of states vis-à-vis their position with neighboring states, when you have politicians who may be in an election year." In general, he says, with most economic development incentive programs, no ordinary economic analysis explains the payoff. "One has to do a lot of manipulation of figures in order to argue a positive cost-benefit." For instance, when Oak Ridge was vying for the Mercedes plant, "We had never calculated that there would be 13,000 'ancillary' jobs, like Alabama has done. . . . [But] I'm sure that they had some bright, perhaps Ph.D. candidates do their analysis."[118]

Still, Young has his doubts about the effectiveness of the whole process in which he is engaged: "Are you creating the kind of jobs that are going to take you into the twenty-first century? I don't know. I don't know at all."[119]

Because efficiency and results are prized above all else, most economic development deals are highly secret. "We've had 902 companies that I've talked to personally, that you sign a confidentiality agreement with them in which you don't tell anybody that they're coming here and what their plans are." Kessell and others defend this secrecy: "There's a good reason for that, because . . . I remember one company that's here came here from Massachusetts or Connecticut, up there, and the unions up there didn't like it because they were moving. Next thing, I'm getting a phone call threatening me that we gave them illegal incentives. . . . They were threatening to sue us, and to cause us trouble with their bonds and everything."[120] This would have stopped the agreement from going through. Accordingly, all the public officials interviewed agreed with Kessell that it was important to keep all of the details of potential arrangements absolutely secret.

When asked to discuss his vision of democracy, Kessell is decidedly disapproving. Democracy is anarchy, he says. "In true democracy, every decision would have to be made by a vote of the people. But in a true democracy, it is only one step away from anarchy. It's organized anarchy, okay? Anarchy is when you have no government, but everybody has a say-so." Kessell, who has been a superintendent of a manufacturing plant and lines his office coffee tables with *Nation's Business, Business Week,* and other business trade journals, clearly sees his job as county executive just as Queener sees his: as CEO of a firm. Democracy is far from their ideal. "You have to have decision makers, people who are willing to take the gaffe, you know, and hope that you live long enough to see that you're right. . . . You know, it's great to have input from people, but if you have anarchy, you can't have government. . . . It's sort of

like a company, you know—if they don't like the direction the
company's going in, they ax the president." [121] This is in the interests of
his constituents, he says, because he understands the economy and pro-
tects their economic interests. Citing incidents where public participation led to canceling economic negotiations with firms, Kessell
concludes that the people should just stay out of government if they
know what's good for them. "Just pure democracy is not in the best interest of people." [122]

Lawrence Young scoffs at the inefficiencies caused by democratic
principles. He vastly prefers the chamber of commerce to the public
sphere. "The fundamental difference is that we have board meetings
during working hours. Government! How many countless, useless
hours I spent from seven until eleven at night in council meetings or
commission meetings." [123] This level of deliberation and participation is
extreme, Young says. "I strongly believe in *representative* democracy,
[not] *absolute* democracy. . . . It's fascinating to me to think about the
ramifications of a generally uninformed public . . . to make decisions."
People are simply not qualified to govern themselves, he says. Experts—
or at least highly educated academics—should make decisions for them.
This is the only thing that makes representative democracy work. "Irre-
spective of what's wrong with our current system and the representative
nature of it, I think virtually all the people that are elected are interested
in generally doing what's right, and they're certainly informed. . . . I
mean it's great to have Rhodes scholars [in Congress]—[Representa-
tive] Jim Cooper is bright!" [124]

Thirty years ago, when Banfield and Wilson warned of the dangers
of the technocratic management style in local politics, they could have
been talking about Steve Queener or Dwight Kessell or Marc Sudheimer. "To govern New York, Chicago, or Los Angeles, for example,
by the canons of efficiency—or efficiency *simply*—might lead to an accumulation of restlessness and tension that would eventually erupt in

meaningless individual acts of violence . . . or perhaps in the slow and imperceptible weakening of the social bonds. Politics is, among other things, a way of converting the restless, hostile impulses of individuals into a fairly stable social product (albeit perhaps a revolution!) and, in doing so, of giving these impulses moral significance." [125] The case studies that follow demonstrate the costs of keeping politics out of local politics.

Conclusion: Grassroots Organizing

Communities have very little to do with the process of economic development, and no say at all in the outcomes. Political elites' faith in the free market's self-correcting abilities has created a crisis for citizens in rural areas and small towns.

Scholars have proposed innumerable alternative strategies for economic development—from job generation to social infrustracture to community-based strategies. But an obvious alternative is for the state to use its power in a traditional way: by regulating the activities of business. In this way the government—whether federal, state, or local authorities—can accomplish progressive economic development goals without becoming directly involved itself in the creation of jobs and management of production. The state can lessen the degree of capital mobility in the local economy, and can even out the costs and benefits of economic development between the public and private sectors. Of course, states and local governments—not to mention the federal government—face stiff opposition if they dare regulate business activity. As Fainstein and Fainstein note with some irony, "While direct state subsidy of business has been a long-accepted American mode, intrusion of the government into the private sector through planning and investment policies has always been resisted." [126]

Even so, as the following chapters will demonstrate, communities have the power to demand some accountability from their governments. Mobilized local groups can do this in several ways. Communities can find out what practices are being used by local and regional governments, and demand enforcement of laws already on the books. Bringing public attention to economic development plans is often enough to stop undesirable deals from being consummated. Democratic awareness can change the entire course of events. Kessell admits this: "For instance, if so-and-so is figuring on moving from New England to here, there's a number of reasons why he doesn't want anything said until he's made the final preparation. Now, if you leave it to democracy. . . . We would have to tell everybody that he's moving, and he would have a fight there, and be expending money and energy there, and he couldn't afford to come here."[127] Protest can be very effective.

Policies can also be used to accomplish larger goals. First, the local government that recruits business enterprises and provides public resources can establish requirements that companies receiving incentives sign specific contracts—including minimum levels for wages and benefits, numbers of jobs that must be created, and a minimum length of stay at the site. When firms violate the agreements, they may be subject to "clawbacks," financial penalties imposed when the economic goals are not met.[128] Many localities in more prosperous areas have implemented a range of "linkage" policies, obligating subsidized industries to contribute back to the community in some way. Other cities have been successful using "eminent domain" takings, condemning existing buildings, claiming them as city property, and making decisions about their best productive use in the future, either using them for municipally owned enterprises or selling them to new owners. Even more relevant to the case studies that follow is the importance of plant-closing laws, requiring advance notice before plant shutdowns and imposing penalties on businesses that close without providing warning or severance pay. Although these laws have mostly been federal initiatives, some local governments have passed legislation to prevent plant closings or to minimize their burden upon workers and the community.[129] All of these legislative remedies impose requirements on the business, allowing the community to demand accountability and a return on its investment, refusing to accept all of the costs of economic development without sharing in the rewards.

Of course, the process of passing and implementing such legislation is arduous. Business groups pose stiff resistance to any attempts to require linkage between incentives and results. Corporate lobbies have often defeated efforts to stop "corporate welfare," despite strong public support for regulations. The real challenge, therefore, is to mobilize a coalition at the local or state level to pressure the government for more progressive economic development policies. The groups discussed in this book attempt to do just that.

In the face of traditional strategies by big business and government agencies, local groups that otherwise have had different or even opposing agendas—including community organizations, labor unions, churches, environmental groups, and others—have banded together to lobby for economic development legislation and to seek economic power. They are taking on a variety of issues: protesting plant closings, fighting corporations' efforts to move freely without warning, challenging local economic development strategies. They are attempting to pass laws regulating the use of temporary employment services for full-time and permanent work. They are lobbying for living-wage ordinances in cities and counties. And they are pressuring economic development agencies at the local, regional, and state levels to respond to community needs and concerns. They reject the idea that *any* business development is good for the community. They differentiate between good jobs and nonmeaningful opportunities. And they insist that their government defend their right to better jobs and working conditions. These groups know that the problem is not a lack of alternatives to the dominant model of business development; other economic development strategies have been discussed, modeled, and investigated for decades. The problem is a lack of the political will to implement them. Political mobilization is the only viable response.

3

You Can't Fight City Hall:
The Closing of Greenbrier Industries

When hundreds of employees at Greenbrier Industries returned from their July Fourth vacation in the summer of 1993, they received a rude surprise. Waiting at their Clinton, Tennessee, homes were phone messages telling them not to report to work the next day. Certain it could not be true, many workers went down to the sewing factory on Monday morning to find out what was happening. There they met supervisors and managers apparently just as confused as they were. The workers were told they would receive calls in a week to let them know when to come back to work. Checking in the next week, and the next, the story was the same.

Little by little, workers discovered the truth. Greenbrier was not reopening. Even worse, the company executives had secretly been siphoning off funds for months. Most workers' last paychecks had bounced. Many payroll taxes had not been paid, suppliers had not been reimbursed for months of deliveries, and the company was behind on its obligations. On July 28, 1993, without informing any of its employees, Greenbrier Industries quietly filed Chapter 7 bankruptcy at its headquarters in New Jersey.

Employing up to 700 people, Greenbrier Industries had been the largest employer in Clinton, a town of only 8,000 people. It was a rather typical factory in the rural South: an apparel plant owned by Northerners, employing mostly women to sit in front of assorted sewing machines for long days. The pay was low; all new workers in 1993 were paid $4.25 an hour. The personnel manager reported that "some hourlies made $5.00, for your more skilled jobs."[1] More experienced workers hoped to be put on jobs where they could earn "piece rates," based on finished production, where they were rewarded for extraordinary speed. But when a worker or a group became too efficient at a particular task—when their earnings neared $6 or $7 an hour—Greenbrier's engineers appeared, to do time studies and recalibrate the piece rate. Sewing machine operators did not get rich at Greenbrier Industries. Yet workers maintain that they liked working there. They were treated well and considered themselves part of the Greenbrier "family."[2]

The large old brick factory building by the river could not have been a more centrally located landmark, just two blocks from City Hall and a stone's throw from the Anderson County courthouse. Although it drew workers from very poor rural Campbell, Scott, and Roane counties, most of the employees lived nearby; nearly everyone in Clinton had at least one friend, relative, or neighbor who worked at Greenbrier. The company had operated for twenty-two years in its current form, but it had a rather checkered history dating back to 1960. Plagued by investigations and allegations of corruption, Greenbrier had been shifted among a series of interrelated owners for many years. Yet it had continued to grow and remain profitable, until now.

Most economists and journalists would understand this plant closing as an inevitable casualty of the global economy. Most observers would say that "the market" logically and inevitably caused Greenbrier to move, or to go under. Economists tell us that plants close because they are inefficient. Production costs must have been too high for the plant to remain competitive, when comparable work could be done at a fraction of the cost elsewhere in the world. Technological developments had made it possible to produce the same goods anywhere, and sewing was a labor-intensive, extremely mobile industry.

A closer analysis of manufacturing at Greenbrier, however, shows the limitations of this argument. The company existed and prospered as it did only with the aid and support of the state, which shaped and structured its corporate decisions from the very beginning. Greenbrier received tangible and explicit government support, such as tax incentives, set-asides, and preferential contracting procedures. It also received implicit assistance, such as the priorities inherent in contracting guidelines and the willingness of federal inspectors to ignore rules violations, as well as their failure to investigate allegations of fraud or enforce any standards of corporate accountability. Despite the high level of government investment in the firm, no one ever evaluated the returns. The state not only fostered the conditions for corporate mobility—which ultimately led to Greenbrier shutting down entirely—but it also created a market for exploitation of low-income workers.

Having created the problem, neither federal nor local governments felt any responsibility to address its profound results. Greenbrier's closing represented a crisis for the town of Clinton. Its largest employer was gone, with hundreds of citizens out of work and a whole array of support services threatened. Although the workers would mobilize and protest the plant closing, they were powerless to win back their jobs. Clinton became a town with high unemployment rates and poor job prospects. The angry, dislocated employees found their elected leaders to be unresponsive or worse. After months of mobilization and resistance, the Greenbrier employees gave up fighting for their jobs and their town. They were defeated, demoralized and disillusioned by the system that had betrayed them.

A Brief History of Greenbrier Industries

The Greenbrier factory's primary customer—for many years its only one—was the United States government. Since the early 1960s two brothers from New York, Howard and Carle Thier, had owned and operated a variety of military-apparel operations in East Tennessee, receiving Department of Defense (DOD) contracts worth millions of dollars. Their plants established themselves manufacturing body bags, and eventually branched out into parkas, bulletproof vests, camouflage suits, tents, windbreakers, and dress coats. The Thiers owned plants in the Northeast and then in Appalachia for over four decades. According to one investigator, they had "maneuvered their apparel business from town to town and region to region, rigging a family of interchangeable companies under different names and apparently different ownerships, which the brothers and their associates insist have nothing to do with one another."[3] But the ventures—Helenwood Manufacturing (which became Tennier Industries), Lancer Clothing, Greenbrier Industries, Loudon Industries, Downslope Industries, Eric Industries, Protective Apparel Corporation of America (PACA)—were in practice a single corporate entity. Besides common ownership, throughout the years the firms shared personnel, DOD contracts, management offices, and even plant space. By the late 1970s the Thier brothers owned three major plants, in the towns of Huntsville, Clinton, and Lenoir City. In 1981 alone they took in $17 million in defense contracts.[4]

Greenbrier's immediate predecessor, Tennier Industries, had been based in Huntsville, Tennessee, the hometown of Republican Senator Howard Baker, Jr. The Tennier manufacturing facility was located just off the Congressman Howard H. Baker Highway, housed in a blue corrugated metal building that sits directly atop an old radioactive waste dump, created when Huntsville's previous military industry abandoned the site. In the early 1980s Senator Baker secured federal contracts for Tennier Industries of up to $10 million per year. This made Huntsville the leading per capita recipient in the country of Department of Defense contracts, amounting to almost $25,000 of federal revenue for each man, woman, and child in the town.[5] The Pentagon paid nearly one million dollars to Tennier to produce body bags alone, and Tennier

Industries produced 34,592 body bags per year—during peacetime. Despite this governmental investment, however, the town and the rest of East Tennessee's beautiful Cumberland Plateau remained overwhelmingly poor.[6]

As we have seen in chapter 2, economic development programs capitalizing on the poverty of the region—and its ready and relatively desperate supply of labor—attracted manufacturers from the North. In addition to high unemployment and low wages, a female workforce trained in apparel manufacture and a plethora of small textile and apparel mills made East Tennessee a magnet for Defense Department contractors. Several counties, used to double-digit unemployment levels, saw official rates soar to 20 percent or more in the early 1980s—not including people who had become discouraged from seeking work. In an effort to stimulate industrial development in areas of high unemployment, the federal government provided incentives for companies willing to locate in poor counties. The Department of Defense conferred remarkable competitive advantages on contractors like the Thiers. Nearly all the contract dollars their company received came as Labor Surplus Area (LSA) preferences. Under this program, when Pentagon projects were being distributed, the Thiers were given preference over bidders in more well-off regions. Thus they obtained "competitively bid" Pentagon contracts even when they were not the lowest bidder, as a reward for locating in high-unemployment areas.

The Thiers also received preferential treatment from the DOD under programs to promote "small business."[7] Despite the interconnections among the many companies, Tennier, Helenwood, and Greenbrier Industries each benefited from small-business incentives and subsidies. Effectively managed as one huge operation, the Thier brothers' three Tennessee companies employed far in excess of the 500-worker ceiling for small-business status. The government never noticed.

The DOD preferential programs, justified as efforts to stimulate local entrepreneurship and to bring economic investment into poor areas, were inadequately monitored and enforced. Large wealthy companies were able to circumvent the regulations easily, violating the spirit but not the letter of the law. The subsidies allowed business owners to take advantage of low-income people and communities desperate for jobs, and the lack of accountability ensured that the programs would not improve conditions in these areas. Companies could receive preferential treatment for operating in poor communities, but there were no requirements that they raise wages, offer benefits, or invest some profits back into the community. The minimum wages they offered were not sufficient to pull a family out of poverty. Workers at Tennier, as in most small Southern apparel factories, toiled in sweatshop conditions. The government programs' benefits accrued to businesses, but never trickled down to the workers or the community.[8]

By the early 1990s turnover rates were extremely high; the personnel manager recalls hiring about 400 people within a six-month period, in a plant with 487 production workers. And "that's not counting temporary people I sent in from At-Work [temporary agency]." Greenbrier began to rely on contingent labor instead of regular workers. "A lot of 'em was from Campbell County or Scott County [very poor Appalachian areas], had to drive far, and they come down there and start at $4.25 an hour. . . . Some of them no doubt couldn't afford it . . . to pay the gas bill from LaFollette to Clinton, a fifty-two-mile trip, five days a week, pay a baby-sitter, they just didn't have enough money." The plant had an absentee rate of nearly 10 percent each day.[9]

Government programs had attracted the Thier brothers to East Tennessee in the first place. From their first venture in 1966, Lancer Clothing Company, a small apparel shop in the Hudson Valley town of Beacon, New York, their empire had grown to a string of factories employing thousands. Because of lax enforcement and inadequate standards, the Thiers profited tremendously from economic development programs. As Schlesinger observed, "Maintaining the fictional lines [between companies] helped the brothers fight unions, win preferences from DOD's contracting system and evade responsibility to a skein of workers and communities."[10] The success of Tennier, Lancer, and Greenbrier cannot be attributed to their efficiency, productivity, or fulfilling a crucial market niche. Rather, the Thiers and their successors were beneficiaries of "corporate welfare." Political deals, federal programs, and the imperatives of military production all shaped the company and allowed its owners to prosper. Communities like Clinton attracted companies seeking disempowered workers, and their disempowerment was only intensified by the chain of events that followed.

Since millions of taxpayers' dollars were at stake, DOD was required to hire inspectors to work inside the plant. Although the workers knew that fraud was rampant, and could have provided many examples, all of this apparently escaped the scrutiny of the DOD inspectors hired for that exact purpose. For example, managers enlisted workers in illegal schemes: hiding shipments of military goods officially being made at a different plant; remaining silent when DOD examiners arrived; packaging inferior goods at the bottom of first-quality boxes. Workers on at least one floor were regularly asked to open boxes of garments sewn in plants in Israel, Germany, and South America—plants owned by the same people who owned Greenbrier.[11] The workers would unload the finished products and sew new labels into the coats, or tents. Bruce Mackrey had been hired by Carle Thier in 1972, and had worked at Greenbrier ever since, through ill health and family crises. Out of loyalty to the company, Mackrey had turned a blind eye to questionable business practices: "They'd ship tents over here, and we would take them out of the sacks that they were in, put ropes in, or put a grommet in it, and then stamp on there 'Made In America.' "[12] Although many workers commented on this customary—and obviously illegal—practice, it apparently went unnoticed by government inspectors. Through its lack of enforcement procedures, and inaction in the face of abundant evidence of fraud, the state enabled Greenbrier to continue its practices.

Perhaps most striking, and most typical, was the extreme mobility of the business. At the same time as Greenbrier was closing the Clinton plant, it was opening plants in Eastern Europe to do the same work. The BBC reported on a new plant in Poland:

> Greenbrier Industries Inc. of the USA, the biggest supplier of garments to the U.S. Army, intends to open a factory at Czestochowa. . . . The company would move its entire production from Germany there, together with some from the USA and Israel. The production costs would be one-fifth of those in Germany, with the product quality unchanged. Other reasons for the decision included the possibility of receiving the tax concessions granted to foreign companies investing in Poland. The factory at Czestochowa is to produce textiles for the armed forces, bulletproof jackets, protective clothing against chemical contamination, and garments of military type for civilians.[13]

Whether production moved to other parts of Tennessee or to Poland, the potential to move out of the community became an aggressive industrial-relations strategy. Many workers testified that the company's greatest threat to workers, strategically used to quell talk of unionization and complaints, was its own impermanence. Greenbrier managers constantly emphasized its capacity to move on. Workers at Greenbrier were often asked to move sewing machines and other large equipment to and from several factories in the region. The connection between Greenbrier and these firms was never clear. Officially there was no connection between this group of "small businesses," for if the links were obvious, the company would not have been eligible for the government contracts. But workers knew differently. Managers warned workers that, at any time, their machines—along with their jobs—could be relocated to other plants.[14] In times of conflict, managers had pointedly remarked, "Two good semitruckloads would get everything out."[15] The threat was very plausible, especially to those who knew the company's history. Delivering on its threat to run away from somewhere else had brought the Thier brothers to Huntsville, and then to Clinton, in the first place. In all those moves, Greenbrier Industries received DOD's full cooperation, subsidies, and the implicit or explicit support of the state.

The Clinton Plant Closing

Before the July Fourth weekend of 1993, there were signs that something was wrong at Greenbrier Industries. Manufacturing output had slowed to a trickle, new contracts were not forthcoming, and finished goods lay on the floors of sewing rooms and in heaps in the hallways rather than being shipped out to buyers. Workers who had been around for years knew that if goods were not being sent out, and work on new contracts not begun, something was drastically amiss. Bobbie Bishop, a white-haired grandmother well respected by managers and workers alike, had been employed at Greenbrier for almost twenty years, working her way up from sewing machine operator to supervisor. She spotted a problem immediately: "Everything's just sitting there. It's still there. It's worth in the millions. The material's real expensive, thread's real expensive. The material for government work is more expensive, better quality . . . water resistant, fire resistant . . . [but] we've got hundreds of those [tents] sitting there."[16] Workers were being shifted around and laid off. For a number of months there had not been enough work for everyone, and many women worked only two or three days each week. Everyone seemed to know business was bad, but management continued to assure workers that new contracts were on the way. Both workers and supervisors were encouraged to believe that the sluggish pace was just a phase between major contracts.

Even after the workers were told they were being laid off, no one knew for how long. Managers had explained that there were some cash-flow problems, since the recently completed contracts had not yet been shipped out and the new contracts were not yet begun. But everyone believed that new work was on the way and that they would resume production shortly. Suddenly, without a word of warning, the plant closed. At first workers were told to come back in a week and were re-assured that they would be rehired then, or in two weeks at most. When they returned the following week, the answers were even more vague. Workers soon realized that the entire plant had shut down, except for the managerial offices. No production was under way. Even more eerie, none of the finished work was being packaged or sent out. It lay in piles in hallways on the factory floor. Rumors began to leak out, mass confusion ensued, and supervisors and workers slowly realized that the plant was unlikely to reopen soon. Besides feeling terribly betrayed, the workers began to understand that they would have to depend only upon each other.

The devastation of being suddenly without work or income intensi-fied as workers gradually found out the details of the bankruptcy. Per-haps most shocking was the huge hospitalization bills being charged to some employees. While they were working, all workers had made mandatory weekly payments for health insurance. Coverage was expen-sive, costing each worker over $30 a week, out of a weekly salary aver-aging less than $200. But without notifying anyone, the company had stopped paying its health-care bills six months previously. Since Green-brier was self-insured, no medical bills had been paid for six months. Some workers were left owing up to $40,000 in hospital bills, for ser-vices including major surgery that were covered by the company's in-surance. By the fall the workers were being hounded by collection agencies on behalf of hospitals, and some began receiving notices that their wages, if they had any, would be garnished to pay Greenbrier's out-standing bills.

Many workers had also contributed voluntarily to a 401(k) pension plan. Greenbrier management had actively encouraged this savings system as a substitute for a company pension, and posters on bulletin boards in the factory advertised the benefits of company-sponsored tax-free savings. The 401(k) plan was the only way for the workers to save enough money for retirement, to ensure that after a lifetime of hard work they would not have to suffer their old age in poverty. Some workers contributed up to 15 or 20 percent of their monthly wages, with the promise that their personal contributions were being matched by equal employer contributions. After the company went bankrupt, employees were astonished to learn that Greenbrier had never made the matching payments. Even worse, their own contributions had disappeared, considered Greenbrier assets and seized by the bank as part of the bankruptcy process. Workers watched helplessly as not only their livelihood but their entire savings disappeared.

After a couple of weeks, when it was clear that the plant was closed for good and the company had filed bankruptcy papers, the Greenbrier workers attended a meeting at which officials of various state agencies explained the guidelines for unemployment insurance and job training programs. Almost 300 people showed up, and after the government presentations, the workers held their own meeting. They compared notes and discovered that all the supervisors had promised they would be returning to work after the summer vacation. One by one, outraged workers stood up and told their stories, of unpaid hospital bills and disappeared 401(k) savings. The group became increasingly angry and discussed possible courses of action. Because the company had declared bankruptcy, no one was optimistic about the plant reopening anytime soon. Still, the workers felt sure that they had been wronged and that if they could bring the company's actions to public attention, they would at least get their back pay and benefits owed them.

At the meeting a woman pointed out that although the workers' bills had not been paid and many of their final paychecks had bounced, all of the managers and office staff were still working and being paid as usual. No one knew exactly what the managers and staff were doing, since the factory had been closed for several weeks and nothing was coming in or going out. But since the salaried managers received paychecks straight from corporate headquarters in New Jersey, they were on a different payroll system, which was still operating. It seemed grossly unfair to the meeting's attendees that managers continued to work while workers were on the streets with uncertain futures. Much of the workers' anger thus turned against the managers, and to a lesser extent against the corporate executives who had made the decision to keep them on. As the workers shared their stories and discussed the situation, they grew increasingly angry.

The group decided to set up a picket line around the building. The picketing had two goals: to force the company to confront the workers' demands, and to garner media attention for their plight. They decided on a picketing schedule of twice a week. They demanded that the company spend whatever money remained not on office staff in an empty factory, but on repaying its debts to the workers. They also decided to continue meeting every Thursday evening in the county courthouse to share information and make further plans.

The decision to picket was a spontaneous one, yet it was taken seriously. Over one hundred workers arrived the following Saturday morning, armed with angry picket signs, and led a lively parade in front of the factory. Local press showed up, and even the Knoxville newspaper and television stations took notice, for picket lines are an unusual sight in the Cumberland hills.

When the Greenbrier plant closing was covered in the Knoxville News-Sentinel, staff members at the Tennessee Industrial Renewal Network (TIRN) wanted to see if they could help. A coalition of labor, community, church, and environmental groups dedicated to organizing around economic issues such as plant closings, TIRN had been involved previously in helping laid-off workers in similar situations. TIRN sent a staff organizer, Bob Becker, to speak with the Greenbrier workers to see if they would be receptive to his assistance in planning strategies and educating people about their rights and opportunities. Becker attended an early meeting, and brought along two women from other plants who had lost their jobs when their sewing factories closed. They discussed with the group the hardship of surviving a plant closing, and filled them in on the various government programs and benefits available to them. The workers appreciated the women's empathy and support, and they were gratified to know that TIRN would commit organizational resources to their cause. Many stayed after the meeting for another hour to talk with the visitors, telling of their individual hardships, injuries, and financial worries.

Becker continued to attend Greenbrier meetings and even walked on their picket lines, for which the workers expressed their appreciation. He contacted lawyers, union directors, and consultants in Knoxville and around the country to get advice on how to begin addressing the workers' problems. He began to work more closely with the group who had been most vocal in the mass meetings. Becker's first goal was to establish a formal organization of workers that would be able to make decisions and act collectively. With Becker's encouragement, the group decided to call itself the Greenbrier Workers Committee (GWC), elected officers, and formally affiliated as a member organization of TIRN. They passed a hat at a meeting to collect the $25 required for official membership status.

In an early meeting, the laid-off workers had discussed possible strategies open to them. Their immediate goal was to secure the money they feared was lost: their final paychecks, health insurance, and pension savings—and perhaps some severance pay. Their initial attempts had been extremely frustrating. When they tried to get back the money they themselves had deposited in their 401(k) accounts, the workers were told to fill out some forms for the trustee. After some weeks they were notified that the paperwork was incorrect and that new forms had to be submitted. At one point it seemed their funds would eventually be released, but then that promise was rescinded. Bobbie Bishop described the futility of trying to track down her own money: "I talked to a gentleman and [he said] he has to go through the bankruptcy trustee before he can release the checks. But it sounds like a stall tactic to me. . . . This guy finally said he wasn't aware, you know, that it was our money, the employees' money. So he had turned it over to another lawyer, which he was supposed to check into. You know when you've got them on the phone like that, they'll tell you anything, to get you off the phone. So we're losers in every way you turn. I don't know what we can do . . . a lot of people were depending on that money for coal for the winter."[17]

Becker suggested the workers contact a lawyer to investigate the situation. Since the group had neither the experience nor the money to look for appropriate legal representation, Becker went back to Knoxville and made some calls. To the next GWC meeting, Becker brought a Knoxville attorney with experience in bankruptcies. The attorney, Jim Lefever, had done some preliminary research and had talked with the bankruptcy trustee in New Jersey to ascertain the status of the Greenbrier estate.

After hearing from the workers about their concerns and needs, Lefever presented the bad news. If he were in their shoes, he told them honestly, he would not spend the time and money either suing Greenbrier or following up on their claims. If the workers were to hire him, Lefever said, it would be prohibitively expensive, since it would require repeated trips to northern New Jersey, where the company was headquartered and where all of its records and the bankruptcy papers were filed. And the work was unlikely to pay off, since the bankruptcy was apparently complete. Greenbrier's individual owners, who reportedly had fled to South America, were protected by American incorporation laws. The company no longer existed, and the executives could not be held personally liable for the corporation's losses.

Becker, the attorneys, and others confirmed the workers' suspicions, informing them that Greenbrier had indeed violated federal law. The company had flagrantly violated the WARN Act, which requires firms to provide at least sixty days' notice before laying off any group of one hundred employees or more. Although the workers were clearly entitled to compensation, again the experts advised the workers not to pursue a lawsuit. A simple cost-benefit calculation demonstrated the folly of paying an attorney to sue a bankrupt company and its executives, who had moved to a different continent and would not have been liable anyway.

Many workers at the meeting resisted Lefever's conclusion. As they explained it, the goal of hiring an attorney would not be to win a large settlement but simply to hold Greenbrier accountable for its actions. As one worker said, "Somebody should be made to pay for all of this." [18] Accordingly, some wanted to explore ways of raising money to finance an investigation. They were anxious to prove management's wrongdoings and to prosecute the offenders.

Joanne James, a tall and articulate woman in her late thirties, had been a sewing machine operator for twelve years at the Health-Tex plant in rural Campbell County, and she had been shocked when that plant suddenly closed in 1990. [19] The personnel manager from Health-Tex, Ed Damiano, had been hired immediately at Greenbrier, and he persuaded a few of his best seamstresses to join him. James accepted the job and the thirty-mile commute, but always worried that her nightmare might repeat itself—and she had seen the early warning signs. Along with other workers, James was certain that mismanagement and fraud were to blame for the Greenbrier closing: "They knew probably two, three, four years ago that they were running into financial difficulties. There's no doubt in my mind that in this time frame, they started taking money and putting it in other companies, changing names, putting it in their own pockets. They really did. And if I had the time, if I had the money, I could prove this with Greenbrier. But I just don't have the money." [20]

All the workers expressed their rage and frustration at the company's behavior and their own sense of impotence. Ann Ritter, an ebullient woman with a loud laugh and a sharp sense of humor, described her outrage: "You know, they took our money. And apparently they'd been taking it a long time." [21] Bob Walker, a large soft-spoken man who worked in the shipping and loading dock, was awed by the imbalance of justice suddenly revealed: "It's like, you've let them steal everything you've got, and there's nothing you can do about it. But now if we—if you or I—go out here and steal something, they'll put us in jail. It's just not fair." [22]

But this tremendous sense of injustice and anger had no outlet. The workers could not dispute Lefever's conclusions, they could not pursue an investigation on their own, and they were forced to defer to his expertise. After the group had finally given up on the possibility of suing Greenbrier, some continued to look for other ways to fight rather than passively accept their fate. Ann Ritter went over to the Anderson County courthouse to see if she could take out a warrant for the plant manager's or the owner's arrest. "He's took money out of our checks and used it for his own." But criminal charges were not possible, she was told. "He's protected by the bankruptcy court." [23]

Most GWC members believed from the outset that if only public attention would bring the truth to light, someone would take action on their behalf. If the community was aware of the outrages perpetrated, if their elected representatives only knew the complete story, they would force the company to make restitution. Ritter described going home from the shut plant in shock and realizing that she had to do something about it. "I watched the news that night, and I thought, you know, this is a human interest story. And I just called them." The news media were interested, and after that "I called Channel 10 News every day. And I said there's something going on. . . . You're talking little town of Clinton, 500 people out of work. Oh, they'd run right out here, you know."[24] Energized by the early attention to their plight, the workers continued telling their stories to the press. They contacted the local weekly newspaper and local radio stations, and got ample coverage in the Clinton area. But the publicity produced no response from the company or elected officials.

Media interest waned quickly, and no one seemed either inclined or able to help the workers, so they attempted to attract political or legal attention. They called their senators and representatives, and contacted county and city executives, asking that an official investigation begin. A few women walked into the local district attorney's office and demanded criminal prosecution of Greenbrier executives. They did not get a meeting but were informed that, in the prosecutor's opinion, nothing could be done. Federal officials responded only by referring workers to the nearest job training and employment offices, and local officials claimed they had no power to intervene with the affairs of a company based in New Jersey. Ritter contacted the office of Tennessee Senator Jim Sasser, a Democrat whom she perceived as friendly to workers and concerned about rights violations. She spoke to the senator's aide in Nashville, who seemed interested and requested more information. Ritter "spent days" writing up everything she knew about the company and the plant closing, and sent it to the senator's office by express mail. Weeks later, having received no response, she left phone messages. Although she tried many times to reach that aide or someone in Sasser's office, she was unsuccessful. She never knew if anyone had read the report she sent.[25] Eventually Ritter gave up.

Other members of the group scheduled meetings with the city manager, county executive, congressional representatives, and other public officials. Bruce Mackrey and Bob Walker scheduled a meeting with their congressperson, Representative Marilyn Lloyd, but were disappointed when she told them she was not responsible for the Clinton district and could not help them. They then called their appropriate congressional representative, Jim Cooper. His office told Walker, " 'We'll get in contact with him and let you know.' I said, 'I want to know something one way or the other. My savings is gone. I want to put my daughter through college, and that's what my savings is for.' "[26] His plea received no response. The workers were sorely disappointed at the results of their efforts to contact politicians. The officials seemed to believe it was impossible to retrieve what Greenbrier owed them, and no one would help them try.

At a later meeting a group of workers reconvened and decided they should continue to try to raise awareness about their plight. They were still saddled with huge hospital bills—one was trying to pay off a $38,000 debt by paying $5 a month, which was all he could afford. They had received no word about their savings. They were still outraged and energetic, but after brainstorming awhile they could think of no real channels by which they could hope to effect positive changes. They decided to do a one-day picket at the county courthouse, to try one last time to move local officials to take up their case and at least investigate, preferably to advocate on behalf of the displaced workers. By then, only about ten workers showed up on the picket line. No city or county official even acknowledged their presence. There was a palpable sense that their cause had been lost and that further actions were unlikely and probably futile.

The picket lines and meetings continued, but as weeks went by, the ex-workers became increasingly demoralized. They had succeeded in getting the office staff out of the empty plant, but it was a hollow victory, winning only more layoffs. They had received no answers about the money due them. The media ceased to be interested in the old news of the plant closing, and politicians no longer returned their phone calls. Clinton's elected leaders seemed unconcerned about their predicament. When the displaced workers wanted to have meetings, they assumed the city government would let them use a room in the courthouse or the community center. They found an available room in the community center, but they were shocked to find that they had to pay $45 to use it. Ann Ritter explained their dismay: "There was 500 people in this city without jobs, and they wouldn't give us a discount or nothing. Forty-five dollars for a room. We had to pay it. We had a shoe box and had to pass it around. And there was lots of people there that couldn't even give a dollar; they didn't have it to give."[27] The workers were slowly learning that the "system" was stacked against them.

Slowly but surely the activists in the group began to lose hope. Some found new jobs, mostly paying less and requiring significant commutes. Many workers were forced to take on two or even three jobs to replace the lost one, and most had no time to continue protesting. When they went out looking for comparable jobs, the workers were surprised to find that the alternatives were mostly worse. Ritter found out about several other sewing factories in the region that were hiring, but none had tolerable working conditions. At the largest, where a few Greenbrier women got part-time jobs after the closing, she only lasted one day. She could not physically tolerate the lack of air conditioning. In Tennessee in the summer, she said, a garment factory without air was "worse than anything in the world. . . . You ain't seen hot." Eventually Ritter had to take on three jobs to replace her Greenbrier salary: sewing, waiting tables, and caring for an elderly woman in Oak Ridge, Tennessee, on weekends. At her sewing job she made $5 an hour, having received a raise from her initial pay rate of $4.50. She drove sixty-two miles each day from her home to the "factory," which was in the owner's house. She said that if Greenbrier opened back up, she would not hesitate to go back to her job there.

Her experience was typical. When the workers began searching for new employment, they experienced the downward mobility that so often characterized work in the 1990s. They could not find employment better than what they had lost. Most of those who accepted jobs at other sewing factories quickly learned to appreciate what they had at Greenbrier. Their new jobs, if they were lucky enough to find them, often started at minimum wage. For experienced workers, who were able to sew quickly for higher piece rates at Greenbrier, this meant accepting salaries considerably lower than they had been earning. Very few employers paid health insurance, according to personnel manager Ed Damiano. "Other than wages, the one thing that people lost that hurts the most is insurance. Because they can't afford insurance. [At Greenbrier] the family plan that we had would have cost over $500 a month." [28] Most available jobs offered no retirement benefits, or would require them to work for many years before qualifying for pensions, which presented a huge problem for older workers. Many had to commute for over an hour to minimum-wage jobs, which barely paid their gasoline bills. And their working conditions were often worse. Although the Greenbrier building had not been new or particularly well maintained, some workers moved to factories without air conditioning or proper ventilation. Others could not find factory work, and accepted work sewing at home, on their own machines, getting reimbursed by the piece. Most workers hoped that Greenbrier would reopen soon so that they could go back to their old jobs. [29]

Other workers were so demoralized by the experience at Greenbrier, it convinced them "to get out of the factory business." [30] Joanne James, unwilling to risk the possibility of yet another plant closing in the garment industry, asked state agency representatives about new career opportunities. They directed her to a job-training program where women were trained for positions as nurses' aides. She entered college, studying science and nursing. James was uncertain what jobs would be available when she finished the program; there were many more women in similar programs in East Tennessee than job openings for nurses' aides. Although many of the displaced workers were persuaded that training would win them good positions in the new high-tech, service-based economy of the future, in reality the women simply moved from one underpaid female-dominated profession to another. They saw that women faced particular economic burdens, although they would not name it as sex discrimination.

With new jobs, school, and mounting financial pressures, the workers could not devote much energy to the stalled effort to fight Greenbrier. The situation seemed hopeless. Many wanted the plant to reopen, and workers continued to get together, speculating about what might happen, and whether they would go back. But it seemed increasingly futile. By early December fewer than ten people came to a Thursday evening meeting, and it seemed unlikely that the group would continue to meet. They decided to hold one more meeting, in mid-January, to see if any progress had been made on tracking down their 401(k) and other funds, and to disband after that. The Greenbrier workers were devastated and bitter. In the end, the workers' sense of powerlessness was intensified rather than abated by their efforts to rectify the injustices of Greenbrier Industries. Hopelessness and despair won out when the workers determined that all the activity they could muster would have no effect on the material conditions of their lives.

Potential for Success

It is easy to understand the sense of helplessness and invisibility that led Greenbrier workers to despair, and eventually to abandon their struggle. And yet, the coming chapters will demonstrate that this outcome was not inevitable. The circumstances of the plant closing, the mobilization that occurred, and the workers' own interpretation of those events all demonstrate a wide range of alternative possibilities. Four factors in particular suggest that the Greenbrier plant closing could have led to a much more extensive, effective, and lasting mobilization. This is not to say that the workers could have succeeded in preventing the plant closing; that seems nearly impossible. Rather, this could have been a much more "successful" failure, a sustained organizing effort that could have generated important outcomes. At a minimum, a real mobilization effort could have educated the participants, involved them in political issues, and brought the workers together rather than dividing them. If the workers had been organized, it is also likely that they would have won back their pension and health benefits, and even severance pay, which they were legally due. Those would have been economically crucial, and the experience of a small victory could have paved the way for future efforts.

First, as many workers testified, there were some obvious early warning signs that the plant was in danger of closing. Many analysts of plant closings have emphasized the importance of early detection in preventing a shutdown.[31] The indications of trouble were abundant at Greenbrier, and workers knew better than anyone else what was happening with production, quality, contracts, and inputs. If workers had shared their knowledge with one another and strategized about a plan of action, it is possible that they could have fought the closing or at least received adequate notice and economic compensation. Bobbie Bishop, a department supervisor, had begun working at Greenbrier in 1979, when Carle and Howard Thier owned the plant. At that time, she says, "It was a well-run plant. It was running like a plant should be run." By contrast, she noticed, "The last two years it really was run like it was going under. . . . We started having all kinds of problems that we never had before. It really did seem like a dark cloud hung on top of us, and it didn't go away, just one thing after another. I knew—because I had worked in a plant seventeen years before I came there, so I know that kind of work—I could see the closing coming. A lot of our good employees did too. It was odd, everybody could sort of see it coming, and yet, they just sort of sat back and waited for it. I don't know why." [32] But there is a good reason why the workers hesitated. Before the plant closing, the workers were afraid of retaliation. If they had questioned the management on its business plans, individually or collectively, they would have been labeled troublemakers and punished or fired for speaking out.

Second, the plant closing represented a community-wide crisis in Clinton, because hundreds of jobs were gone and because so many families would suffer severe and unexpected economic repercussions. And the workers clearly had been wronged. Everyone, including the lawyers and the county officials, agreed that the company had acted in bad faith, reneged on important commitments, and broken the law in a variety of ways. Managers had literally stolen money from employees, in the form of final paychecks, health care premiums, and 401(k) investments. Criminal acts had taken place, and early legal advice could have alerted workers to this fact. The company had disregarded the WARN Act. It had apparently shifted equipment and materials to other plants before declaring bankruptcy. It had induced workers to lie about the origins of various products. Greenbrier and its predecessors had a long history of corruption, fraud, and abuse, if not outright criminal activity. The workers had on their side an invaluable organizing tool: justifiable rage. They were angry at the way they had been treated; their anger was legitimate; and they were willing to speak publicly about the wrongs that had been done to them.

Third, the immediate mobilization and activity that followed the Greenbrier plant closing was impressive. Apathy was not a problem. Large numbers got involved without any inducement: recognizing and naming the injustice done to them; asking the right people for help; attracting the attention of the community through effective use of the media; and using direct action such as pickets and protests to highlight the urgency of their plight. Although none of them had ever been involved in anything like this before, the workers were not scared to protest. In a quiet, rural, Southern town, this was a remarkable sign of the magnitude of the crisis the plant closing represented.[33]

Fourth was the leadership potential within the group itself. Several individuals demonstrated an obvious capacity to lead. One was Ann Ritter, who was influential early on in deciding to set up picket lines and to attract media attention. Ritter took a very visible leadership role in the protests: "I said, I don't care who gets mad at me—and they were mad at me—but I was no better than any of those people, you know, and what happened to them ain't right . . . My friend that works for the city of Clinton, he said, 'Give 'em hell, give 'em hell.' You know, if you don't stand up for what you believe in, there's nobody else ain't gonna do it for you."[34] Ritter had obviously been a leader even before the plant closing put her into the spotlight. She was respected by her co-workers and willing to put herself on the line for the group. "I've always been forward anyway, and I say what I'm thinking." Besides being press spokesperson, picket captain, and government lobbyist, Ritter also acted as personal counselor to her co-workers. "That first month my phone rung from morning till night. It didn't quit. People that worked at the plant, that I knew, but never even really had nothing to do with: "I'm so-and-so, do you remember me? What's going on?" People were scared to death. . . . I was a supervisor and I led those people. I mean, I was supposed to be somebody they looked up to. I was supposed to have the answers to their questions. A lot of people didn't even feel like they worked for Greenbrier, they felt like they worked for you."[35] Ritter stood up to the owners, the bank, politicians, and local agencies. She took on battles over unemployment compensation denied; cars and homes repossessed; personal bankruptcies; people trying to pay off $38,000 hospital bills at the rate of $5 a month, and more. Other workers exemplified different models of leadership. Many workers mentioned Mackrey, Walker, Bishop, James, and others as individuals they respected and looked up to.[36] All of these workers were articulate and assertive. If they had worked collectively as a group with a sense of purpose and vision, with some guidance on possible courses of action, they could have launched a campaign with far-reaching results.

Explaining Failure

Although the workers turned out in impressive numbers for the early meetings and picket lines, displaying initiative and rage, this early initiative died down rather quickly. Protest could not be sustained. Anger and outrage turned into bitterness, pessimism, and hopelessness—rather than into righteous intensity, protest activity, and mobilization. Although there was a precipitating crisis, intense interest within the affected community, and clear legal and moral violations to be addressed, nothing resembling a social-movement organization emerged.

Some of the reasons for the GWC's failure to emerge as a force for change or as a lasting community organization are obvious. As research on social movements correctly predicts, for example, the lack of resources presented a huge barrier to mobilization.[37] The Greenbrier employees were low-income workers scattered over several counties of East Tennessee. Many of the workers lived in trailers in rural Appalachian counties, and did not even have telephones in their homes, making it difficult to mobilize for any type of activity. Once the plant had closed, they had no obvious system for communicating with one another and making plans. Many lived with relatives and were responsible for taking care of children, elderly, or disabled family members on a daily basis. Some took on home work, sewing for low piece rates. Others became overwhelmed with new jobs. No one had extra income or leisure time to spend on what was likely to be a losing political battle.

Financial resources were also lacking. The workers could not afford to rent meeting space, send faxes to the media, make picket signs, do research, or hire attorneys to investigate Greenbrier and win settlements. No one had the skills or the connections to attract resources from outside the relatively poor Clinton community. Unlike other workers' organizations, particularly affiliates of national labor unions, they had no access to consultants or groups with expertise on plant closings. They had no connections with unions or other labor organizations, which could have represented the workers in the bankruptcy proceedings. They did not have contacts in state politics or in the media who could help keep pressure on elected officials. All of this made it impossible to mount a large-scale campaign to fight Greenbrier's illegal actions or to push for more responsible economic development policies in East Tennessee.

The importance of a minimum level of resources was painfully evident in the very early stages of organization, when workers met to discuss possible courses of action. The group wanted to gather information about their options and about Greenbrier's financial situation. They wanted to call the Internal Revenue Service to find out if the taxes taken out of their paychecks had been paid, and if not, who was liable for the debts. They wanted to contact the bankruptcy trustee in New Jersey to find out what was left in the Greenbrier corporate estate, who had claims upon it, and the level of priority of workers' claims. They thought about tracking down the plant manager and the owners, whom some of them had known personally, to find them in South America and challenge their actions. They wanted to research Greenbrier's other plants and corporate affiliations, both within Tennessee and in other countries. If they could document the close connections they knew existed between companies, they could show that Greenbrier was part of a larger firm that was still extremely profitable and could be held liable for everything they were owed. In the end, none of this research was possible because the workers did not have the money for it—not even for a series of follow-up phone calls to the trustee in New Jersey. Organizing to fight corporate decisions in the global economy is nearly impossible without even enough money for long-distance phone calls.

Other, less tangible factors were no less essential. There was no tradition of community organizing or mobilization in Clinton. There were no other community-based organizations or groups that had been active in politics or in self-help activities. There were no socially active networks and no strong unions in town. The lack of an organizational history, tradition, or culture among workers and community members—and the failure to make strong connections with a group that had the knowledge and expertise—made it nearly impossible to start up a group successfully in a time of crisis and uncertainty.

TIRN, based in Knoxville, was the one organization that offered help, sympathy, and advice to the GWC. The Greenbrier workers greatly appreciated their moral support and shared outrage. The endorsement of an established statewide organization strengthened their resolve and seems to have sustained GWC activity over difficult months. In some ways, however, TIRN's intervention in the Greenbrier situation was actually experienced as disempowering. Despite its good intentions, TIRN's ability to bring in attorneys and other "experts" reinforced the workers' assumption that they themselves were powerless to affect the results of Greenbrier's actions or the Clinton economy.[38]

The attorney who came to speak to the GWC acted as an expert and an advisor, and he focused his comments on the viability of a lawsuit and the possibility of recovering money. Lefever used a rough cost-benefit economic analysis to assess possible action. Obviously, since the company was bankrupt, it was not cost-effective to pay lawyers to pursue something that would never pay off. This was the same advice the GWC had received from local politicians. All the experts treated the company's decision to close as an economic one. They also assumed the workers would base their decision to fight it on a "rational" economic calculus.

Political officials, attorneys, and even TIRN leaders therefore advised the workers that it would be irrational to sue a bankrupt company. But the workers themselves had concerns other than retrieving money. These concerns came out clearly in their interviews, and would have been obvious to any organizer interested in helping the group achieve its own goals. As Joanne James said, "It wasn't the money that we wanted. I think we would have been satisfied with an apology." [39] "I'll be satisfied—and I think most of them would have been—if they could get those doctor and hospital bills paid," said Bobbie Bishop. "Even though I didn't owe any." [40] Seeing justice done was almost more important than their material self-interest.

To maintain their dignity and sense of justice, the workers wanted a public hearing of their case against the Greenbrier management who had betrayed them. They believed strongly that they knew what had been done wrong, and they had received official confirmation that the company's actions were clearly illegal. To be told by all the experts— even those who were ostensibly on the workers' side—that they should do nothing felt like a further betrayal. TIRN's help unintentionally added to the workers' disempowerment. Another expert—an accountant married to one of the laid-off workers—was brought to a subsequent GWC meeting to provide the workers with information about their lost 401(k) savings. He presented his research to the workers. He concluded that while there were several technical avenues that he would continue to pursue, it seemed unlikely that anyone would see his or her retirement money. The workers listened silently to his presentation and accepted his advice: wait and see. Let the bankers, lawyers, judges, and accountants do their work; they will notify you with the results.

The point here is not that experts have no place in a struggle. The question is the appropriate role of expertise and professional advice in political organizing. It is one thing to allow experts to dictate the course of action, as the Greenbrier group did. It is very different to encourage the group to consider its own options, and to use expert information to apprise a group of available possibilities. In this case, the dominance of experts, especially those with legal or economic training, mainly convinced the workers that what they knew and what they wanted was unimportant and impractical compared to the experts' knowledge.

In contrast to the meetings led by experts, both of which resulted in quiescence and discouragement, at one meeting the workers themselves brainstormed possible courses of action. They considered holding a sit-in at the offices of local officials until someone agreed to discuss with them the county's response. They considered further mass actions, including mass picket lines or demonstrations. Trying to narrow down the issues they would address, the group eventually focused on the huge hospitalization bills facing some of them. One ex-worker, Jimmy, captured the attention and sympathy of the group. Jimmy admitted that he could not pay a $30,000 outstanding bill from his daughter's surgery—a bill he had assumed would be covered by the payments he had made regularly for health insurance but that Greenbrier had neglected to cover. Jimmy was going to be brought to court, and the Oak Ridge Hospital would then begin to deduct payments from his unemployment checks.

Another worker, outraged that the burden was now on the formerly insured worker to pay for Greenbrier's fraud, suggested a plan. The bills they all owed were rightfully the company's responsibility, for Greenbrier had promised the workers coverage in return for the high premiums they paid. If the hospital wanted its money, she argued, it should "get in line and wait" for its share of the estate when the Greenbrier bankruptcy was settled—just as the workers were waiting. When Jimmy came before the judge, she proposed, 400 of his fellow laid-off workers should come with him as support and to show the court: "This is not just about Jimmy. This is about all of us."[41] She received resounding support from the assembled workers; some suggested they march directly to the hospital, and hold a sit-in or a press conference to demand debt forgiveness for all Greenbrier workers. The group was excited about the possibilities for action.

But the TIRN staff member believed their plans to be unnecessarily confrontational, and therefore discouraged workers. Again using an implicit cost-benefit analysis, he suggested that the proposal was too risky and time-consuming, and unlikely to result in the desired benefit. Afraid of leading them into a strategy that could turn out to be a failure, Becker urged more patience. He encouraged the workers to rely upon the advice of experts rather than act collectively on what they knew. The workers never marched into the courtroom or had their sit-in at the hospital. They believed the experts: they would never accomplish their goals.

Although it was intended to protect the workers, the experts' calculus was not ultimately in the workers' best interest. Becker minimized the number of meetings, assuming that workers' time was valuable and scarce. He did many tasks himself rather than ask anyone else to take care of them. But the workers reported that they liked to meet, that they would rather have more opportunities to work together, and that they appreciated having jobs to do and ownership over their campaign. As Bishop said about the meetings, "People could get their frustrations out. . . . Not a whole lot happened . . . but I still think they did some good." She mentioned the task of filling out reports for the bankruptcy court, which had occupied the workers for several weeks after the closing. "Whether it does any good or not, at least you feel like you did something."[42] After the shock of losing their jobs, the workers' sense of efficacy was fragile. The ability to act, and to be supported by others in their same situation, was comforting and even empowering.

Another factor contributed to Becker's aversion to the proposed strategy: apprehension around his leadership role. When suggestions such as the hospital sit-in were made, Becker was reluctant to endorse them or even to discuss them unless there was absolute consensus among the group. After an action was proposed, Becker typically asked if anyone at all would like to disagree with the idea, and he repeated the question until someone spoke up or expressed reservations. At that point Becker seized upon the objections and urged the group to explore them further. When the idea proved divisive, it was dropped. Becker was trying to be democratic and collective, believing that consensus was necessary for a successful action. But underlying this dynamic is an ideological hesitance about leadership roles. Becker ended up validating people's fears rather than helping them overcome their concerns and act. Those most timid and hesitant imposed their will on the entire group. This was no more democratic and egalitarian than accepting leadership from those with confidence and ideas about how to win.

Many of the workers had better instincts. They reacted positively to the idea of a demonstration at the hospital because they had done a similar thing just after the plant closed. A young woman came to the picket line in tears because her doctor had notified her that he had not received payment for services previously rendered, and she did not have the money to give him. The group of women picketing at that moment, outside the empty building, suggested to their distraught co-worker that they all march right over to the doctor's office, explain the situation to him, and demand that he either write off the charges as indigent care or wait for the Greenbrier bankruptcy settlement to come through before forcing the woman to pay. They did so, and the physician agreed to their demand. Their action was successful, and it gave the women a sense of power, which led them to suggest a similar plan when the problem came up again. But Jimmy had no such luck, for the workers were dissuaded from acting collectively on their own behalf. The young woman's example indicates that the cost-benefit analysis used by Becker may have been wrong—when the workers felt inspired and acted together for themselves, the result had been successful by every measure, even by a purely rational economic calculus.

Failing to Organize

The GWC, isolated and overwhelmed, failed to create a permanent structure and vehicle for collective action. But it also failed to provide something even more basic and potentially transformative for the workers involved—an alternative analysis of their situation. With no apparent options, the Greenbrier workers were forced to accept the experts' simple analysis: a company had declared bankruptcy, and there was no recourse. Their solution? Give up. There was nothing to be gained from fighting the inevitable. Because there was no analysis of politics, the economy, or power—but instead a reliance on experts and technical solutions—the Greenbrier Workers Committee became an example of a "failed failure." It did not succeed in the most basic goals of political mobilization, which other failed organizing efforts achieve. It was not a social-movement organization in its early stages, facing huge barriers but still demonstrating the potential eventually to grow into a real political struggle. Rather, it was an effort that could have become a proto-movement, but did not.[43] The failure of the GWC caused the Greenbrier workers, angry and wronged, to turn their rage against the obvious targets: themselves, each other, the supervisors and the plant managers who had made mistakes, lied, or otherwise misbehaved and let them down. For nearly all of the workers, the analysis ended there. They understood their situation as a highly personalized betrayal of trust. No change in consciousness or culture resulted. Despite a huge and painful upheaval in their lives, the status quo was reaffirmed.

Outsiders would be surprised how the loss of Greenbrier devastated the workers. Objectively the work seemed less than desirable, and local political leaders did not mourn the loss of such "bad jobs." Besides being difficult, extremely tedious, repetitive, and very low-paying, work at Greenbrier was dangerous and physically taxing. Injury rates—including carpal tunnel syndrome, nerve damage, severed fingers, lung problems from lint dust and poor ventilation, and back injuries—were astronomically high.[44] Nevertheless, workers attested to loving their jobs and finding the work challenging and personally rewarding. Ritter had moved from a line position as a sewing machine operator to jobs in the cutting room, quality control, training department, inspection, and finally a supervisor. "Here I just learned. I learned the cutting procedures, how they cut things, and patterns, and how all that works. . . . I just learned so many things, I just loved it."[45]

The women who sat together every day on the assembly lines grew to know each other well and care deeply about each other. Until the closing they had great respect for one another's work and dedication to the job. Nearly all talked about how terribly they would miss their co-workers, and about the close relationships they had formed at work.[46] Bishop, a supervisor of about sixty sewing machine operators and seam inspectors, recalled, "You would work with your operators, train the new girls, work with them some. . . . You listened to their problems. We had a lot of personal problems, maybe problems with their husband, or their children. You run into a lot of problems where the women didn't have a husband, or they were pregnant. You listened to them, you done what you could."[47]

Margaret Jones never expected to stay in the sewing industry for so many years, enduring "crippling" work and low pay. "I just liked working with the girls. . . . I'm kind of hoping that something will come back over here [and open a sewing factory in the old plant], so I can come back."[48]

Most workers felt extremely loyal to the company and proud of their product. Workers who were around in the early 1990s during the Gulf War, for example, talked about the hard work and exhaustion, the unpredictability of their schedules, and the sheer overwhelming volume of material waiting to be assembled. But they also spoke with pride of their dedication and commitment to the shared project that was Greenbrier Industries. Like most industrial manufacturing workers, they were proud of the actual goods that they produced. They enjoyed describing their products and production processes in great detail. They used high-quality materials and produced strong and durable apparel.

The Greenbier workers showed unusual dedication. Louise Gessing and Lois Palmer described walking out to their cars in the parking lot, exhausted after a grueling sixteen-hour double shift, only to find the floor supervisor running after them, imploring them to stay for one more shift. They could not refuse.[49] At times, managers had everyone working long overtime hours for days on end. Workers slept on cots while others ran their sewing machines. Like a modern version of Rosie the Riveter, they were excited about doing their part for the wartime effort, and felt good about creating the goods—tents, parkas, bulletproof vests, camouflage suits—that would protect American soldiers in the Gulf. Caught up in the spirit of urgency, some workers even agreed to do extra tasks and to work overtime hours without pay. They saw it as a favor to managers and as their own contribution to the group effort. "We made bulletproof vests, 'frag vests.' You've seen it on TV, the Marines wear them . . . these camouflage vests. We made a cold-weather parka—I worked on that—and a coverall, and a dress raincoat, and helmets. All of this was military contracts."[50]

Even in quieter times the workers considered both management and workers to be integral parts of the Greenbrier "family." This was a traditional family, one in which the authority of the parental figures—the owners—was never challenged. "We didn't question them. We thought everything they were doing was right."[51] The company encouraged this family atmosphere, acting as the generous parent to its employees. "They had parties, showed everyone a good time. They had Christmas parties for the employees, they bought lots of gifts for the kids."[52] In return for their efforts under harsh working conditions and low compensation, the workers believed, the affection and respect of the plant managers was their best reward.

The plant closing was therefore experienced as a terrible shock and a personal betrayal. Ritter described her very last encounter with the plant manager: "The day that we left for vacation, I went to Virginia Beach, and I went into my boss's office, which was the plant manager, and I said, 'you going away on vacation?' and he says, 'Yeah, I'm going camping.' I said, 'Well, you guys'—him and Gail, his wife—'You all have a good one.' And he said, 'Yeah, you too, Ann, we'll see you when you get back.' And I told him that we was having problems with the bags. And he said, 'We're going to get our bags straightened out and we're going to roll them out of here.' And I said, 'I'm ready.' . . . There was never a clue that we ain't coming back to work."[53]

Bob Walker, who worked on maintenance and security for eighteen years at Greenbrier, described his deep loyalty to the plant manager: "He was like a father to me . . . I would have done *anything* for him, really. I was always a company person. . . . I cared about the place and wanted to see it grow." In fact, after being seriously injured on the job several years ago, Walker decided not to file a workers' compensation claim or to ask for sick pay. "No pay, no workmen's comp, or anything. . . . I felt at the time that it would just hurt the company."[54] Walker believed in the company's rhetoric of family and personal loyalty. He went out of his way to help and support the managers, and expected they would do the same if asked. Like the other workers, Walker was astonished to learn that the managers did not have equal respect for him.

The plant closing changed the way workers saw their roles in the firm. Bruce Mackrey, who had been close friends with the plant manager and often did personal favors for him without compensation, later regretted his relationship with Hetzel. "He was the type of guy that would . . . cut your throat behind your back." In hindsight he blamed Hetzel for the closing. Mackrey, who had been at Greenbrier for twenty-two years, moving with the company from Knoxville to Huntsville to Clinton, suffered a serious heart attack right after the plant closing and could work no longer. He says about the whole experience, quite literally, "it made me sick." [55] Thus most workers personalized their blame and anger, and expressed their sense of extreme betrayal by the plant managers who had been like parents to them. "We knew they was in trouble. We were not surprised they were going to close. We were just surprised at how they treated us. That it was done so dirty." [56] Joanne James elaborated: "I think it wouldn't have bothered any of us near as bad if they had said, 'Hey, we don't have a job for you anymore, we don't have your 401(k), we don't have this.' But they didn't say anything. And that's what bothers you so bad. It is terrible. And it takes a long time to get over that. Because you have the devastation of being without employment, you know, just the financial aspects of it, you have no health insurance, but then you have to deal with being treated that way. And that, for me, has been the hardest part. I'm not over that yet. Because I feel like somebody that they had no respect for whatsoever. And that has been very difficult for me." [57]

As is common in plant closings, the blow to workers' self-esteem and confidence had repercussions in both their work and personal lives. Ritter took a job at a tiny sewing factory near Knoxville, and although she likes the work, she will not trust anyone. "They're all liars. . . . What guarantee do I have that the company I work for is paying my income tax? And then you think, what guarantee do I have that I'm working for who they say I'm working for? Especially in a place like this, you don't know who you're working for." She says this feeling has carried over into her personal relationships; people who treat her well remind her of the plant manager, who was so good to her and then betrayed her. The lies and the closing itself were a huge blow to her self-respect. Before it happened, "I cared about my job. I tried to always do the best I could do and be as fair as I could be with people. I felt like I *was* the company; they were paying me to do what I seen best to do." Now, she says, "I feel like I was nothing." [58]

The Greenbrier workers' tendency to place blame on individuals, and themselves, reflects the lack of a broader analysis in which to understand the plant closing. The workers are unanimous in their view that bad management caused the closing. And there is ample evidence for this theory. Some blame the plant supervisors and personnel managers; others place fault with upper management and owners in New Jersey. Some, in retrospect, believe their bosses to have been devious and manipulative; others guess that they were merely incompetent and lost money by planning and running the factory poorly. The workers had observed the production system closely, and could identify numerous flaws in the process, as well as poor attitude and poor decisions on the part of managers and supervisors trying to cut corners. They believed that fraud and corruption had played a part in the Greenbrier debacle, in the final year if not for much longer. Managers had clearly lied to the employees about many things.

The workers believed that the plant was profitable, efficient, and productive, and that it closed unnecessarily. Many believed that disinvestment must have been intentional: "It could've been a plan to go down." [59] The workers knew that Abe Silvershatz, the owner, had been shifting machinery and materials between a number of plants with different, but interlocked, ownership. This included plants in South America, Israel, and Europe. Some of the workers had become friends with managers, and they had helped load machinery from Greenbrier onto trucks bound for other plants in Tennessee. "We had to go to Maryville to work on their machines, and go to Sparta to work on theirs. . . . The mechanics did that. When they got something that they couldn't fix, the president called here and sent two of us down there."[60] There was obviously a close connection between Greenbrier and a number of other establishments, both locally and internationally. The workers knew that the owners had gone to South America to continue producing outerwear. "It's unbelievable that they were allowed to get away with it."[61] Bruce Mackrey explains the plant closing: "They had some bad supervisors on the floor. . . . [They would] act like they was doing their job and they wasn't. . . . I feel that we would have still been in business if we'd had a little better management."[62]

The workers were correct in their assessments of mismanagement and fraud, but their analysis stopped there. Although Greenbrier Industries had survived entirely on government contracts and every worker worked closely with government-employed inspectors overseeing every aspect of their production, the workers did not hold the Defense Department or the government responsible for what happened. Mackrey says, "I don't think they contributed to it."[63] The workers did not consider themselves employed by the government, although every garment they assembled was bought directly by the federal government. They had no response when asked about the role of the state in the plant's troubles or its closing. When asked if she holds the government responsible for anything, Bobbie Bishop answered, "No. We should've been able to change with the times."[64] Some seemed unwilling even to consider alternative ways of thinking about the situation: "You can't figure it out really. It just closed."[65]

All they would ask the government to do differently is to punish the "thieves"—the corporate officials who took their savings and health premiums without providing the promised benefits. This attitude corresponded to the workers' individualized and narrow understanding of the crisis at Greenbrier, which was never challenged by the organizers from TIRN. None of the workers had ever been involved in political campaigns or issues, and many had never even voted. The plant closure and their elected officials' inefficacy only reinforced a very old and deep-seated sense of powerlessness, and a belief that the political system is ultimately unresponsive and stacked against them.

Many fired workers blamed their co-workers. One supervisor attributed the closing to the high turnover rates, which compromised both efficiency and product quality: "I really don't know why we had such a turnover. . . . When I first started to work, you wouldn't have any turnover. . . . People worked every day." She blamed the workers and their "poor work habits." "People don't take any more pride in their work. They're really not that ambitious, you know . . . especially young people. I guess they're spoiled, probably. I think a lot of them are satisfied with welfare and that kind of help." [66]

Workers and supervisors also blamed other workers for submitting excessive workers' compensation claims—even while acknowledging that work-related injuries were rampant.[67] When asked who should bear the costs of workplace injuries, many workers blamed other workers for lying and cheating. For example, "I don't think it was all injuries. People took advantage of it. A lot of it was carpal tunnel, which I never heard of until 1985. . . . I wonder what happened to all those ladies who were working for fifty years before that time." [68] Bishop has similar suspicions: "I'm not saying all of them, because some of them were legitimate . . . but it got so that you could say your wrist was hurting, or your back or something, and most of the time the company doctor [who had to verify all workplace injuries] was on their side. . . . It was abused." When asked for specific cases, she could think of no concrete examples of fraud.[69] But she was angry and hurt, and her co-workers seemed a legitimate target. Bishop was typical in this regard; even after the hardship foisted upon them by the company, the workers often blamed one another for hurting Greenbrier.

Some workers cited the problem of drug use at Greenbrier as a reason for the high turnover and poor quality of work in recent years, although again, no one provided evidence.[70] Greenbrier workers expressed contempt for minority groups, single mothers, and welfare recipients. Ed Damiano expressed typical sentiments about African Americans. "Greenbrier Industries was, you know, a government contractor, so you've got to have an affirmative action [program]. . . . We're an affirmative action company, we hire minority and handicaps. . . . And I made every effort to hire blacks."[71] "I hired some good black people, really, they would've made great employees. But I couldn't keep 'em." When asked why, he did not hesitate, "Welfare." The availability of public assistance, he says, "penalizes people for working, and they quit. . . . They didn't have any initiative, they just didn't. They were in this little rut here and they just didn't want to get out. No, it didn't make no sense. . . . They wouldn't give themselves a chance."[72]

The Greenbrier workers also have very traditional ideas about gender-based divisions of labor. Bobbie Bishop's analysis reveals views similar to those found in the public relations materials for Latin American or Asian free-trade zones. They accepted biological explanations for industrial segregation. Men can't sew: "They don't have the knack for it. You know, it takes a certain type to handle sewing machines; some of those machines are hard to run. And women are better at it. You need good hand movement, mostly. A lot of it is tedious work too. Men's hands are bigger and it makes it harder for them, I think. . . . The men carried work, they were the service person, our shipping and receiving was men."[73]

Like most of the women, Joanne James had never considered questioning the fact that, in all of the factories she had seen, only women worked as sewing machine operators. But when asked why she thought it was this way, she had a ready answer: "They're lower-paying jobs. I think men would feel that type of job is beneath them. I think men have been geared to probably holding themselves a little bit higher than women—and I think these *are* menial jobs. They don't pay anything."[74] Even Bishop acknowledged, "Men don't want to do that work. . . . They'd think it was sissy, or whatever. . . . The men made better money, I think, than some of the women did." Unlike women, if men didn't want to do the tedious assembly work, they could do other work. Back on the job market, the women knew they were facing a poor set of choices.[75]

Single mothers also received blame for Greenbrier's problems: "You have to put up with a lot from them. . . . A lot of them come in that's not married, got two or three kids. . . . If they got a gripe, you gotta listen to them; they come in mad in the morning, you try to soothe them down, because if they're mad, they're not going to sew." Mackrey seems to blame the workers for their troubles and even their poverty: "You can walk out in the parking lot, and you see junky cars." He faults Damiano for "hiring [people] off the street."[76]

Bobbie Bishop argued that Greenbrier's problems started with the new managers hiring the wrong type of people: "They started hiring just anyone."[77] There is a racial or ethnic implication in this statement, but also a class distinction. Bishop and the others believed themselves to be "working class" or "middle class" and thus far above a social sector they would describe as "lower class." They made this distinction as if it were obvious and indisputable, although in reality it would be extremely hard to define. As the workers themselves knew, people on welfare often earned more than they could earn at the factory. Even most full-time workers earned wages that placed their families considerably below the poverty line. Yet nearly all the workers disparaged people who receive welfare benefits. Of course, this perspective is not unique to the Greenbrier workers or to Southern white workers. White workers under capitalism had always found incentives to stigmatize African Americans. As Roediger says, "The white working class, disciplined and made anxious by fear of dependency . . . constructed an image of the

Black population as 'other'—as embodying the preindustrial, erotic, careless style of life the white worker hated and longed for." [78]

The workers' contempt for people on welfare, usually racially coded, was especially intense. It was also ironic, since everyone knew that Greenbrier wages were so low that many women who worked at the factory still had to accept welfare benefits in order to support their children. Even Bishop acknowledged, "A lot of them drawed welfare and worked. And they got more if they drawed welfare than if they worked." [79] And after many months without work, many more Greenbrier employees were forced to apply for food stamps, housing assistance, energy assistance, and other welfare programs. If they themselves had not, every worker knew someone who had been on welfare for a time, either while working or after the plant closing. They did not seem to blame their friends and relatives who needed it. Still, these same workers claimed to be absolutely "against" welfare, and frequently derided people who received welfare or relied on government subsidies of any type, seeing themselves as fundamentally "different." The Greenbrier workers believed that unlike other recipients of aid, they were more than willing to work. They saw themselves only as down on their luck, victims of sudden misfortune rather than structural realities of the political economy. [80]

Indeed, the welfare system was a favorite target of the Greenbrier employees in the aftermath of the plant closing. When asked what was wrong with the government or politicians, they seemed to forget their most immediate experience, which had been one of attempting to influence officials to act in a situation of clear injustice, to no avail. Instead they focused on the evils of welfare—a program that had not hurt them in any apparent way, as other public policies had. They recited a litany of anecdotes about perfectly capable, able individuals they knew who were receiving public assistance through fraud or deceit. One worker even reported that "some of them was into thieving and stuff. You feel sorry for them, but if you let it get to you, it takes its toll on you." [81] It is not clear who "they" are, but the workers all identify some problematic group different from themselves. These "other" people were often said to be living better than the hardworking Greenbrier employees and their friends and families. They were lazy or immoral, yet they were successful. This was an untenable situation to the workers, for it violated strongly held norms of justice and merit.

Their commitment to values of individual effort and self-reliance (even after those values had failed them in many ways), is also evident in the Greenbrier workers' attitudes toward unions and collective action. Greenbrier's managers and owners had been vocally anti-union, and had communicated their feelings to the workers. When there had been talk of unionizing, in the early 1970s, management had made it clear that they would go "all out to fight it." [82] Like many Southern factory owners, they argued that the workers were treated well and did not need a union, and that an "outside" union would disrupt the Greenbrier "family." [83] The plant owners told workers bluntly that if they unionized, the owners would surely close the plant. They had done this before, they claimed, when they had faced unionization attempts in other locations. They would rather move the entire plant than be forced to negotiate with a union. Workers believed the owners were serious about this threat. "It was a known fact that they wouldn't tolerate a union, that they would close down if a union came in." [84]

Bobbie Bishop explained that although she was not ideologically sympathetic to unions, she would make an exception in the case of Greenbrier. "I guess a union may have been the best thing—it may have handled some of the problems that we had with employees, problems with discipline, things like that. . . . In our situation, I'd say a union would have helped more than it hurt—the company, not the employees. 'Cause it had gotten to the point where the employees had . . . no one to stand up to them." [85] The Greenbrier workers remained firmly committed to traditional hierarchies and belief systems. The role of unions, like the role of government, was primarily to punish people who broke the rules, and thereby to restore order. This seemed to be their only solace in a world that was otherwise disintegrating around them.

The Greenbrier workers present many apparent contradictions on the subject of labor unions. Joanne James had worked in a unionized plant, and on the one hand she saw clear differences between organized and unorganized workplaces. In addition to better pay, benefits, and insurance, the contrast was apparent in "just the way you were treated. The working conditions were better. Just basic cleanliness, for one thing. Basic cleanliness, safety measures. Over at Greenbrier we worked with the floor falling in. We worked with the ceiling leaking water on the electrical machines. Just safety was better with the union. . . . It's just a fact that it really was." Wages were also higher, and processes fair and well established. Despite all the evidence, however, James was not pro-union. Her old, anti-union ideology remained strong, for although her experience had changed dramatically, no new analysis had replaced the old. "I'm not especially for unions, you know. I don't think a unionized [shop] is the answer. . . . Had Greenbrier been under union contract, there would have been a lot of things they couldn't have gotten away with. Oh yeah, it would have helped. But I don't necessarily think that a union is the answer to everything. I think the employees could accomplish things on their own."[86] James was vehement in this last assertion, even though it was directly contradicted by her own experience and her previous statements about that experience.[87]

These explanations are particularly striking when compared with the experiences of displaced workers in the next two case studies. Those who had participated in a significant and sustained struggle, worked on organizing drives, and engaged in campaigns in solidarity with other groups had a very different analysis. Most important, they could articulate some analysis of power relations, in the workplace, in their community, and in the nation as a whole. They could state their reasons for voting a certain way, or for supporting a particular political party or program. By contrast, most of the Greenbrier workers had no party affiliation and few ideas about political issues or candidates. Bobbie Bishop said she had voted Democratic in the last election—in this respect she was in the minority—but when asked why, she admitted, "Well, you know, it's probably who makes the best speeches, I guess, or who looks best on TV." [88]

The Greenbrier workers also had confusing ideas on the subject of NAFTA, unlike the workers who had been through the other plant closings. [89] Bruce Mackrey discussed Greenbrier's international dealings in detail, and speculated that they were making money by farming out production tasks to different countries. "They come around and say that they're doing us a favor by trade agreements, [but] I don't believe it." But his reasons for this opinion did not relate to the outsourcing he had seen at Greenbrier. Mackrey said, "The only thing that I can see coming out of that trade agreement is we're going to be flooded with people coming over here, more than what we've got now. . . . They'll come over here and work for nothing." [90] Immigration was seen as a bigger threat than more lost jobs. Bobbie Bishop similarly expressed contradictory opinions about NAFTA. She first said, "I don't think it hurt us, it may help us in the long run." But in the same breath, she went on to express the opposite view: "When they make products in another country, they should pay dearly when they bring it back into the United States to sell. . . . That would be fair, if they got cheaper labor." [91] This type of contradiction characterized the Greenbrier employees, and differentiated them strikingly from the groups who participated in the more organized struggles around plant closings.

One of the most important deficiencies of the Greenbrier organizing effort, therefore, was the absence of broader political analysis. An alternative analysis would have situated the events in Clinton in a context of national and international political economy. It would have placed the action of the plant managers and even owners within a system of economic pressures and political forces, showing the workers that concrete decisions were made, but without demonizing or personalizing the individuals responsible. In addition, a contextualized political analysis would have identified the agents responsible for the workers' plight— including the government agencies and corporate executives—and demonstrated to workers that their situation had historical roots, but new complexities because of hypermobility of capital and the new international political context. Finally, leaders could have shown the workers that their individual powerlessness was not essential, but could be changed through collective action.

Because of the lack of a broader analysis, the workers continued to believe in ideologies that did not reflect the facts of their situation, and were counter to their own interests. They also became confused, depressed, unsure of themselves, and disgusted with everyone else. This demoralization had concrete political consequences. The workers lost faith in the politicians they had elected but also in the larger system: the political and judicial systems that would not consider their interests nor give them a hearing; the media that tired of their story after a single day of picketing; the community leaders who seemed more loyal to business leaders than to the people. The plant closing and surrounding circumstances convinced most workers of what they had already suspected: that politicians do not care about people like themselves and that the simple rules of justice do not apply to those in power. The workers who had tried to contact politicians for help were bitterly disappointed and said they would not attempt to influence them, or even vote, again. As Margaret Jones said, "It wouldn't do me no good, they'll just do what they want to. . . . I feel it really wouldn't make any difference." [92]

This extreme sense of disempowerment, victimization, and fatalism is not altogether surprising, for it is not altogether inaccurate. As the history of DOD involvement with Tennier and Greenbrier shows, the federal government itself has benefited from passive labor. Although they were not aware of the entire history, the workers' sense of powerlessness stemmed in part from the reality of the political economic structure. For state entities had helped create and perpetuate the problems in their community—and there was no point in appealing to the government for help when it had been part of the problem. The state had disempowered these workers; how could it be expected now to empower them? Unlike protesters during the civil rights movement or other struggles in American history, the Greenbrier workers could not feel that they had American values and national principles on their side; longstanding national policies had caused their predicament.

The failure of the protests, publicity, and appeals to public officials was extremely demoralizing. Joanne James was certain that someone— she wasn't sure who—should have held Greenbrier's management accountable. "You know, I'm not saying the government is at fault for this, but we *were* working on government contracts. . . . It has been made so easy for—I don't know if I should say companies, or owners, or whoever, it's just been made so easy for them to get rid of their responsibilities. . . . It's obscene what they're doing." James wanted to hold the government accountable, but after being told so many times that it was just the owners' financial decision, it seemed pointless. So, like the others, she stopped fighting and gave up on politics. "They have been allowed to get away with this; not just one time but numerous times. . . . And I think that's what's wrong with our country. . . . As long as your leaders, whether it be in a plant or in the Congress, or whatever, as long as they have no morals, and they're going to say, 'You know, we can get away with this,' I don't think things are going to get any better."[93]

Because of the organizers' lack of political analysis, the workers were angry but could not identify the source of their predicament. This problem is not surprising, for the forces of global economic change are complicated and relatively invisible. Lacking a more subtle explanation, most workers indicted the political system as a whole, extending the personalized analysis of the plant closing to the government also. "We've got too many politicians, I know that. And every time they want to pass a bill, they stick about fifteen amendments to it. . . . You can bet that somebody in the government is going to profit on it. [Congress-people are getting] payoffs. . . . Just think of the money they make." [94] Margaret Jones echoes Mackrey: "They're sitting high on the hill, they've got it made, and they don't care about anybody else. . . . They'll get what they want, regardless." [95] Ann Ritter was shocked when government officials told the workers their only option was to retain a private lawyer. "I said, the state shouldn't make a law that they can't back up; that ain't right. We shouldn't have to get a lawyer, the state ought to back us. If I steal something from you, the state will back you up, and get you a lawyer, and protect you. . . . We shouldn't have to go out and get a lawyer and worry about paying one. . . . The state should have stepped in." With others in the group, Ritter tried to contact every political official she could think of, to no avail. In the end she could only feel hopeless and disgusted. "Through every bit of this, the people were done wrong, and there's nobody that just stood up for the people." Ritter described her sense of violation and powerlessness in the face of the politicians' inaction and apparent complicity in Greenbrier's criminal acts. "When they claimed bankruptcy, it made me so mad I wanted to die. I said, it's like standing on the courthouse steps being raped, and the police driving by and just waving." [96]

Analyzing Power

The bitterness, hopelessness, and sense of worthlessness and futility expressed by the Greenbrier workers is very different from the workers in the next two case studies. The workers in the next chapters, who mounted serious political mobilization efforts in the wake of their plant closings, initially felt just as the Greenbrier group did. But their attitudes and behaviors were transformed through their actions. Many of them vowed to continue their political involvement, and believed that they had learned some valuable lessons in their experiences during the plant closing, including a more realistic understanding of government, the economy, and power relations in their own communities. This broader, structural analysis was essential to the workers' ability to move forward, politically, collectively, and in their own lives.

The story of Greenbrier reveals that power is transmitted and perpetuated in many ways. One is through the political system and traditional institutions, the locus of power typically analyzed by political scientists and theorists. Power is also exercised through the economic system, which empowers some and makes mere survival difficult for others. Of course, political and economic power are tightly linked. The structure of the political economy shapes power relations and opportunities. As the history of Greenbrier Industries and the involvement of the federal government shows, Clinton was targeted in the first place because of its powerlessness.

Finally, power flows through ideas. The Greenbrier workers were not wrong in their understanding of their place in the political system, or the extent of mismanagement at the plant. But their interpretation of these facts only reinforced a dominant interpretive framework, one in which the workers' powerlessness was accepted and legitimated. One myth that served this purpose was the powerful idea of the Greenbrier workforce as a family, which evoked a model of helplessness—childhood—that was also warm, friendly, and protective. Another was the ideology of individualism, which suggested that independent effort was more important than other goals; the workers vehemently denounced anyone who needed welfare or public assistance, or even col-

lective representation through unions. Self-reliance was most celebrated.

Closely related, as David Roediger and others have shown, is the crucial role of racism in white working-class culture.[97] White workers'
sense of superiority over African Americans, immigrants, and workers
of other ethnicities signifies what Roediger, following W.E.B. DuBois,
describes as "the wages of whiteness." The ideology of racial superiority, fostered by the managerial class, allowed employers to pay white
workers poorly and exploit them as necessary. As Roediger says, "The
pleasures of whiteness could function as a 'wage' for white workers.
That is, status and privileges conferred by race could be used to make up
for alienating and exploitative class relationships."[98] No matter how deplorable their objective conditions, they were always better off than
blacks. Corporations—as well as local governments and economic developers—benefited from the passivity that resulted. Economic and political powerlessness was advertised and named "good business climate."
Even the federal government benefited from a culture of acquiescence.

Why did the Greenbrier workers blame each other for the economic
crisis that resulted? Why did they not band together, recognize their
common interests, pursue their goals collectively? Why would they di-
vide themselves against each other? The case studies in the following
chapters suggest some interesting hypotheses. In the absence of an alternative analysis, the workers' identities were defined through hierarchy
and inequality, including racial inequality, class distinctions, and the gender hierarchy implicit in their descriptions of the workplace "family."
This very divisive, individual, and personalized system undermined the
possibility of collective response, making it nearly impossible to achieve
the goals that the workers themselves set forth.

The communities in the following cases live within the same cultural
systems of meaning as the Greenbrier workers. And yet their actions
show that changes in consciousness are not only possible but wide-

spread if the conditions are appropriate. These changes come about through the experience of collective action, and through challenges to power relations within a community or workplace. A history of such experiences—whether those challenges have failed or succeeded—can significantly change the dominant framework in which the group begins. And as the next two chapters demonstrate, a process of grassroots involvement and political mobilization within a larger context has the capacity to transform the political, economic, and cultural underpinnings of a community, as well as to create the potential for future politically transformative struggles.

4

Resisting the Great Sucking Sound:
Acme Boot Workers Take on a Runaway Company

At one time the Acme Boot Company owned and operated five large boot-making plants in Tennessee. The company employed thousands of workers to carry out the various tasks of sorting, cutting, stamping, stitching, piping, repair, shipping, and receiving. The employees in rural Tennessee created the very best quality casual, dress, military, and cowboy boots. Made by Acme workers, they were then distinguished with such famous brand-name labels as Dingo, Dan Post, Corcoran, and Luchesse. The boots were sold throughout the United States and Europe, and promoted in expensive advertising campaigns featuring celebrities such as Joe Namath and O. J. Simpson.[1] Acme boots had a loyal clientele in each sector of the boot market. Its higher-priced boots were especially admired, and Acme was known as "the Tiffany's of the western boot business."[2] As any Acme employee could tell you, Acme Boot was the largest manufacturer of western boots in the world.[3] Its corporate headquarters and largest plant were located in Clarksville, Tennessee, a small city on the Kentucky border. As recently as 1990 the Clarksville plant employed about 1,500 people.[4] The county seat of Montgomery County, Clarksville was the heart of an area between Tennessee and Kentucky sometimes called Tuckessee, and best known for its proximity to Fort Campbell Military Reserve. In Montgomery County, Acme was not only the largest employer but a source of pride and recognition for the community.

By 1993 this company had ceased to exist. Acme Boot Co. was still, by all accounts, a viable and extremely profitable corporation. But it was not making boots in Clarksville, or anywhere else in Tennessee. Acme had moved nearly all of its production offshore, and subcontracted most of it to other manufacturers. Acme workers mobilized and challenged a seemingly inevitable sequence of events. Their efforts in Clarksville, Tennessee, exemplify a "successful failure," one that led to individual transformations and the potential for future victories for global economic justice, in Tennessee and beyond.

A Brief History of Acme Boot

The company had begun manufacturing shoes and boots in Tennessee in 1929. Its original owners, Jessel and Sidney Cohn, moved the Acme Shoe Company from Chicago to Tennessee, in an early example of capital mobility—"to take advantage of an exceptional work force."[5] As Barry Bluestone and Bennett Harrison showed, "Management can move capital by completely shutting down a plant. . . . In a few cases it may even load some of the machinery onto flatcars or moving vans and set up essentially the same operation elsewhere. This last option earned the epithet 'runaway shop' in the 1930s, and again in the 1950s, when industries such as shoes, textiles, and apparel left New England for the lower-wage, non-unionized South."[6] Acme was a pioneer in this trend, and its beginnings in Tennessee were an omen. In 1992 Acme would leave Clarksville to become a "runaway shop" once again.

The Cohns turned Acme into a profitable and productive company. By the late 1930s they were selling millions of shoes and boots, shipped all over the world. After running their business for nearly thirty years, the Cohns sold Acme to the Philadelphia and Reading Corporation in 1956.[7] That company changed the name to Acme Boot Company, Inc., continuing Acme's production standards and expanding production considerably, building a huge state-of-the-art plant to replace the old

Clarksville factory in 1964. Philadelphia and Reading sold Acme to Northwest Industries in 1969. Northwest, in turn, added an automated warehouse next to the enormous manufacturing plant in Clarksville.[8] Besides the Clarksville headquarters, Acme Boot Company plants were scattered throughout the state's rural areas, in small towns including Waverly, Ashland City, Springfield, and Cookeville. All of these factories produced, finished, repaired, or shipped boots of different styles and labels. Mostly because of Acme Boot, the region of Middle Tennessee was the nation's major source of cowboy boots, producing up to 90 percent of the nation's supply.[9]

In Clarksville, the Acme Boot Company was proud to be the county's largest and best-known employer.[10] Everyone in the town of Clarksville knew where the Acme factory was located, and most knew someone who had worked there. Acme was not just a large corporation, it was an important fixture in Clarksville's economic and social landscape. The company was considered a good citizen and a responsible employer. People in Clarksville remembered how, during the Great Depression, other factories were shutting down. At Acme, as elsewhere, demand had dried up and production was halted. Rather than lay off their employees, however, Acme's owners sent the workers out every day, to cut the grass or paint the building, in order to keep them on the payroll as long as possible.[11] To them, this symbolized the company's commitment to its workers and their families. Unlike other businesses, which came and went with mixed records, Acme was seen as a distinguished participant in the Clarksville community.

Unlike most factories in rural Tennessee, Acme Boot had been unionized for over three decades. When the Philadelphia and Reading Corporation purchased Acme in 1956, it began cutting wages, from about $46 to $42 a week.[12] In response, the workers began a unionization drive, with support from the United Rubber Workers International Union (URW).[13] After several failed organizing campaigns, they succeeded in negotiating their first contract in 1962, and became Local

330. The URW eventually represented Acme workers throughout the state. Working through the union, the workers achieved steady gains in wages and working conditions. These gains did not come easily, but instead were the product of much struggle. Throughout the 1960s and 1970s the union was forced repeatedly to demonstrate its strength. Walkouts and other job actions were not uncommon. The longest strike, in the mid-1970s, lasted eighteen weeks. Alan Buckner, a Clarksville native in his early fifties, was a leader of the union at that time, although before the plant closing he had left Acme for a job as a traveling salesman. Buckner remembers with pride, "We stood up for the union then, and that's when we got most of our recognition at that time. They didn't doubt us no more." [14]

By 1980 Acme's employees had decent working conditions and insurance; they were treated fairly and relatively well paid. Many of the experienced workers, those with the quickest fingers and the most seniority, did well on piecework. Wilma Mittendorf was one of Acme's best workers for sixteen years, until she became disabled and had to undergo several surgeries for severe carpal tunnel disease. "There were a lot of those girls down there making $10 to $15 an hour, [until] they cut their production and put them on time." [15] The work was dangerous and tiring, as at Greenbrier and most apparel plants. Edna Luttrell was fifty-six years old and had moved to Clarksville with her entire family thirty-four years before, from a farm in rural Stewart County. She had never finished middle school, but she was a hard worker and one of Acme's most senior and valued employees. Luttrell operated a huge boot-assembly machine. "When you put that piece of work underneath that old needle, sometimes the pressure foot would come down . . . and some of them sewed their fingers. I mashed my fingers . . . and I put a nail in my foot one night. It went clean through my shoe." [16] Nearly every worker had horror stories: "I saw one guy lose about this much of his finger. He was new and nobody was training him." [17]

Carpal tunnel syndrome was a big problem at Acme. During her sixteen years working there, Wilma Mittendorf had needed braces, nerve blocks, and two operations to enable her to continue using her swollen hands. By the time the plant closed, her hands were nearly paralyzed. "I don't have any grip. I can't lift. I spill stuff . . . I can't even clean very well. It turns blue [and] it feels dead." [18] Betty Schmidt, who had worked at Acme for twenty years along with her husband, Charles, also had serious health problems: "They had me sitting in front of an air vent, and I had a sinus infection all the time . . . I've got stiff fingers, tennis elbow, rheumatism in my neck, my shoulders hurt. It's all job-related." She explained, "The muscle damage and back damage and stuff like that was [caused by] repetition." [19] Many workers became disabled and were forced to take early retirement. Others were in severe pain but kept working as long as they possibly could, mostly "on account of the insurance." [20]

Still, compared to what they had known, Acme was an excellent opportunity. Many workers had been enticed to leave family farms or coal mines to work at Acme, and they in turn encouraged their relatives and friends to join them in the factory. Acme employees had migrated to Clarksville from an extensive area covering middle Tennessee and southeastern Kentucky. They had come in search of relief from the unending toil, dangerous conditions, and lack of mobility that characterized decades of labor in farming or mining. Jobs at Acme promised a better wage, shorter hours, health insurance, the protections of a union contract, and job opportunities for family members in Clarksville.

By all accounts the workforce in Clarksville was extremely dedicated and loyal. Unlike Greenbrier, Acme had a very low absentee rate and a low turnover rate. In 1992 average tenure at the company was twenty-two years. Workers accepted the fluctuations in hours and occasional layoffs when production sagged, and worked overtime when needed. At times, according to Edna Luttrell, "we put in fifty-eight hours a week. We worked ten hours a day, [including] Saturday." [21] They also worked fast. Mittendorf had worked on piping for sixteen years: "It's real tedious work . . . *You* do seven cases an hour, forty-eight shoes in a case, and see how you feel like!"[22]

Nearly every worker who stayed at Acme Boot for more than a year or two was retrained at some point. By 1992 much of the assembly work had been computerized, and longtime employees had learned how to use the new technologies. Luttrell described the process: "Each [boot] pattern has a cassette tape, and you just punch a little button, just like a radio tape recorder. . . . All you have to do is punch the Start button, and it would start sewing. You had three machines, so while that one was sewing, you'd go to the next one, do it the same way, and get it started, go to the third one, and do it the same way. By the time you do that, you get back to the first one, it's done stopped—you put another piece in, and take off again. . . . It's amazing to see that."[23] Like most workers, Luttrell expressed pride in her accomplishments at Acme. She had begun working there on April 7, 1960, as a "floor girl." For about fifteen years she delivered work to the sewing machine operators. Eventually she bid on a new job and moved to computer operations. "It was different from what I'd been used to. It was a challenge. It was hard at first . . . [but] it was fine. Right at the last, before they closed the plant, I learned to set the machines up by myself. That was fun."[24] She worked hard and received positive feedback from her superiors.

Many attest to the closeness they felt with their fellow workers. Like the Greenbrier workers, the Acme Boot workers refer to their co-workers as "family."[25] When Acme workers are asked why they enjoyed their exhausting and dangerous jobs on the production lines, they all give some version of the same answer: "It was just like family . . . We had a lot of fun. We always had Halloween parties, or Christmas dinners, and Thanksgiving dinners, and if any of them had a birthday, we'd always make cakes, and pies, and turkeys and hams. . . . And anybody retires, we'd always give them a big dinner. Anybody quit, we'd give them a big dinner. We were always just a happy bunch. We really enjoyed it." [26] Says Edna Luttrell, "I had friends over there, it was just like family. It was fun; I enjoyed it. I miss it . . . A whole bunch of 'em. Seem like sisters . . . When you come out there now [to the empty plant], you could just squall your eyes out. You miss 'em. I miss the whole crew." [27] Sally Kellam, who was forty-eight at the time of the closing and had worked at Acme for over twenty-five years, had just bought a relatively costly new home with her new husband, assuming she would stay at Acme until she retired. "When you're working around people like that, you have your ups and downs, and you fuss with each other . . . For years we have fussed and argued . . . [but] we all knew each other, and we knew our ways, and our family's problems. Everybody knew everybody. It was pretty close." [28] Besides good relationships, skills learned, and the sense of community at work, Acme workers also enjoyed the pride and satisfaction of creating an excellent product. They were gratified by the unsurpassed quality of the product they turned out every day. They say that Acme boots were the best in the world.

Downsizing and Closing

In 1985, Northwest Industries was taken over by Farley Industries, a privately held Chicago conglomerate owned by industrialist William Farley, a high-profile takeover specialist who already owned several large companies. [29] Farley bought Northwest Industries, a far-flung conglomerate, for $1.4 billion, in the largest leveraged buyout to date. The sale, which included only $14 million in equity and the rest in debt financing, was financed by Michael Milken of Drexel Burnham Lambert. A diversified company with interests in automotive components, railroad parts, apparel, and footwear, Farley Industries' annual revenue in 1990 was over $3.5 billion, and the company was responsible for the employment of approximately 50,000 people. [30] Farley Industries was best known for its Fruit of the Loom brand name. Farley received considerable personal publicity, and his $2.5 million advertising campaign for Fruit of the Loom featured Farley pumping iron in a T-shirt, denouncing the "uncaring attitude" of American management and extolling "feeling good about yourself and your company . . . the only way to win." In the industry, by contrast, Farley was known as "Chicago's poster boy for the demise of junk bond–financed leveraged buyouts." [31]

Acme Boot, however, was considered a productive and modern factory in a booming industry, a safe business investment and a wise addition to Farley's footwear holdings. [32] In 1991 Farley had been threatened with a bankruptcy petition, and he negotiated a reorganization to mollify his bondholders. This was one of several bankruptcies and reorganizations that afflicted Farley throughout the 1990s. Immediately after the takeover, accordingly, Farley had begun selling off all non-apparel divisions of Northwest Industries, earning about $630 million to pay down his debt. [33] But along with Fruit of the Loom and the textiles giant West Point–Pepperell, Acme was always considered to be "financially strong and viable and . . . not involved in the bankruptcy proceedings" that would affect so many of Farley's holdings. [34]

The parent company, however, was burdened with tremendous debt. Anxious to boost productivity and sales, and to elevate profit levels in his most promising subsidiaries, Farley planned to reorganize Acme. He notified the workers and their union representatives that the shoe and boot industry in the United States had begun to change dramatically, and that Acme Boot must change along with it. Part of Farley's prescription was accurate. The industry and Acme both had already changed considerably over the decades, especially through mechanization and computerized production methods. But the international market was not as dire as Farley's managers suggested. On the one hand, the domestic footwear industry may have had a gloomy outlook; industry experts called the sector "beset by low-wage competitors."[35] Lower-cost imports were popular, and American-owned companies competed with contractors hiring low-paid workers in developing countries. Many shoe manufacturers believed the simplest way to match low production costs was to move the work from relatively well-paid, unionized plants to areas with less costly labor and looser regulation.

But the western boot business was different. As *Nashville Business Journal* reported, business was booming; most western boot plants in Tennessee were expanding, not downsizing. "[International competition] isn't a problem on the western side of our business," said an executive of Georgia Boot Company in Franklin, Tennessee, in 1992. "There's very little in the way of imports." An executive of another western boot manufacturer concurred: "Domestic manufacturers . . . have an inherent advantage in that they are closest to the marketplace . . . Construction workers and dyed-in-the-wool cowboys, they like that 'Made in America.'"[36] In this context, the rapid downsizing at Acme Boot was unusual—it was pioneering an unfortunate national trend. For while other boot manufacturers were increasing production, Acme decided to base its strategy on global mobility. It began to close its Tennessee plants and opened non-union, lower-wage plants to produce boots in Texas, Mexico, and South America, returning boots to Tennessee for finishing, repairs, and shipping.

Although Farley's public statements assured Acme workers that his company would continue the excellent production standards set by previous owners, his actions suggested otherwise. The parent company analyzed the situation and concluded that the most profitable role for Acme Boot was as a marketer of western boots, rather than a producer. Other shoe companies had demonstrated the profit potential of subcontracting all of their production work to developing nations and free-trade zones, using U.S. operations only to market and sell merchandise.[37] Farley decided to follow their lead. According to corporate spokespeople, long-term restructuring plans for Acme favored "outsourcing," contracting out manufacturing tasks to a variety of plants on the basis of a competitive bidding system. As Acme Boot Company president Mike Vogel explained much later, moving production to lower-cost sites was "part of our strategic marketing plan to put more emphasis on global sourcing and less emphasis on manufacturing."[38] Acme would become a boot-marketing company. At the same time as workers were being laid off and plants closed in Tennessee, Acme Boot Company was dramatically expanding its national advertising budget. In 1992 alone the ad budget doubled, bringing "strong increases in sales of all of its brands."[39] Eventually the company's primary activity would be to buy low-cost boots from makers in Latin America and elsewhere and then to sell them under Acme labels.

Farley's business decisions exemplify a national pattern of corporate disinvestment in the 1980s and 1990s. As Bluestone and Harrison explain it, "The essential problem with the U.S. economy can be traced to the way capital—in the forms of financial resources and of real plant and equipment—has been diverted from productive investment in our basic national industries into unproductive speculation, mergers and acquisitions, and foreign investment."[40] Farley undertook all three with a vengeance, and Acme workers in Tennessee felt the strategy's impact. By 1990 only the Clarksville plant remained, and many laid-off Acme workers from other parts of Tennessee had relocated there in order to keep their boot-making jobs.

Many of the workers were suspicious of Farley's plans. As Kellam said, "Things started to really change when that Farley Industries bought it out. When he came in here, he told us that he wasn't for the union, but he wouldn't work against it. [But] he must have really been against it, because he started making big changes."[41] Mostly through the union—which represented all Acme workers in Tennessee—the workers were apprised of changes in the other plants as well as their own.

When Acme closed its factory in Waverly, Tennessee, in 1991, the workers were told that the layoffs were only temporary, between contracts. But when it reopened, it had become Stetson Boot Co., apparently unrelated to Acme. Stetson Boot bought the Acme plant in Waverly in 1992, and hired 250 people in the first year.[42] The Clarksville workers suspected the plant was still owned by Farley. "They called it Stetson, but it's still Acme," said one longtime Acme employee. "Some of the supervisors from here are working there. And before the plant closed [in Clarksville], we were sewing boots for them. And they would come out here and get their supplies, come to the leather room and get their leather. . . . It's just under a different name. It's always been Acme."[43] The workers also have a theory about why this happened. "They closed that plant in Waverly, and opened as Stetson. It's non-union. They make, I think, $5 something an hour—and then they got to pay for their insurance . . . They didn't like the union. That's all there really was to it."[44]

Meanwhile, Farley was instituting big changes within the Clarksville factory. In his first round of contract negotiations with the union, in 1986, Farley demanded wage concessions. The union agreed to forgo wage increases for a full four years, until 1990, and some workers took huge cuts. Alan Buckner, who had been there thirty-years, suffered a severe wage reduction: "I went from piecework to hourly work. I went from $13.22 an hour to $5.35."[45] He and others were indignant. Sally Kellam recalled, "People with top seniority was making the same as the person with five years. . . . They took bonuses from us, they dropped the amount. I was making $9.42 an hour when my wages started dropping."[46] As Emma Luttrell said, "As long as I've been here, thirty-four years . . . when they closed the plant [in 1993], I was making $7.50 an hour."[47] In the early 1990s, Clarksville presented few other employment opportunities.

Farley then cut benefits, and the union protested but went along, convinced it would save members' jobs. The workers also conceded to major changes in work rules, which resulted in considerable speedups in the production process. At the same time, managers were being added. Management set up a new department, "Value Engineering," to improve efficiency and "shelf appeal." "We are trying to refocus the way in which we look at containing costs and how we go about reducing costs," said Vice President John Petrovich. "It will be the first time that we have an entire department devoted to taking the costs out of the boot." [48] In addition, new management teams were hired to coordinate the operations of the Dingo, Dan Post, and Acme lines of boots, eliminating existing workers' positions in purchasing and scheduling. And a new senior vice president, Chuck Truckenbrodt, was hired to "work on special assignment to president Mike Vogel to develop projects designed to improve efficiency and profitability." [49]

Even while cutting wages and benefits and laying off hundreds, Farley continued advertising both himself and his company as committed to communities, and family oriented. He visited the Clarksville workers. "He said his daddy belonged to a union—he worked at the post office—and he didn't have nothing against the union." [50] He promised the workers that all the changes he was making were in their best interests. Alan Buckner remembers, "I go back to what [Farley] told me when he first took over. He patted me on the back, he said, 'We're one happy family—and we're going to grow.' . . . I never forgot it." [51]

Farley persuaded the union to agree to concessions by warning of a move. "They threatened us, right away: 'Well, we'll just go to Mexico, or El Paso, or wherever—you take what we got to offer, and that's it.' And we did . . . We could grouse and mumble all we wanted to, but it wouldn't do us any good." [52] Buckner, Local 330's chief steward in the 1980s, remembers one particularly harsh round of negotiations, conducted while several other plants were still in operation. "We went through negotiations to give concessions to keep the plants open. I tried at that time to get him [the union president] not to do it. I said they're going to close the plants anyways. But cuts and concessions came." [53] As Sally Kellam said, "We did this, you know, to save our jobs. We did everything to save our jobs. We made a lot of concessions." [54] This was not unusual in the downsizing epidemic of the 1980s and 1990s. Even the strongest unions were under extreme pressure to cut their own pay and benefits. The members did not protest. As a *New York Times* survey showed, a great majority of workers across the country—82 percent of those polled—said they would work more hours, take fewer vacation days or accept lesser benefits to keep their jobs.[55] At Acme the bottom line showed the impact. By 1990 profits were higher than ever, and productivity had increased by 35 percent.[56]

In November 1992 the bomb fell. Acme suddenly announced plans to close its last manufacturing plant, in Clarksville. The workers were shocked. "None of us ever *dreamed* Acme Boot would close." [57] The company would lay off nearly 600 people, mostly within three months, and production work would shift south, especially to a new plant in Puerto Rico. Some management and supervisory personnel would move to Puerto Rico immediately, to begin operations there. Vogel reassured the community that although no manufacturing operations would remain in Clarksville, they would retain over eighty managerial employees in corporate headquarters there. "Acme will continue to be in Clarksville . . . Clarksville is home," he said.[58] The workers saw it differently.

The decision to close the Clarksville plant was made in Farley's corporate offices in Chicago's Sears Tower. By 1992, Farley Industries was in serious financial trouble; it had defaulted on $3 billion in junk bonds (from a hostile takeover of West Point–Pepperell textile company), and Drexel, which had collapsed, was unable to bail out the company. Farley Inc. was liquidated under Chapter 7 bankruptcy, but Farley retained control of Fruit of the Loom and remained chairman and CEO of West

Point–Pepperell Inc.[59] Farley Industries reorganized under Chapter 11 as a smaller conglomerate, retaining Acme as a subsidiary. Industry analysts were unanimous about Farley Industries' troubles. "Farley is in this fix partly because he used debt to solve his past deals' problems. There are signs that this habit is wearing thin with investors."[60] Acme had to pay off Farley's debts. Managers were cutting costs wherever possible. Acme Boot production was booming in El Paso (with much of the actual assembly work done across the border in Mexico for much lower wages), where the two Acme plants had doubled their employee base and tripled production in the previous year.[61] And production facilities in Mexico and Latin America were proving very profitable. There was no longer any compelling reason for Farley to maintain relatively costly plants in Tennessee. The Clarksville boot-making operations would be relocated to Puerto Rico.[62]

Explaining the decision to move, Acme Boot president Mike Vogel was quite frank about the anticipated surge in profits. He explained, "It's better for us to do it there. It's less costly." He cited the tax advantages, lower costs of wages and benefits, and employee training incentives Acme would receive from the government. Vogel did *not* say that the Clarksville plant was closing because it was doing badly. Indeed, Acme was doing extraordinarily well; the fiscal year 1992 was Acme Boot's second-best profit-making year of all time.[63] Sales of all brands were on the rise. Acme's sales of women's boots had been up 50 percent in 1991 over the previous year, while men's sales rose as well. Acme director of marketing Mike Duncan exulted, "We're very happy with our business and we're having an excellent year."[64] The decision to close their flagship plant was apparently unrelated.

Both the Puerto Rican government and the United States government had directly encouraged Acme's decision to move the plant to Puerto Rico, in several ways. After discussions with Puerto Rican officials, Acme Boot had been given a building in Toa Alta, Puerto Rico. It was invited to begin production in the building immediately, at no cost whatsoever. The structure was owned by the Puerto Rico Industrial Development Company (Pridco), a governmental entity. The Toa Alta plant and its surrounding roads and utilities had been built with federal government money, and had been occupied previously by a pharmaceutical division of Baxter International, Inc., which had subsequently moved. In return for the free building, Acme had promised to invest $1 million in production equipment and machinery in Puerto Rico, and eventually to hire 600 workers.[65] Puerto Rico was overjoyed at the prospect of bringing hundreds of jobs to island residents. Acme's move was touted on the island as a major economic development coup.

This great boon for economic developers in Puerto Rico was a tragedy for workers in Clarksville. The closing hit the community hard. Although the jobs at Acme Boot were not extremely well paid, and the work was dangerous, they were some of the best jobs available. When the plant closed, the average employee was forty-seven years old and had been there for twenty-five years. The loss of work was an awful blow. "It is horrible. You know, people don't realize what it's like to be in a situation like that, but you can't go out on the street and pick up a job . . . Some of 'em's too old to get out and go to school . . . The only thing you'd probably find was a fast-food restaurant, like McDonald's here . . . [Even] some of 'em that's got education can't get a job, unless you're working for minimum wage. And you can't make a living off of that."[66] State agencies encouraged job training, but the workers were skeptical. "Jobs are really scarce around here. Everybody I've talked to so far, I don't think a lot of them have even gotten jobs."[67] Education and training did not help much. "We got people that's been to college; they can't find no job."[68]

The situation was even more dire when an entire family worked at Acme Boot. Edna Luttrell's sister, father, brother, two nephews, and niece earned their livelihoods at Acme. In the early 1960s they had all

moved into Clarksville, from a farm in rural Stewart County. Her elderly parents now depended upon her income, and her siblings had families too. Luttrell said, "I don't know what we're going to do."[69] Sally
Kellam's daughter had worked there too. "She still hasn't found a job.
And her unemployment's running out. You know, we lost a lot."[70]

Even those who found new work lost something. Kellam found a
warehouse job that was much more physically demanding than her previous job as a boot piper. Her salary was significantly lower than before.
"I only make $5.86. And that's not much. But I knew when I lost Acme,
I knew that I would never make what I was making before . . . I have to
work seven days a week to get what I made at Acme in forty hours.
That's hard to accept. . . . Everyone keeps saying, 'Well, it's a job, it's a
job.' Yeah, it's a job! But that can be very depressing."[71]

The situation was as difficult emotionally as it was economically. As
in every plant closing, laid-off workers became scared, depressed, and
mistrustful. They had not anticipated either the material change or the
feelings that went with it. "When I got laid off, I got depressed, moody.
. . . Then you get bitter. It really was very hard. . . . I had a hard time
adjusting. I got so depressed that I couldn't even clean my house; I didn't
go noplace; I didn't even do nothing. I was just so upset and worried
that I wouldn't find a job. It was a real hard time."[72]

Most workers had believed their jobs to be absolutely secure. They
had worked at Acme for their entire adult lives and had no training in
anything else. Moreover, Clarksville was in the middle of a serious re-
cession—a depression, according to most workers—and they knew
other jobs would be scarce and low-paid. Even with a strong union, the
highest pay bracket at Acme in 1992 was $7.95 an hour, or approxi-
mately $16,000 a year—for workers who had been on the job more
than thirty years.

In a letter many of the workers signed and sent to President Bill Clinton, they wrote, "Three-fourths of the Acme Boot workers are women,

and they only earn $7.95 an hour. The job market in our area is very poor now, and hardly any new jobs offer better than minimum wage." Moreover, they wrote, they had worked hard for President Clinton's election, at their union's urging, and now they were counting on him to live up to his promises. "In your campaign, you often expressed sympathy for the 100,000 U.S. workers who lose their health insurance each month. Many of the Acme Boot workers are farmers' wives who definitely need their insurance coverage for their families. Most are in their 40s and 50s, and will have great difficulty finding another job."[73] As in other rural communities, the closing of a large manufacturing plant would reverberate throughout the regional economy.

The Union Fights Back

For about ten years prior to Acme Boot's closing, management had been telling the union—URW Local 330—that times were tough. But even as the other Tennessee plants were downsized and shut down, the Clarksville plant had never been a target of cuts. So when the company announced that the Clarksville plant would close, the union leaders were surprised and angry. They had seen Acme's other Tennessee plants close, and had been reassured that the Clarksville factory—Acme Boot's first and flagship plant—was doing better than ever. Suddenly they were told that within two months from the announcement, half the employees would be laid off. Even worse, managers were being relocated to Puerto Rico almost immediately, to hire 250 workers for the brand-new Acme Footwear Inc.

The union began a campaign to protest the closing. The effort would last for nearly a year. Immediately after the closing was announced, the workers began an effort to gain public attention to their plight. Exactly as the Greenbrier workers did, the Acme Boot workers believed that an outraged public would rally to their side and exert moral and political pressure, forcing the company to reconsider its plans. As the Greenbrier workers had done, the Acme group began its struggle immediately after the closing was announced, holding meetings, brainstorming, and notifying the local press and local officials of Farley Inc.'s intentions.

Forced by media and politicians to respond to the workers' charges, company officials assured the public that Acme intended to be a "good corporate citizen" of Clarksville. They promised to provide more assistance to workers than required by law, and they said they would do everything possible to minimize the impact of the changes. Managers congratulated themselves on saving the jobs of the small group of associates who would remain in Clarksville. They also argued that the closing was inevitable—not a decision made by Farley or his creditors but a direct consequence of the global economy. They claimed that the company could not survive in Tennessee any longer, and that if it had stayed it would have been bankrupted. Even with all the union's concessions, Acme executives said, in a context of international competition the costs of doing business in Tennessee were simply too high. The closing was an economic necessity. Directly contradicting earlier statements, Vogel now said, "The last 5 or 6 years have been very tough. What we are trying to do is make this company well so we have jobs for the remaining employees." [74]

The workers, who had just received their highest production bonuses in thirty years, knew differently. "They were making money! We can't understand why they closed down on us, because they were making money. They were selling boots. . . . Western wear is *in!*" [75] Mittendorf was right; even the company spokespeople acknowledged that the Clarksville plant's profits were higher than ever before. The workers saw the move to Puerto Rico as an executive decision to boost profits and relieve corporate debt—not to save jobs.

The union leadership did some research into Acme's proposed move. They found that the company was taking advantage of the Possessions

Tax Credit, also known as Section 936 of the U.S. Internal Revenue Code. This credit, established under the Tax Reform Act of 1976, allowed Puerto Rico–based subsidiaries of U.S. corporations to send their profits back to their American corporate parents without paying federal income taxes.[76] Federal taxes were waived on profits earned in U.S. territories including Puerto Rico, Guam, and the Virgin Islands, giving multinational corporations a legal 100 percent tax break. Under Puerto Rico's Industrial Incentives Act of 1948, an American company was also exempt from most Puerto Rican taxes. Between these two programs, according to the U.S. General Accounting Office, "since 1948, most U.S. subsidiaries in Puerto Rico have been completely or partially exempt from Puerto Rican taxes as well as from the U.S. income tax."[77] The island provided a very attractive tax shelter for corporations, and Farley Industries could profit from it.

When President Mike Vogel was first asked about the closing, he said he was looking forward to the tax breaks, which gave Acme a chance to increase its profit margin dramatically. In particular, he said, "There are some tax code advantages to doing work in Puerto Rico."[78] The most important of these was clearly Section 936.

The Campaign Against Section 936

Fighting Section 936 itself—and specifically opposing its use for "runaway shops" like Acme Boot—became a major focus of Local 330's campaign to prevent the plant closing. The loophole in the IRS code was not only siphoning jobs away from states like Tennessee, it was also costing taxpayers millions of dollars. For example, four companies with Puerto Rican subsidiaries—Merck, Coca-Cola, American Home Products, and Pepsico—enjoyed nearly a half-billion dollars in annual tax savings, but employed only 3,100 people on the island. The cost to mainland taxpayers was approximately $156,000 per job, per year. The thirty largest beneficiaries of the 936 tax credit all showed similar subsidies.[79] Senator David Pryor called Section 936 "the Mother of All Tax Shelters."[80] In years of recession and budget cutting, the URW believed it could attract considerable political support to stop "corporate welfare."

The Acme Boot workers became centrally involved in a national movement to amend or eliminate Section 936 of the tax code. The union worked closely with other organizations, particularly the Oil, Chemical and Atomic Workers (OCAW)—which had just been through a similar struggle when Whitehall Pharmaceuticals moved its plant from Indiana to Puerto Rico—and the Midwest Center for Labor Research (MCLR), which provided research and strategy assistance. The coalition found that the footwear industry in the U.S. had declined rapidly in the 1980s and 1990s, with the help of Section 936. OCAW identified 30,000 jobs that had moved directly from the States to take advantage of these incentives.[81] The unions did not object to economic development in Puerto Rico, but they made a powerful argument against government-sponsored transnational corporate capital flight and job destruction.

Acme workers organized a delegation to Washington, including Local 330 president Mitchell Tucker, Local 330 vice president Sam Self, URW International vice president and Tennessee native Michael Stanley, and Thurston Smith, a URW International representative and twenty-three-year Acme Boot worker. In an intense five days of meetings they met with the staff of most members of the House Ways and Means Committee, where all tax legislation originates. They also met with most members of the Tennessee congressional delegation, including Senators Mathews and Sasser.[82] They encouraged officials to support President Clinton's proposed reform of Section 936, to make it a wage credit. Clinton's plan would benefit companies that hired more workers and paid more wages. It would also restore to the U.S. Treasury an estimated $4 billion annually in lost taxes—revenue that instead accrued directly as profit to transnational corporations.[83] The Acme delegation believed their representatives were amenable to the idea of amending or eliminating Section 936.

The URW was key to a coalition—including a number of mainland unions, the AFL-CIO, MCLR, TIRN, and others—that organized an impressive array of activities. They held lobbying days, press conferences, public demonstrations, rallies, leafleting, legal challenges, public hearings, and other actions all aimed to put pressure on elected officials to rescind or amend 936. But the coalition's efforts met a strong counterattack. Industrial and governmental leaders quickly mobilized to defend their subsidies. Their resistance was particularly strong in the economic and political climate of the early 1990s. Global production and outsourcing were increasing sharply, with the support of institutions such as the IMF and the World Bank. Political decisions expanded opportunities for trade and investment in developing countries. Business leaders had become bolder about demanding incentives and subsidies from both state and federal governments, and moving elsewhere if these were not granted. Over seventy Fortune-500 companies, manufacturers, and bankers with more than a trillion dollars in assets created an organization, the Puerto Rico–USA Foundation (PRUSA), to uphold 936 and other incentives. PRUSA argued aggressively that most manufacturing companies "would leave the island over the next several years if Section 936 tax breaks are slashed."[84] Its sister organization, Puerto Ricans Organized for Section 936 (PRO-S936), mobilized Puerto Rican citizens, in Puerto Rico and on the mainland, warning "Puerto Rico Is In Danger!" Eliminating the tax break would have dire consequences: "Families may lose homes. Some family members may have to relocate in search of jobs. Stateside communities will be taxed to provide support for increased populations coming from Puerto Rico."[85]

PRO-S936, PRUSA, the chamber of commerce, and the Puerto

Rico Manufacturers' Association (PRMA) organized rallies in San Juan and New York, busing in hundreds of thousands of working people to protest any cuts in 936. They ran expensive media campaigns, petitioning and letter-writing campaigns, and lobbied intensely for their tax incentives. With over a million dollars of corporate investments, New York City's 1993 Puerto Rican Day Parade was "turned into a save-936 media event."[86] Working people in Puerto Rico were pitted against workers on the mainland, including the Acme Boot workers, trying to save their jobs. The Puerto Rican workers were encouraged to see their employers as allies, protecting their interests and livelihoods.

In fact, the situation was much more complicated. Workers' organizations and community-based groups on the island, as on the mainland, supported amending or cutting Section 936 incentives. The Puerto Rican Federation of Labor passed a resolution opposing 936: "The practice of accepting 'Runaway Plants' in Puerto Rico has undermined the well-being of workers in both Puerto Rico and the United States, putting [sic] workers in both countries against each other."[87] The Puerto Rican community and its leadership was deeply divided, just as Americans would be divided over NAFTA a year later.

The pro-936 corporate campaign was a good example of what William Greider refers to as "mock democracy" or "democracy for hire,"[88] when corporations, lobbying firms, and business consultants take on expensive campaigns on a range of issues. In the past, these campaigns were most often carried on within the Beltway. Now the lobbying efforts expanded to include "ordinary" citizens in a multipronged attack, to broaden the appeal to Congress. As Greider says, "Only those who have accumulated lots of money are free to play in this version of democracy. Only those with a strong, immediate financial stake in the political outcomes can afford to invest this kind of money in manipulating the governing decisions. . . . This is democracy and it costs a fortune."[89] A Washington-based corporate lobbyist working on Section

936 confirmed Greider's argument: "The companies have been work-ing very actively [to retain 936 benefits]. But they can't show their faces because in today's Washington they are seen as the bad guys."[90] Puerto Rican citizens were therefore mobilized to do the political work for them. And their appeal was successful. Three Puerto Rican members of Congress told President Clinton they would not support his budget un-less Section 936 was saved.[91] By creating the appearance of unified grassroots support, as well as representing some very powerful corporate lobbies, the well-orchestrated campaign dissuaded President Clinton and congressional leaders from their plans for reform. The 1993 budget passed with Section 936 completely intact.

The Acme workers and their allies had mounted an impressive na-tional campaign, and met with formidable resistance. Yet the coalition maintained the pressure for several more years. Although their efforts were not immediately successful, in 1996 they would see major victory. Section 936 was eliminated. Acme Boot workers were pivotal in ending a major corporate welfare program and permanently changing federal policy.

Clarksville's Struggle Continues

While the political fight about the future of Section 936 was under way, Acme Boot workers were also pursuing more immediate strategies to stop the plant from moving. Unlike the Greenbrier workers, the Acme workers did not become demoralized and give up when a particular tactic failed. With the help of the union and other organizations with national and international connections, they pursued an array of cre-ative strategies, devising an ambitious and multifaceted campaign.

The group's primary focus was on public policies, especially financial incentives, that facilitated Acme's move. In addition to Section 936, the company's decision to move had apparently been influenced by the availability of local subsidies in Puerto Rico, so the workers attempted to fight Acme's plans by blocking the company from taking advantage of Puerto Rico's existing tax breaks. Acme Boot had been offered job-training funds, a free building, and infrastructure improvements in Toa Alta, Puerto Rico. Local 330 did its homework and found that Acme Boot was probably ineligible for many of the lucrative incentives it was slated to receive. The union relied primarily on two legal provisions. First, a 1987 Commonwealth law prohibited local officials from waiving local corporate taxes if a company's move "would substantially and adversely affect the employees of an enterprise under related ownership operating in any state of the United States." A question on the tax-break application asked if the jobs coming to Puerto Rico would cost jobs anywhere in the U.S. If the answer was yes, the company was ineligible for benefits. Acme had answered no. Lying constituted tax fraud, punishable by fines and imprisonment. Second, Puerto Rico was legally forbidden from offering tax exemptions to firms opening plants on the island if they were moving "to avoid contract obligations with labor unions on the U.S. mainland."[92] Local 330 believed it could show that Acme was doing precisely that.

The URW vowed to save Acme Boot in Clarksville by convincing either the U.S. or the Puerto Rican government to review the case and deny the company's claims. Neither governmental entity had ever refused tax exemptions to any company before. In order to build its case, the union amassed proof that the move to Puerto Rico was harming mainland workers and the state of Tennessee. They gathered evidence that equipment had been shipped directly from Clarksville to Puerto Rico, and that the work planned for Puerto Rico was exactly the same as the Clarksville operation.

Union leaders contacted Puerto Rican officials and met with them in Washington, D.C. They urged the officials to enforce their law prohibiting tax benefits to manufacturing companies whose relocation on the island contributed to job losses in the States. They found some sympathy, especially from Carlos Romero Barceló (Puerto Rico's "shadow congressman"). Clifford Myatt, administrator of Puerto Rico's Economic Development Administration, promised to recommend to Governor Rosselló that a formal hearing be held on the Acme Boot situation. This would be the first hearing ever held on an exemption application. Myatt assured them that Acme Boot's tax exemption had not been approved, and he pledged to weigh Local 330's evidence before granting any credits.[93] But for the most part, Acme had already been received with open arms by local politicians desperate for new jobs at any price.

Local 330 president Mitch Tucker wrote Puerto Rico's governor Rosselló to ask that he deny tax benefits to Acme Boot. "We state to you unequivocally that this is a runaway shop. . . . If an exemption has already been granted, you must revoke it. . . . If an application is now pending, it should be denied." Tucker wrote to Rosselló that Acme "plans to perform Clarksville production processes on Clarksville brand name boots with equipment shipped from Clarksville. . . . Any attempt by Acme Footwear, Inc. to represent the facts otherwise, especially on its application under the Puerto Rico Tax Incentive Act, would be fraudulent."[94] Tucker also sent letters to Carlos Romero Barceló, and to Vice President Albert Gore. Both expressed sympathy, but declined to intervene. The URW decided to escalate its campaign. It initiated a process by which the Commonwealth Government's Office of Industrial Tax Exemption would hold public hearings "to determine whether Acme Boot Co. Inc. should receive a tax exemption decree for its planned Puerto Rico manufacturing operations."[95] The Puerto Rico Office of Tax Exemption scheduled hearings for May 26, 1993.

While waiting for the hearings to begin, the URW pursued other strategies within the political system. Back in November, when the closing was announced but layoffs had not yet begun, the Local had contacted the Tennessee Industrial Renewal Network (the same

Knoxville-based organization that had worked with the Greenbrier Workers Committee) and asked for its assistance in thinking about ways to fight a plant closing. TIRN sent staff and members who had been through plant closings to a meeting in Clarksville, at which they brainstormed ideas and discussed various legal options with the workers. One idea was getting the state to fund a "pre-feasibility study," authorized under the federal Economic Dislocation Worker Adjustment Assistance Act (EDWAA), enacted in July 1989 under the Job Training Partnership Act (JTPA). EDWAA, designed to prevent plant closings, had two important provisions. First, it required Dislocated Worker Units in each state to perform pro-active "economic monitoring for potential dislocation," also known as early-warning monitoring. This had not been done at Acme. Second, in situations where new ownership (either employee ownership or traditional entrepreneurship) could potentially result in job retention, the state could use EDWAA funds on a pre-feasibility study. TIRN contacted Greg LeRoy, research director of the Midwest Center for Labor Research, and a leading expert on corporate accountability and employee ownership. LeRoy believed a pre-feasibility study would cost $15,000 or less, and would inform the workers whether or not job retention was a good possibility if new ownership could be found. He also believed that employee ownership might be a good option for Acme Boot, especially since the majority of workers had been there over twenty years and knew boot-making well. LeRoy wrote Local 330 president Mitch Tucker suggesting that the union look into the possibility. Employee Stock Ownership Plans (ESOPs), he said, "enjoy significant tax advantages which can make an otherwise unprofitable business viable."[96]

Tucker contacted local state senator Riley Darnell and initiated the application for state funds. A group of workers wrote to Clinton and Gore, Governor Ned McWherter, and Senator Jim Sasser, asking that the Dislocated Worker Unit fund a pre-feasibility study for alternative ownership. The workers pointed out that funding the study—which could potentially lead to the plant being saved—was less expensive than one week's worth of unemployment benefits for all the workers at the plant. But the state refused to fund the study—never giving a clear reason—and the union decided that it would not spend any more of its scarce resources pursuing it. Local 330 turned instead to its community-wide campaign and legislative activity around tax breaks.

The union also challenged the legality of the shutdown itself, claiming that officials at Acme Boot violated the federal WARN Act, which requires companies to give employees sixty days' advance notice of any potential layoffs or plant closings, by not telling the employees who would be laid off at each stage of the closing. The union then discovered that the Tennessee Department of Labor was given a list of workers to be laid off in each phase, but the workers had not received the same notice.

TIRN looked into other legal options as well. Bob Becker contacted the Tennessee ACLU to investigate the possibility of age-discrimination lawsuits. Since the average age of the laid-off workers was forty-seven, it seemed possible that Acme's closing was partly motivated by its unwillingness to cover the pensions and health expenses of an older workforce. Indeed, Acme had been sued once before on these grounds when Jerry Castleman was fired eight months before becoming eligible for a pension. Acme Boot was found guilty of age discrimination, and a U.S. Appeals Court upheld the ruling.[97] Moreover, many of the workers—primarily older women, including women of color—would experience further discrimination in their search for new employment. As Wilma Mittendorf said after being laid off, "That's just all I've done all my life since I was eighteen and I'll be fifty-eight next month. . . . Ain't nobody gonna hire you out there at that age."[98] Becker asked about keeping track of such discrimination in order to improve the law in Tennessee. But the ACLU and other agencies declined to get involved.

Faced with equivocation and obstruction within regular political channels, the workers focused on a public boycott, to increase pressure on Acme's parent company. By making their story public, the workers hoped to gain sympathy, but also to exercise power. As Greg LeRoy explained, "Acme Boot's customer base is rural and Southern. . . . Word of the plant closing will result in consumer decisions to buy other brands. Already, some dealers have returned shipments, and Clarksville-area outlet stores are vacant of shoppers."[99] The workers had to spread the word. If they could call into question Acme's (or William Farley's) reputation and public image—and perhaps even threaten the company's bottom line by affecting its sales—then the company would find it in its interest to negotiate a settlement with the workers. In this way the workers hoped to persuade the company to abandon its plans to move to Puerto Rico.

In January 1993 the union held a mass rally in Clarksville. The event was very well attended, by community members as well as by the workers directly affected. People gathered to hear charges that Acme was a runaway shop, possibly illegal and certainly immoral. Individual workers told their stories and wondered what they would do after being laid off from one of the best jobs in Clarksville. Mitch Tucker vowed, "We want to send William Farley a message: We intend to fight this illegal shutdown." Tucker called on Farley to fulfill the promise he made at the time of purchase that Acme Boot would maintain manufacturing in Clarksville.[100] The rally featured Connie Malloy of the OCAW, a laid-off worker from Whitehall Pharmaceuticals and a rank-and-file leader who had helped fight Section 936 in Elkhart, Indiana. It also featured Ricky Mullins, a dislocated worker from Decaturville Sportswear, which had moved from Decaturville, Tennessee, to El Salvador, with the support of the Agency for International Development.[101] The Decaturville plant closing had been a major campaign issue in 1992. Vice presidential candidate Al Gore had visited Decaturville and denounced the pattern it represented. The Administration had invited Ricky

Mullins himself to the "Faces of Hope" luncheon at the Clinton inaugural. The URW pointed out the connection and asked for Clinton's support.

Local 330 urged all area unions, community groups, and churches to attend its rallies, demonstrations, and events, and to participate in its campaign. "We need all of Clarksville to help us stop this illegal shutdown," said Tucker.[102] TIRN invited its member groups—organizations from all parts of Tennessee—to participate in the campaign as well. Everyone was urged to write their representatives about Acme's future, and to come to Clarksville for major demonstrations of support for the Acme workers.

The media, and some public officials, began to take notice. Once Local 330 had presented its case publicly, government officials could not condone the blatant violation of the law, but they still withheld direct criticism of Acme and outright support for the union. A spokeswoman for Vice President-Elect Al Gore made a rather weak statement. Acme's proposed move, she said, was "an unfortunate use of the existing tax law, which was intended to create jobs."[103] Similarly, the *San Juan Star* quoted Puerto Rico's new chief of economic development, Clifford Myatt: "If it is a clear case [of a runaway], then we will be obliged to make a decision in accordance with the facts." But Myatt also cautioned that, while his agency would take a close look at the Acme application, there is "a very thin line" between runaways and normal plant closings. "We will have to see the reasons for the closing, whether the company thinks it makes business sense, and if it does not relocate in Puerto Rico, if it intends to relocate somewhere else."[104] None of these criteria were included in the law.

With other groups from Clarksville and elsewhere, the Acme workers planned event after event. They held demonstrations, press conferences, and marches. They held a 300-car motorcade through the small downtown. Workers stood in front of Kmart and Winn-Dixie supermarket every weekend, distributing fliers explaining their plight and encouraging community members to contact decision makers. On May 4, 1993, the union sponsored a mass public boot-burning, to which hundreds of Clarksville residents brought their Acme-made boots and burned them. This dramatic gesture inaugurated a national boycott of Acme, Dingo, and Dan Post boots. A boycott flier, "The Anatomy of an Acme Boot," designed by award-winning labor cartoonist Mike Konopaki, was distributed by labor unions nationwide.

The URW International Executive Board had declared the boycott, which would be coordinated out of Akron, Ohio, by Michael Stanley, URW International vice president. URW International president Kenneth L. Coss urged all AFL-CIO members and supporters to observe the boycott: "URW Local 330 members at Acme Boot in Clarksville, Tennessee, have done everything possible to save their jobs," he said. "In return, they have been stripped of their jobs and their dignity. Acme's actions are an affront to the local community, the state and the nation."[105] The workers' spirits rose when the boycott was announced. They had asked the AFL-CIO to endorse the boycott, and it agreed, making it officially a national campaign. Local 330 was optimistic that Farley would act to prevent a sizable drop in sales of Acme's boots. As Coss said, "It is the URW's goal that a boycott, in conjunction with efforts to amend Section 936 . . . will convince the company to reopen the Clarksville facility."[106] The boycott, rallies, and demonstrations in Clarksville encouraged the workers for another reason. With all the activity came an outpouring of support from outside the plant gates.

Unlike the Greenbrier workers, who were isolated and forgotten, the Acme workers felt the support of a much wider community. The national labor movement was a constant source of support and motivation. The local campaign also involved other groups within Clarksville, who had become aware of the workers' plight through their mobilization and public activity. All the workers had stories of their friends and neighbors expressing sympathy and even helping out. Wilma Mitten-dorf's friend donated a pair of Acme boots to the cause: "Yes, I took a pair of Dave's boots and burned them. We burned boots, we done everything." [107] The boycott especially helped the Acme workers feel that they had the community on their side. As Alan Buckner said, "I was talking this morning with a man . . . and he always wears cowboy boots. And I didn't bring the subject up, he did. He said, 'Well, I'll tell you one thing,' he said. 'I'll never buy another damn pair of Acme boots.' And see, he had nothing to do with it. He's never worked a day at Acme. He's just a hardworking man and that's his feeling. And I'm glad to hear it." [108] This external validation was crucial to the workers as they continued their struggle. The Greenbrier story shows that this type of support does not materialize spontaneously—the Greenbrier workers felt more disdain than sympathy from their neighbors. Community support happened because of the mobilization at Acme Boot.

A crucial component of Local 330's strategy involved attracting media attention. Because the union connected its plight to a national political struggle—and because of Clinton and Gore's attention to the issue during their campaign—they were extraordinarily successful. Local media coverage, including both written press and TV, was extensive at the outset, and continued at a slower pace for many months. Even the national press paid attention, especially at the height of the struggle around Section 936. Dan Rather reported on Acme Boot in a CBS News segment on job loss in the global economy. *Prime Time Live* and *This Week with David Brinkley* both covered the situation at Acme and the general problems with Section 936 and related plant closings. The Associated Press picked up Acme's story as the "human interest" side of the political battle being waged in Congress. And Nashville's NBC affiliate produced a special week-long investigative series, including in-depth interviews with many of the Acme workers, and an analysis of the effect of the plant closing on the Clarksville community. This media coverage was impressive, and very unusual for a plant-closing story.

On May 29, 1993, the *Walter Cronkite Report* covered the shutdown of the Clarksville plant. Invited by the URW, the TV news attended the boot-burning and other events, including the last day of work at Acme Boot. The *Cronkite Report* aired extensive footage of interviews with dislocated workers and showed the devastating impact of job loss on workers in the already depressed Clarksville economy. It emphasized job flight, the lure of Section 936, and the connection between tax policy and job loss. Members of Local 330 were tremendously encouraged by the outpouring of public support for their cause. They received mail and support from individuals and groups around the country.

Just after the boot-burning and motorcade, the union and the workers learned of a major victory. At least one prong of their strategy had succeeded. Acme suddenly announced that it had withdrawn its application for federal income tax incentives under Section 936. Its press release announced simply, "Officials at Acme Boot have decided not to seek income tax exemptions offered for the company's operation in Puerto Rico." [109]

Why had Acme given up? A high-ranking Puerto Rican official cited "corporate exhaustion" as the reason for Acme's withdrawal of its tax-exemption application. And Clifford Myatt said, "I think the union has been so vociferous and unfair in its attack on them that they [Acme] don't want any more bad P.R. Also, they've been inundated with so much paperwork and expenses that they decided to forget it." [110] The workers' struggle against Acme's decision had paid off. Rather than endure the barrage of negative media attention, the continuing boycott, and potential harm to its image and sales, Acme decided to forgo a very lucrative opportunity. The elated union was triumphant.

Then came the bad news. Acme was going to move anyway. Vogel explained that although the company was distancing itself from the 936 controversy, it would still receive local economic development subsidies and was continuing with plans for production in Toa Alta. Acme still refused to concede that the new factory would be a "runaway." Vogel claimed that the Clarksville plant closing and the establishment of a new plant in Puerto Rico were "nonrelated, coincidental issues."[111] No one believed him.

Acme's decision to forgo benefits under Section 936 was a major victory for the workers. The U.S. taxpayers had saved some money. Yet the workers had failed to save their jobs or their community. The Clarksville plant closed on schedule. The company, with fewer but still considerable tax breaks, moved the work to Puerto Rico. After months of mobilization, coalition-building, public education, media attention, political lobbying, and protest, the Clarksville community lost Acme Boot.

Months later the workers learned that the long battle against Section 936 had ended in a compromise. Instead of a 100 percent tax break, corporations would enjoy only a 60 percent exemption. The companies had managed to preserve the type of credit that Clinton and congressional leaders had deplored publicly. Companies would continue to be rewarded on the basis of their incomes, not for jobs created or wages paid. As the *Wall Street Journal* analyzed it, "Despite the fact that they were the first—and an especially vulnerable—target of the new president's desire to change Washington, the drug companies escaped with much of their coveted tax break intact."[112] Corporate executives and Puerto Rican officials were delighted with "the rescue of Section 936."[113]

The centerpiece of the unions' campaigns—the provision to prevent runaway plants—was never enacted. The Puerto Rican government and economic development establishment had lobbied heavily against the provision, and Clinton had declined to press for it. The corporations' political campaign had been expensive and ingenious.[114] PRUSA lobbyists had convinced even proponents of tax reform, such as Senators Bill Bradley of New Jersey and Pat Moynihan of New York, to maintain the loophole.[115] Two journalists concluded, "The key to [the corporations'] success appears to have been their ability to escape the administration's special-interest wrath by encouraging 'grass-roots' efforts among Puerto Ricans. In part, the Puerto Rico government and masses of Puerto Ricans here and on the mainland became a willing front for some of the largest corporations in the country."[116]

Even after it became clear to the workers that Acme had moved its production out of Clarksville and was not coming back, they still wanted to pursue other options. Before the official closing date of May 21, 1993, the URW spread the word that it was looking for another buyer for the Acme plant. The workers and the union believed that the plant was productive and profitable, and a skilled and highly experienced group of employees was available. They did not want a new owner, like Farley, to wring some profit out of Clarksville and move on; the workers wanted to be involved in every aspect of production, including plant ownership.

The union quickly received a response from John Sisk, a Jacksonville, Florida, businessman with personal connections to Tennessee. Sisk presented a plan to reopen the Clarksville plant as American Boot Company, rehire 160 former Acme workers, and begin making boots again.[117] The boots would be sold to a number of contractors, including Acme itself.[118] As more buyers were found, employment and production would increase. After meeting with union representatives and workers, Sisk signed a letter of intent that American Boot would buy the plant and remaining equipment from Acme "with the intention of re-opening the facility to once again make footwear."[119] Acme was willing to participate in the deal, Sisk explained, because "the company has moved from manufacturing to retail, with a significant portion of their profits derived from their 50 retail outlets. . . . Acme has elected to

purchase boots from outsources and to concentrate on sales and marketing."[120] Acme would become a customer, not a competitor.

Sisk sent a letter to the workers whom he had met, outlining his plan.
"We are all in this together," the letter promised. "It is important for
each of you to make suggestions as to ways to run the plant more profitable [sic] and make the work environment more harmonious for each
of you. Opening up communications is dynamic and I truly believe this
represents American Boot Company's contribution to a new style of
American Management—a **Renaissance!**"[121]

The workers were initially interested in the possibility of becoming
owners of the new company, and keeping their jobs. But as more of the
details became available, union leaders began to have doubts. Greg
LeRoy, who had worked closely with other employee-ownership projects, conveyed "very serious misgivings" about Sisk and his plan.[122] First,
there were problems with Sisk's business design. The worker-ownership
was not structured as an ESOP, which meant it would forgo huge tax
savings and low interest rates designed to encourage employee-owned
firms. Sisk seemed to know very little about employee-ownership plans.
Second, there were some signs that Sisk himself was perhaps not as reliable as the workers had hoped. He had been closely associated with at
least five bankruptcy proceedings in Florida and South Carolina, and he
had outstanding judgments against him totaling perhaps $7 million.[123]
And as a real estate developer and investor, Sisk had no manufacturing
experience whatsoever. Finally, Sisk demanded serious concessions from
the workers. Sisk believed Acme's wages had been too generous at $7.95
per hour plus health insurance.[124] Moreover, as an initial payment, each
worker was asked to contribute a lump sum of $8,500—more than half a
year's gross income. For many of the workers, "such a sum represent[ed]
a large share of their life savings."[125] This premium was mandatory for
all employees. The workers' investment would cover the initial costs of
$1.5 million; Sisk would not contribute his own equity. The state of

Tennessee agreed to contribute $400,000 in "reimbursement for salaries paid during the training and startup period," and a low-interest loan of $500,000 for equipment financing.[126] In return, Sisk said he "anticipated" paying out 50 percent of the company's after-tax earnings as dividends, to be shared among the worker-owners. There was no guarantee that the workers would recoup their initial investment, or even be employed beyond a year or two. And a decision to sell or close the plant could be made by Sisk alone. The workers would be assuming a huge share of the expense with very little of the power.

For all of these reasons TIRN, LeRoy, and Tucker eventually advised against the Sisk plan, and the workers rejected his offer. There were not 200 workers who could have afforded the initial payment on a salary that had been cut substantially. And even if they could, it was too risky. If the union advised workers to invest their money, it could expose itself to a Duty of Fair Representation liability.[127] There were too many signs that Sisk was doing just what Farley had done. Rather than investing his own capital and creating a personal stake in boot production, he was asking the workers and the state of Tennessee to assume the costs and the risks of manufacturing. The workers feared that after the contract with Acme expired, Sisk would close up shop and go back to Florida, leaving the employee-owners in debt. They rejected the bid. Acme Boot closed on schedule, never to manufacture boots again.

Acme as a "Successful Failure"

Although the Acme Boot campaign failed to keep the Clarksville plant open, it was nonetheless victorious in a number of ways. Acme Boot is a story of what I call a "successful failure." Although the workers were sadly disappointed with the final outcome, they had created a very important struggle and a meaningful political process. The impact of the campaign can be demonstrated in four ways. First, the workers affected

Acme's decisions and corporate behavior, which is an unusual and notable accomplishment. Second, the Acme workers developed a contextualized analysis of the closing itself. Rather than blame themselves or each other for their misfortune, the Acme workers learned their place within the global economy. Third, the Clarksville workers evaluated unions, and collective action in general, much more positively than the Greenbrier group did. Fourth, the workers who got involved in saving their plant learned a lot about politics, and translated these lessons into future activity. Thus the impact of the struggle in Clarksville went far beyond the boundaries of Middle Tennessee. Each of these points is elaborated below.

First, the workers' capacity to mobilize to defend their rights had a significant impact on the company's behavior, and on politicians' behavior as well. The workers won some concrete victories. Acme did not receive the federal tax exemptions it had sought. Because of the union campaign, the company rescinded its application. The union also succeeded in changing Section 936. In December 1993 the exemption rate was cut, forcing corporations to pay approximately $3.75 billion in additional federal income taxes over five years.[128] And only two years later the coalitions of unions succeeded in eliminating Section 936 completely. The Small Business Job Protection Act of 1996 repealed the Possessions Tax Credit as of December 31, 1995.[129] Given the intensity and expense of the pharmaceutical and other industries' campaign to defend Section 936—and most politicians' capitulation in the face of corporate pressure—the defeat of 936 was a remarkable victory. If the labor movement, with the URW in the forefront, had not kept up a grassroots campaign, Section 936 benefits would have remained intact. The union and its allies had countered an aggressive corporate campaign, and won a national policy change.

Second, the solidarity between workers and the community was striking. While the Greenbrier plant closing ended with divisiveness, scapegoating, and self-reproach, this did not happen at Acme. The union's nine months of intense mobilization provided the workers with a larger analysis of the situation they faced. Ironically, while unions are usually blamed with antagonizing relations between workers and management, the opposite happened here. Unlike the Greenbrier workers, no one from Acme Boot blamed their immediate supervisors or managers. Instead they blamed Acme's owners and the federal government, which helped corporations more than it did workers. As Alan Buckner says, "It wasn't management here. It was Farley Industries, a corporate giant. He just wanted more, more, and more . . . to correct his mistakes."[130] Kellam says, "I don't blame the supervisors. . . . I blame our government for giving them the tax breaks to allow it to happen. They shouldn't make it so easy for them to go. . . . If they're over there, why shouldn't they have to pay these high taxes? We have to pay the taxes to make up for them. That's not fair—we've lost our jobs, we have to pay higher taxes, and they're sitting over there paying no taxes. I blame the government for that."[131] The workers were educated on the national and international political decisions that led to the plant closing. They understood Acme's move as a strategic corporate decision made possible by a series of governmental policies, influenced by other transnational corporations.

The workers were understandably furious with William Farley. A paragon of Southern politeness says, "He was a you-know-what."[132] "Farley—when he bought out Acme . . . he wanted to get rid of the union. He's got money, he's a millionaire, sitting up there in the Sears Tower in Chicago, he's got money. He don't care whose throat he cut."[133] They offered various explanations for his behavior. Buckner thought it was simple: "Greed. Greed of the owner. He wasn't satisfied with what he was making here. He wanted more. He didn't care about his fellow workers, shall I say? It was in his financial interest to close us down."[134] Mittendorf believed he had moved the work to El Paso and

Puerto Rico "to get the union out. They didn't like the union. That's all there really was to it." [135] Luttrell conjectured, "He [said] he didn't have nothing against the union, but I think that's the only reason why they done it, to get rid of the union." Acme wanted to escape not only high wages and benefits, she said, but rules. With the union, "they had to do things legal, that they wouldn't normally do. . . . They had rules to go by." [136]

In the process of their struggle, the workers became more critical of ideologies they had always accepted. They began to analyze their workplaces and communities in different terms. After the closing, Sally Kellam felt lucky to have found a new job in a warehouse, but didn't think of the employer the way she used to. "Where I'm at here, they talk about 'family.' I said, 'I don't want to hear none of this 'family' stuff out here now. I've been through this 'family.' . . . Your family will mess on you before anybody else!" [137] Although the Acme workers had once considered their co-workers to be "family," they were now discriminating in their use of the term. None used the metaphor of family to describe the company as a whole. They had come to understand their interests as distinct from those of their bosses.

Also in contrast to Greenbrier, not a single Acme worker I interviewed blamed herself, other workers, or some "other" group of people. As Kellam said, "I'm not bitter toward other people. I'm just bitter with the way things happened with our jobs." [138] They expressed respect and empathy for their co-workers at the plant. The workers also did not blame the union for the plant closing. Although some of them wondered if they could possibly have received more severance pay, more notice, or more benefits, they did not think the union could have prevented or stopped the shutdown itself. As Luttrell said, "I thought they could have done more than they're doing, but . . . no matter what the union done, [Acme] weren't going to change their minds. . . . They was just trying to get that tax cut, is what they were after. Lying dogs, they said that wasn't the reason they went to Puerto Rico—but everybody knows better." [139]

The workers understood the political and economic context in which Farley had decided to close the Tennessee plants. When asked if they hold the government responsible for not better regulating the economy, the typical response was, "Yes I do. I think our government should stop it; don't you?! I mean, why take our jobs and give it to them?" [140] The workers expressed disappointment in local politicians as well as national officials. Luttrell had been shocked that the mayor of Clarksville had been unwilling to assist the workers more in their effort to keep the plant open. "What we've had to go through with the mayor, to help us out! . . . They [city officials] said they went to see Farley, but I don't believe that either." [141] Buckner agreed: "I didn't see any good come out of Acme's people—our mayor and county government—for Local 330 when the plant started closing down." [142]

Because of their experiences, the Acme workers understood complex economic issues. Buckner explained why capital mobility should be regulated: "Puerto Rico's government let [Acme] save $20,000-some per employee that they saved by not paying income taxes there. . . . And prices have definitely not gone down for the consumer. They have stayed the same. . . . Just look at the pharmaceutical firms down there. Look at how medicine prices have risen in the last ten years—the cost of medicine has tripled. They don't pass the savings along to people here." [143] As Kellam said, "Major companies are getting richer and richer, and we're getting poorer and poorer." [144]

Third, the Acme workers' ideas about labor unions and collective action differed dramatically from those of the Greenbrier workers. The Greenbrier group expressed unanimous disdain for unions. They believed in their ability to defend their own interests—even after their experience contradicted that belief. The Greenbrier workers insisted, for example, that it would have been inappropriate for outside parties to insinuate themselves into the "family" of Greenbrier. The Greenbrier workers perceived labor unions to be just another set of powerful institutions, far removed from their concerns and unlikely to protect them or represent their interests. The Greenbrier workers expressed staunchly individualistic anti-union attitudes, typical in Appalachian Tennessee. The Acme workers, by contrast, had more nuanced understandings of unions' role. They freely expressed disagreements with union decisions and policies, but they also appreciated the indispensable support of the union and community groups.

This difference between the two workforces was not based in ideology or culture, for neither group was ideologically or culturally predisposed to support unions. Rather, the Acme workers had developed their attitudes during the process of struggle. They understood the union as a pragmatic entity, as opposed to an ideal one. Like most workers in Tennessee—even after Acme's long history of struggle—they are not reflexively pro-union. But the Acme workers unanimously appreciate the benefits and work environment created by a union. They see a sharp contrast between their experiences at Acme and that of workers at non-union plants. Their most serious complaints at their new (non-union) jobs involved layoffs, favoritism, unequal treatment, discrimination, and mandatory overtime. With a union, Edna Luttrell saw, "they treated you like human beings, they couldn't push you like they normally would, without the union. The union dues are a little high, but I didn't mind it. . . . It's well worth it, knowing that they couldn't shove you out the door."[145]

The Acme workers' experiences convinced them of the need for collective action and the support of a powerful union. "The main thing I see is that if you have no union, you have no seniority rights. . . . You can work at a company twenty years, but if you're non-union, they can come in and say, 'Hey, we don't need you anymore.' And as you get older—this is what hurt me—when they put those people out, it's harder to get a job. And you can't get insurance." Alan Buckner believed this was a change from corporate practices of the past. "Now, the people at the top, all they think about is gimme gimme gimme. It's greed." [146]

With the union at Acme Boot, workers had come to expect fair treatment, open and agreed-upon procedures, and reliable avenues for redress of grievances. "It wasn't the old buddy-buddy system, you know, you pat my back and I'll pat yours. Everybody was more treated equal. They had to treat us equal. They done away with a lot of patting on the back." [147] This general expectation of fair treatment fueled the workers' political campaign as well.

Fourth, the mobilization in Clarksville transformed the participants' political behavior. Compared with the Greenbrier workers, the Acme workers who had participated in union activities were significantly better educated about American politics. Throughout the plant-closing campaign, they had written letters, phone-banked, met with politicians, followed the events around Section 936, and learned much about politics in general. Unlike the Greenbrier workers, the Acme workers—with the help of their contacts at national organizations—had succeeded in eliciting a response from their representatives. Congressman Sundquist met with the union's leaders, and Vice President Gore and Senators Sasser and Mathews made public statements in support of the Local's campaign. This support was vital, not in terms of political outcomes but because it made a big difference to the workers involved. Instead of feeling absolutely powerless, demoralized, and despondent, the Acme workers knew that they were not alone. Even if their political representatives capitulated to corporate pressure in the end, their vocal support indicated to workers that their troubles were important, that they were on the right side, and that they could be heard. All of this was essential to their ability to continue mobilizing and acting politically. When 936 came to a vote, the Tennessee congressional delegation was split. The union had changed some minds and solidified some votes in opposition to the existing system. By contrast, the Greenbrier workers never received a hearing from their own congressional representatives, and after all their efforts, Senator Sasser's office did not even return their phone calls.[148]

When other economic issues arose in national political debates, the Acme workers applied the lessons they had learned. While most of the Greenbrier workers who knew about it believed the North American Free Trade Agreement (NAFTA) would probably be "a good thing," *all* the Acme workers interviewed could speak quite knowledgeably against NAFTA and its effects on both American and Mexican workers. At a minimum, they said, it would take jobs away from places like Clarksville. "That NAFTA—I don't like that!"[149] "Clinton—what's he doing to us? Taking all of our jobs. This deal he passed with free trade, it ain't gonna do anything but move our factories out. . . . I don't think he should have went along with Bush on the free trade agreements."[150] Charles Schmidt had worked at Acme for twenty years along with his wife, Betty, packing boots onto trucks in the shipping department. Schmidt had never been involved in political issues in his life, but he had done his homework on NAFTA and found he had strong opinions: "This is a Republican treaty. It was drawn up by the Bush administration. . . . All that time, they were strictly antilabor, strictly."[151] "I get hot under the collar when it comes to this. . . . Before long, there will be no manufacturing in this country—it's coming to that. Just slowly, it's all creeping off. Which has been going on for years. But I didn't even realize how bad it was until this happened to us."[152]

Accordingly, when NAFTA came up for a congressional vote in the fall of 1993—and then with the General Agreements on Tariffs and Trade (GATT) and other "free trade" proposals—many of the Acme workers became involved in the political campaigns to defeat them. "I can't see anything good out of that NAFTA. . . . They say there will be high-tech jobs, but I don't see many of them. For every 500 workers at Acme Boot, they may create a hundred, if that many, but you can't sacrifice four out of five jobs. You can't give away four jobs to get one, regardless of what the pay scale is." [153] When the workers heard news reports on issues related to international trade, they paid close attention, relating the stories to their own experience. Kellam said, "You turn on TV all the time and you hear about a plant closing and part of it going to Mexico. . . . You know, I didn't realize it was that bad [until Acme closed]. I just did not realize at all." [154]

The union's campaign had an even deeper impact on the workers' ideas about international issues than their opposition to NAFTA and GATT suggests. The Acme workers fit exactly the demographic profile of Pat Buchanan's supporters in 1995: mostly white, working-class, disillusioned Democrats, culturally conservative, Christian, in the South. As victims of a plant closing, they might have been persuaded to place the blame on immigrants or on the Puerto Rican people for "stealing" their jobs, as Buchanan and other right-wing leaders were advocating. But not a single worker interviewed believed this. As Mittendorf said, "I might blame the government of Puerto Rico, [but] the poor workers are like us . . . there ain't nothing they can do about it. The Puerto Ricans can't do anything. All they could do is refuse to work, and they're not gonna refuse to work if they're starving to death and need jobs." [155] And while Kellam deplored the impact of NAFTA on U.S. workers, she also felt for the Mexican workers. "I just can't believe that these Mexican people are living like this. . . . They make nothing compared to what we were making. And that's sad. . . . You think about all the children in the world that's growing up; where are they going to get jobs?" [156]

Although the Acme workers had participated and learned much by doing so, they were not necessarily more sanguine about the political system. They had learned that their representatives did not take workers' needs and interests very seriously. Sally Kellam said, "We [the URW workers] went out here and worked for this man [President Clinton] to get him in office. Now we feel like we've been let down. So, I don't think I'm gonna vote again. What's the point?" [157] Mittendorf agreed: "I thought Clinton would stand up for us, as hard as we worked for him. I politicked for him—'cause I was a Democrat. But I done resigned. I ain't gonna vote no more. I'm sick of politics." [158] Charles Schmidt learned "the power is with these corporations; *they've* got the power." [159]

Despite their disillusionment, however, the Acme workers actually maintained their political involvement after the plant closed. Kellam acknowledged that her cynicism was unlikely to last, given her previous activity. "Now, maybe I'll change when the time comes again." And whether or not she participates in electoral politics, Kellam's political behavior was clearly changed by the Acme Boot campaign. She had not been active before the plant shutdown. Now, she says, "I've gotten more involved in a *lot* of things since this plant closing. . . . I've gotten more involved. I had never in my life wrote letters to congressmen and the White House. I never was like this." An important kernel of optimism remained: "I feel like we need to stand up because that's important. They need to *know* how the people feel. It could make a change. It could make a difference." [160] Buckner wanted to pressure Clarksville politicians to revive the defunct plant: "They could float some type of bond issue to help the *people* out." [161]

Unlike the Greenbrier workers, who mostly did not express a party preference or a commitment to a particular political ideology, the Acme workers knew what they were looking for in a political leader. They nearly all identified as Democrats, or at least they were Democrats until the Clinton administration let them down. And they had high standards for a candidate they would support. Mittendorf explained her disgust with Clinton: "I don't think he's trying to help the working-class people. I think he's out more for the rich, and the big wheels. . . . Before he was elected, how he went on . . . all this stuff about the poor working class. But he forgot; it's all gone now." [162] She is looking for a leader who stands by his word and is committed to "creating more jobs," raising wages, and improving the lot of the working class. Betty Schmidt had a similar standard: "Say John Doe voted for NAFTA. Are you going to vote for somebody that gave our jobs away? . . . I think people get it." [163] The Greenbrier workers, by contrast, did not "get it." They could not connect their wrenching and life-altering experience with any political issues or outcomes.

The Acme workers' year of struggle, protest, and collective action did not save their plant, but it may have saved their dignity, and it certainly changed their politics. They did not feel the same sense of helplessness and disempowerment that were so tangible at Greenbrier. Although they had lost, they had also learned that they could act to affect their own fate. And they continued to act, even after the campaign to stop the shutdown had ended. Mitch Tucker consulted with other union leaders considering fighting their companies' tax exemptions. Unlike the Greenbrier workers, the people at Acme found ways to use their new knowledge and to retain a sense of agency in their own lives and in the political economy. As Kellam said, "I think I have changed a whole lot." [164]

Jane Hutchins and Jane Pryor walked up and down their streets ringing every doorbell to get their neighbors to sign a petition against NAFTA. They went to TIRN meetings, and eventually were chosen to participate in a delegation from Tennessee as part of an exchange with Mexican workers. The delegation, made up predominantly of women, was designed to counter the message from companies that workers in the Southern Hemisphere were "stealing the jobs" of workers in the southern U.S.[165] Along with other workers who had been through plant closings or other profound and rapid economic change, Hutchins and Pryor traveled to Mexico to witness the conditions of work and to speak with workers in the *maquiladoras* (free trade zones). This was their first trip on an airplane, and they expressed great trepidation before the trip. But they returned with a much fuller understanding of the similarities between the situations in Mexico and Appalachia, the impact of the global economy, and the corporate agenda. They joined TIRN's Fair Trade Committee, and through the labor/community coalition, they became leaders in the anti–NAFTA campaign, the anti–Fast Track campaign, and future trade and globalization issues.

By mobilizing workers to analyze their situation and to act, Local 330's campaign had lasting ramifications in the wider political world. The Acme workers' willingness to take on the challenge of fighting some of the most powerful corporations on the globe was an inspiration to other unions and political organizations. To attempt this type of struggle was extremely rare at the time. Local 330's fight was one of the first cases in the country of a union taking an active role in protesting the unregulated mobility of capital. What later became known as corporate welfare, subsidy abuse, or the global assembly line was absent from the public debate in 1992. Words like *globalization* had not even entered the lexicon.

No one had expected the URW or its allies to fight Section 936. The *San Juan Star* noted the bewilderment of corporate executives and government officials at the mobilization in 1993. "When Puerto Rico defended Section 936 tax breaks from proposed cuts in the mid-1980s, U.S. labor unions hardly made a peep. Yet today, labor's voice is shrill in the 936 debate on Capitol Hill." [166] As Dick Leonard of OCAW said, "Section 936 is a very obscure part of the tax code and also the most complex . . . We put out an all-points bulletin to other unions and said, 'This is going on and let us know if it's happening to you.' " [167] The URW and others were ready to act.

The coalition that formed against Section 936 is a perfect example of a successful failure—a campaign that failed to meet its explicit goal at the time, but sowed the seeds for later mobilizations and major victories. The Acme Boot activists and their allies laid the groundwork for the national mobilization around NAFTA only a year later. Two years later they defeated 936 completely, ending a major corporate loophole. The following year, to everyone's surprise, they defeated Fast Track legislation in Congress. These were the first victories against corporate globalization in fifty years, and they motivated a new generation of activists to get involved in future fights around international economic justice.

During Acme's campaign many unions and other groups either participated in the coalition against Section 936 or watched with interest, and an intensive process of political education took place within the working class across the country. People learned about the importance of the tax code in job creation, about economic development incentives that pit workers and localities against each other, about "runaway shops" and taxpayer-financed job destruction. Workers and organizations began to pay attention to the phenomenon of transnational corporate capital flight. When NAFTA and future trade agreements came up for debate, the very same issues were at stake. Free trade no longer seemed like an arcane economic policy sphere, as it easily might have. Instead it was a hot topic with important ramifications for workers' lives and communities. When the Acme workers moved on to talk about GATT, Fast Track, the WTO, and the issues in Seattle, the groundwork for the movement had been laid.

Because it failed, the Acme Boot campaign—and NAFTA right after it—also taught the labor movement what it was up against. Relatively small unions like OCAW and URW had fought some of the wealthiest corporations and their powerful political allies, and lost. The power of money in U.S. politics was not news, but the willingness of corporations to spend so heavily on issues like this, and to win congressional support through a faux grassroots campaign, was unexpected. The unions learned that if they hoped to regulate corporate mobility in the global economy of the 1990s, it would require continued pressure, resources, and true grassroots mobilization across state and national boundaries. Acme Boot workers developed the arguments and built the early stages of a coalition, which the national movement against NAFTA would revive one year later. Acme's campaign—and others like it all over the United States—permanently changed the landscape of political possibilities, in small but important ways.

Explaining Success

Why was the Acme Boot campaign able to achieve so much? What explains the ability of Local 330 to organize a sustained and large-scale mobilization around economic issues, and in the process creating change in Clarksville and beyond? Why could the Acme Boot story end as a relatively "successful failure" while Greenbrier ended in total defeat?

The most obvious and significant difference between the situations at Greenbrier and Acme Boot is the presence of a strong union. Most important was the union's ability to mobilize, and its proven record of doing so when necessary. The Greenbrier story shows that laws alone cannot protect workers from secret and unfair corporate decisions. Greenbrier Industries, like innumerable corporations before and since, violated the law in numerous ways: by failing to notify workers of the plant closing, surreptitiously transferring equipment and materials between plants and between countries, failing to insure them for the health care they had purchased, failing to contribute its portion to the 401(k) fund, and confiscating the workers' own retirement savings. Some of these violations were certainly extreme, but others were not. In violating the WARN Act, for example, Greenbrier is not unique—it is actually in the majority. In most plant closings in the U.S. in the past six years, companies have not complied with the federal law.[168] Acme Boot was one of the few that not only complied with the letter of the law but even went beyond the requirements stipulated in its contract with Local 330. The reason for Acme's compliance, and for its repeated press releases and public statements to reassure the community of its good intentions, lies with the union's capacity to mobilize, publicize, and actively protest corporate wrongdoing.

Thus the Acme workers received many protections that the Greenbrier workers were denied. Besides fair warning before the closing, the Acme workers received severance pay. It was not a large sum; most workers received less than $1,000, before taxes. But it was negotiated between the company and the workers' union representatives, and it was a form of recognition for their years of service and their abrupt termination. It was far more than the Greenbrier workers received, more than the GE workers in the following chapter received, and more than most victims of plant closings in America receive. The Acme workers were not merely lucky, nor were they protected by the legal provisions of their contract, although those helped. The workers' history of organized union activity, demonstrations, and long strikes protected them the most. Acme knew what the union had done in the past and what it was capable of doing again. Rather than face organized resistance, as it often had, Acme Boot calculated that it would be less costly to negotiate a settlement.

The structural relationship between the company and the union local influenced the workers' ability to mobilize and the outcome of the plant closing itself. Because the URW was negotiating contracts with the company on a regular basis, the union's leaders had access to financial reports and other information, and the union was contractually entitled to receive fair warning before major changes. This was particularly important at Acme, where there were very few of the traditional "early warning signs" unions look for. Unlike at Greenbrier, production at

Acme had been continuing apace. The workers knew that Acme had been afflicted by layoffs and cost-cutting since 1985, but since the introduction of computer technology and expensive modernization at the factory they had good reason to believe that the worst was over. Even in hindsight, they could not name the typical signs that usually provide an early warning of trouble. When asked what had changed in the months before the closing was announced, almost none of the workers could think of anything significant: "You got me on that one."[169]

The company's early notification to the union leaders before the plant closing was essential to the campaign that ensued. Because they knew what was going to happen, the workers could strategize and discuss the issues among themselves while they were still at work and able to communicate with each other easily. The rallies, demonstrations, press conference, and other large-turn-out events all took place while the plant was still open. Compared with the work of the GWC, Local 330's job was much simpler. Workers found out about plans and events at work, as they always had, and often went to rallies together, straight from work. Mobilizing a group with a common workplace was much easier logistically than reassembling workers who had been dispersed and were busy trying to earn a new living. The early notification about the plant closing was important for another reason. Psychologically, it was far easier to mobilize people to save an existing, well-functioning plant. When the Greenbrier workers were faced with a locked factory, it only deepened the workers' sense of powerlessness and despair. By contrast the Acme workers were angry and worried, but optimistic; success felt attainable. In this case the closing had only been proposed, and the workers believed it possible to change the company's plan. Because they were starting early, they felt they had a good chance of mustering sympathetic forces on their side and persuading Farley to keep the plant open. The stakes were high: a successful campaign would save their jobs. The workers had a strong incentive to participate in any way they could.

The contrast with Greenbrier reveals another important point: Knowledge is not enough. The Greenbrier workers had information, and some of them confronted their supervisors or managers, began asking questions, and shared their suspicions with family and friends, but the situation at the plant remained unchanged. In order to be effective, information had to be coupled with the experience and leadership to act, immediately. At Greenbrier, workers knew of fraud and abuse—and that the plant was very likely to close—but never acted on their knowledge. Because the Acme workers had acted collectively in the past, and seen positive results in such action every time they won a new contract or resolved a grievance, they were prepared to do it again. They knew from experience that collective action—and no other strategy—could stop the plant from closing.

Because the union had an organizing structure in place, the Acme workers could be informed and involved almost immediately as events unfolded. This was essential to the success of the mobilization. The rank-and-file employees were up-to-date on the situation and informed about any course of action their leadership was undertaking. They knew what was happening with Farley, they knew about Acme's tax breaks in Puerto Rico, and they understood the legislative campaign around Section 936. Because of the union's structure and its ability to disseminate information and an analysis of the events effectively from worker to worker, the Acme workers were less likely to blame one another for what happened.

The difference between Acme and Greenbrier is remarkable in this respect.[170] Every one of the Greenbrier workers interviewed commented on the "other" workers and their problems, although not every one had the same "other" group in mind. They blamed single mothers, minorities, people on welfare, and young people for the company's failure. Although Acme was more racially diverse than Greenbrier, not a single Acme worker brought up scapegoats. Buckner expressed the typical attitude: "Ninety-seven to 98 percent of the workers at Acme worked *hard*. There always were and always will be a few who don't, but most of 'em worked hard. . . . All people are doing is trying to survive."[171] And Kellam added, "I don't see how a single parent can make it. . . . Cause I couldn't. I don't think I could do it."[172] This expression of empathy was rare at Greenbrier. The solidarity and sense of mutual purpose provided by the union is at least partly responsible for the culture among Acme workers. This was not a mysterious phenomenon; rather it grew directly out of the existence of a grassroots organizing structure within the workplace, by which union stewards shared an analysis with the workers. Sharing information meant much more than providing the facts, relaying data, or leaving a newsletter in people's boxes. Instead the union played a crucial role in helping the workers process the information collectively. Union leaders explained the current situation in context, and shared their understandings of its causes and likely effects. The workers discussed it with their stewards and then with one another. They were forced to consider how any proposed changes would affect not only themselves as individuals but also each of their co-workers who was in a different position from them. This process of collective discussion and analysis was essential, for it united the workers, despite their differences, into a strong coalition. Receiving updates and discussing the situation together on a regular basis prevented the workers from looking at one another in suspicion, or starting rumors, or debating whom to blame. For the union had already identified the enemy—Farley and the public policies supporting his interests—and there was no need for scapegoats. The true stories of corruption, greed, and political deal-making were dramatic enough.

The Acme workers had experience in protests and strikes, and the union knew how to launch a public campaign. Local 330, and other unions they knew, had held marches, parades, rallies, boycotts, and other events—unlike the Greenbrier workers—and they knew how to organize actions. They had dealt with the press on a regular basis. Union leaders and members had been active in political campaigns before, so they knew which officials to call first. But the union's experience meant more than just the acquisition of technical skills. Because workers had the memory of previous strikes and struggles, and had seen positive outcomes from these, they were willing to participate in the campaign. Many workers had been around for the conflicts of the 1960s and 1970s, and they were proud of their bravery during that period. Edna Luttrell said, "I got a picture—I cut it out of the newspaper when we went out on strike [for recognition]. I guess that was back in '62 and '63." [173] Buckner remembers that drive also: "We met in a tiny little service station over on Cumberland Drive. Yes, I was one of 'em that helped organize. I took those little cards around, got 'em signed." [174] He went on strike more than once, and he was proud that he had made an important difference in his work life at Acme. "It took a long period of time for things to change after we had a union, but it worked out well." [175]

Besides recognition drives and contract struggles, the union had also been active in political campaigns. Every four years the Rubber Workers had endorsed a presidential candidate, and Local 330 worked on his behalf in Clarksville. When particularly appealing candidates were running, the union had also worked on congressional races and local campaigns. Political campaign posters and banners from years back adorn the "union hall"—a small shack at the edge of a hay field. When Clinton and Gore ran for election in 1991, Local 330 pulled out all the stops. The union encouraged the workers to volunteer in the campaign, and many did. Luttrell worked hard on the campaign: "We made signs and things. Held rallies. Bought all kinds of shirts, buttons, and pins." [176] Experience in this type of activity made a difference when the plant was threatened. Workers who had worked to elect their own representatives felt a stake in their actions. They felt strongly that the politicians owed them something; the workers deserved a hearing. And so when officials they had helped elect—not only by voting but by donating their scarce time, money, and energy—rejected their claims, they were angry. "I'm sorry [I worked on Clinton's campaign]. A lot of people are. I never thought he would do something like that." [177] They wanted to hold their leaders accountable.

Finally, the URW—unlike the Greenbrier Workers Committee—had access to resources from outside the immediate community. They could pay people to fly in for rallies; send union representatives to Washington to lobby; create leaflets, posters, and banners; and take out advertisement space in local newspapers. Local 330 was able to pay Greg LeRoy of MCLR for hours of consulting. Acme Boot workers' entire campaign assumed a basic level of resources. By contrast, the Greenbrier workers had difficulty scraping together enough money for a meeting room or posterboard. [178]

The union's connections to larger organizations—especially to the URW International Union, other labor unions, relevant divisions of the AFL-CIO, coalitions like TIRN, and research and advocacy institutes like the MCLR—were crucial. Staff and members from all of these organizations consulted people at other organizations who could help. By the end, an impressively wide and diverse circle of individuals and groups had assisted the Acme workers, providing crucial support at various stages of the struggle. The support was not only financial or tangible. The organizations also provided assistance in brainstorming, research, thinking through possible tactics, locating relevant information and applicable precedents. Most of this help was provided at no cost to Local 330. TIRN staff and members worked on the Acme campaign for months, asking no remuneration or reciprocation. [179] Greg LeRoy of MCLR continued researching and strategizing even after the plant closed, dues funds dried up, and Local 330 could no longer pay a consultancy fee. MCLR provided the workers with more than a hundred pro bono hours of consulting assistance.[180] And the other labor unions used their own resources to fund their work with Acme—because they believed that Acme's campaign, whether it ultimately succeeded or failed, would strengthen their own prospects as they faced similar challenges. This is a model of solidarity for the entire labor movement to emulate.

Building a More Inclusive Movement

The Acme Boot workers created success out of failure by transforming themselves and their community, and creating the possibility for further political action around the issues they had raised. At the same time, however, Local 330's campaign had some weaknesses, which will become clearer in comparison with the final case study. The most important shortcoming of the Acme campaign was its failure to involve large numbers of workers in the lobbying and legislative activity around Section 936 and the plant closing. This was partly a question of resources— only two local leaders could travel to Washington, D.C., and naturally Local 330's president and vice president elected to go. But the problem was deeper. The union leadership did a good job of educating members on the problem and keeping them informed, but did not involve many members in decisions about strategy or tactics. Local leaders did not place a high priority on their responsibility to bring forward new leaders from the rank and file, and they accordingly lost touch with a significant group of members.

This lack of vision and inclusiveness at least partly explains why the Acme workers were not more successful in the long run. Some workers were mistrustful of the union, and this attitude made them less likely to become involved in a range of political activities. Some workers resented the union for taking their dues money while leaving them out of the important decisions. As Mittendorf said, "I feel like the union has done us wrong in one way by not calling us together for meetings enough, and telling us what's really going on. Because we were union members. We paid our dues for sixteen years." [181] Although she knows all about Section 936, the Puerto Rican tax exemption, the union's lawsuit, and Acme's withdrawal of its exemption application, Mittendorf felt left out of the process. Not surprisingly, workers who feel this way are suspicious of the union's leadership. They wonder if they could have done more than they did, or if the workers could have won more through a different strategy. "Sometimes I think the union done us wrong, you know, letting us settle for what little we got." [182]

Because of this, the leadership of the union did not reflect the membership. The union president and chief stewards were always men, although the workers were more women than men. As with Greenbrier and Citizens Against Temporary Services (CATS), the women did the lion's share of the work in the campaign—phone-banking, leafleting, letter writing, gathering signatures on petitions. They remained loyal rank-and-file members. Yet they were not rewarded for this work within the structure of the union. This had real costs for the collective effort. Workers who showed tremendous leadership potential, who had generously contributed their time and energy to the union for decades, were not recognized as leaders and did not think of themselves that way. Instead of becoming responsible for future campaigns, they remained in the background. Some of the women who worked at Acme later became involved in TIRN, where their leadership potential was recognized and taken seriously. Jane Hutchins and Jane Pryor—who, through TIRN, became leaders in the anti-NAFTA campaign in Clarksville—were all but ignored by their own union. Ingrained sexism prevented the organization from being as strong and effective as it could have been.

The next case study shows the importance of fostering new leadership, especially among women and citizens who have been marginalized and invisible. It also suggests the transformative potential of a campaign that has a broader vision, and an analysis of the political economy that goes beyond workers' immediate self-interest to make connections with other political and economic-justice issues elsewhere. The Acme Boot workers were able to accomplish an impressive amount within the structure they had created, and the General Electric workers in the next chapter demonstrate that even more successful efforts are possible.

5

Seeds of a Social Movement:
General Electric and CATS

All major plant closings—especially unexpected ones—create hardships for displaced workers and for their community. Those who lose their jobs and livelihoods are angry and frustrated. The community's response, however, is not nearly as predictable. In the wake of crisis, some individuals and groups are quiescent, while others create organizations and pursue ambitious activities that would have been unthinkable just months earlier.

When a General Electric plant closed in Morristown, Tennessee, in 1989, factory workers did something remarkable: they created a community-based workers' organization to take on state and local public policies. They called themselves CATS: Citizens Against Temporary Services. This chapter begins with the story of General Electric's plant closing in Morristown, and culminates in the creation of CATS. CATS identified temporary employment as a systematic economic trend in the East Tennessee region, and decided to tackle this problem through concerted collective action. During the ensuing five years, CATS pursued change in at least four realms: through local political officials, legal strategies, a community-based campaign, and finally statewide legislative and lobbying efforts. Although CATS did not succeed in passing legislation or otherwise regulating contingent work, the organization played an important role in an emerging social movement. CATS members went on to participate in political activities, and used their experiences to support other groups and to pursue political and economic change. The participants in CATS' struggle not only educated themselves politically, they also transformed an array of local institutions and laid the groundwork for a nascent national political effort to regulate the increase in contingent and temporary work and the rise of sweatshops. This work was not the result of luck or good timing. Rather, the accomplishments are directly attributable to the organizers, the coalitions that supported CATS, and the local history and tradition of community organizing in East Tennessee. Because of all these indigenous resources, CATS created lasting change. The failure to prevent a plant closing in Morristown was only the beginning of a political effort, the results of which are just being seen, as far away as Seattle, Quebec City, and Genoa, Italy.

CATS presents a fascinating example, for it suggests that there are opportunities to transform issues of economic injustice into an agenda that involves a wide cross section of the community. It also reveals the importance of labor-and-community coalitions to take on these issues. CATS' experience demonstrates the potential of a "successful failure." A sustained organizing effort that failed to achieve its immediate political goals, the group nonetheless was able to transform its members, its Tennessee community, other nongovernmental organizations, and ultimately the national political agenda. The story of CATS suggests the possibility of mobilizing a local social movement around issues of the global economy.

General Electric in Morristown

In Morristown, Tennessee, a town with almost 20,000 residents in a mountainous rural Appalachian region, a job at General Electric was one of the best jobs a person could hold. Like all of upper East Tennessee, Hamblen County had been hit hard by plant closings and layoffs in the 1980s. Unlike most small companies in the area, GE was considered a progressive employer and an invaluable asset to the community. Its wage scales were significantly higher than those of most local factories. Morristown had a very low rate of unionization, and a mostly unskilled rural workforce, and GE's average hourly wages of between $9 and $12 were high for the area. Most workers had worked for the company for many years and considered themselves fortunate to have secure, permanent jobs. Alice Rollins had moved to Morristown when she was eighteen from the coalfields of Kentucky, where her father was a miner. She recalls about GE, "It was a wonderful place to work. We got good wages, and we had good benefits."[1] Kathy Muller, a wiry and vivacious redhead in her fifties, who had also settled in Morristown after growing up in a rural farming area, says that being a GE employee enabled her to see herself as middle-class. Having moved up in the world, she looked down on her less fortunate neighbors. "I got up every day, and I went to work, and I made good money, and a lot of times when I went to the grocery store, and I saw somebody that had food stamps, I always thought, you know, 'Oh, that *little* kind of people, they ought to get a job and go to work.' "[2]

Besides the good pay and benefits, GE was considered a friendly and generous employer. Ernest Gardiner explains that, besides the excellent benefits, including medical, dental, and eye care, he appreciated the confidence he felt "knowing you was working in a big company, knowing it was solid, business is good, GE is worldwide. It just gives you a better feeling than maybe working somewhere where you think it might shut down the next day."[3] The workers felt appreciated and rewarded for their efforts. Every year the company held an employee picnic at Dollywood, the theme park near the Smoky Mountains. Workers and their families were invited to attend, and GE paid for the entire day.[4] GE sponsored baseball and softball teams, and the different shifts competed on Friday afternoons. At Christmas time, one employee remembers, "They gave gifts. We got all kinds of stuff. . . . We had Christmas parties at the plant. If you wanted to go home, you went home, but you got paid . . . We worked like dogs, [but] it was the best time of my life. I had more fun when I worked at GE than all the time when I was in high school." [5]

As a result GE workers were loyal and hardworking. Unlike Greenbrier Industries, GE had an excellent attendance rate and very low turnover. A supervisor at the factory for nearly twenty years, Calvin Brown says, "Records show GE had a very dedicated group of employees in Morristown. Sixty percent of all employees had either *perfect* or *excellent* attendance, meaning they missed less than sixteen hours during the year." [6] Ernest Gardiner was one of these employees. "I think for about five years in a row I had perfect attendance, meaning I didn't miss one minute's work." [7] Joe Perkinson recalls, "They'd give out prizes if you had a year of perfect attendance, without missing any work—I even missed [winning the prize] one year because I clocked in one minute late." [8] Jobs at GE were so coveted, people did not risk losing them. Openings for full-time positions at the plant were very rare. Once someone had won a job at GE, their future seemed secure.

In 1988 a new management team introduced new efficiency standards, and labor-management relations worsened. Calvin Brown traced the changes back to 1983, when Jack Welch took over as CEO at GE corporate headquarters. Welch achieved recognition as one of the first major CEOs to institute drastic downsizing and corporate restructuring in the name of competitiveness. Brown had seen "Neutron Jack" in *USA Today* and on the cover of *Business Week,* "boasting of how he eliminated 125,000 manufacturing jobs. Under the old management, they boasted of how many employees they used to employ. Today, they boast of how many employees they eliminate. That's it in a nutshell." [9] The character of work and working conditions at the plant deteriorated, and workers say they felt increasingly harassed, vulnerable, and powerless. Alice Rollins, who had developed close friendships with her co-workers since moving from the coalfields to Morristown, described the change: "In the beginning it seemed like we were over there for a purpose. We were there to work and make a living; they were there to pay us and make a living. Somewhere along the line it just changed, we was just there to make *them* a living. They changed the supervision, and then after that just everything went downhill. . . . They started cutting back on the little extras. . . . It just killed everybody's spirit. They took the camaraderie out of it. I reached a point where I didn't think they really appreciated my effort; it seemed like all that you heard about was just lining their pockets."[10]

Brown noticed a dramatic shift in managers' attitudes. "The old management cared about the employees; the new management had no respect whatsoever for their employees. . . . As a matter of fact, the new plant manager made the statement that he didn't want to see any employees in his office. Period."[11]

The quality of the product suffered, and workplace accidents increased. Muller remembers that over a friendly cup of coffee the new plant manager confided to her, "I don't agree with seniority. I think you should lay people off on management's discretion, on who they think they should." Muller recalls, "That shocked me! I just jumped, because I thought, if they do that, the first person that'll go is a bunch of women. I *knew* that."[12] More layoffs occurred. "At first, they eliminated the over-road drivers. Then they eliminated the security guards. Then the jobs were closing inside the plant, such as the plating system—those jobs were being farmed out to other companies, where they were getting it done for a lot less. And some jobs transferred to Mexico."[13] Many of the changes seemed completely irrational to the workers. "We were making parts in Morristown, sending them to Maine to be plated, and from Maine they went to Mexico to be subassembled, and then from Mexico sent back to Morristown to be put back in the finished product. I had a hard time figuring that out; I thought I might be able to think of a better way of handling that if I was in charge. But you know, you can't argue with a large corporation any more than you can with the government, and when both of them are in cahoots, you may as well forget it." [14]

A Union at GE?

Beginning with Jack Welch's appointment as CEO, the Morristown workers began a long series of efforts to challenge GE. The workers' first reaction to the changes in the workplace was to contact a union, to see if they could secure collective bargaining rights to protect their jobs and working conditions. Labor unions were not popular in East Tennessee, and the GE workers had been typical in avoiding union representation. But when management changed, the workers decided the company was no longer protecting their interests. In June 1988 a group of workers called the International Brotherhood of Electrical Workers (IBEW) and asked them to launch a union-organizing campaign at the GE plant in Morristown. From the outset there was substantial support among workers. Linda Yount remembered that "in June through September 1988 we were in a heavy union campaign." [15] One group of mostly assembly-line workers formed an organizing committee. They divided up the workforce among themselves and began to talk to their colleagues about the possibility of building a union to protect their jobs and acquire a say in plant decisions and changes. The organizing committee found a receptive audience. Within a short time they had signed up a majority of their co-workers on union membership cards.

Once the word was out, management actively began to counter the union campaign. Yount, employed at GE for sixteen years, recalls, "The company spared no expense to mislead the employees to believing that everything would be great if the union was voted out. I was one of the employees that voted no on the union because I believed so strongly in the company."[16] Management treated employees to parties and gifts. The company asked the workers, "Why should you pay union dues when you get all of this stuff from us?"[17]

Workers were shown films describing how the union would hurt them and the plant. The union was depicted as an outside agitator and a divisive force, more concerned with politics than with helping the workers. The workers were warned that unions brought strikes, plant closings, and Mafia corruption. Meanwhile the company produced its own promotional video, devoted to "the GE family." The film featured shots of many workers, with families and friends, enjoying recreation in the beautiful surrounding area. For this film an original country-music song was commissioned, dedicated to the people and countryside of Morristown and stressing GE's commitment to the area. The company promised that GE would protect Morristown's workers and their community more than any "outside" union could.

Kathy Muller was amazed at the company's all-out effort to defeat the union. "They snowed people. They showed us that film of how we were family, and showed it the day right before the election, how we were family and they were going to take care of us. . . . Another thing they did—they brought in these hunks—you know, because there was a lot of women, they knew the women were going to swing the vote, so they brought in these good-looking guys. . . . They made us sit through hour after hour of propaganda."[18] Some propaganda was positive about GE; some was negative about unionization. Workers were warned that they could lose their jobs if a union came in, and that their comfortable work routines would become more regimented and beyond their control. Muller remembers: "They scared people bad, too. They said that the union would take people's money, and would go to Hawaii and spend it, they had big homes down in Florida that they lived in off of the people, throwed big parties and stuff."[19] Brown remembers the company saying that with a union, "certain people would have 'super seniority'—the shop stewards—and how unions cost jobs. . . . And if you filed a grievance, it would always be thrown in the garbage can. . . . And that you would have to go on strike, and you wouldn't get paid during the strike."[20]

By September 1988, by instilling some mixture of fear and complacency, the company had won. When the election was held, the union was voted down by a three-to-one margin. One observer noted that the majority of "the employees beamed with pride because they thought this would demonstrate to the company how they believed in General Electric."[21]

In their worst nightmares the workers could not have predicted the chain of events that followed. Only one week after the vote, and with absolutely no warning to anyone, GE summarily laid off nearly 200 people—the overwhelming majority of those same workers who had supported their employer in the vote. They were told that there was no work, that they should stay home, and that they probably would be called back to work early in 1989. But the next week they learned—only by listening to radio and television reports—that they were losing their jobs for good. The Morristown warehouse was closing. The workers were devastated; they had often been told that their future with GE was secure. "Our company did not even have the decency to let the employees that supported them for sixteen years have the news before they released it to the news media. How do you suppose we all felt about this news and the way we found out? An employee such as myself that worked for this company for sixteen years, only to have their dreams taken away."[22]

The news got even more confusing. The distribution center warehouse was moving thirty miles, literally down the road, to the town of Mascot in adjacent Knox County. The press reports the workers heard featured spokespersons for Knox County government boasting about the "new" jobs the county had attracted. They claimed that the GE plant would be the anchor for a new industrial park, a renaissance of economic development in the region. And the final shocker: GE had received economic development incentives from Knox County to encourage the move, as well as state funding to train the new workers.

The workers could not believe it. They called the radio and TV stations to say there was a mistake. Many called their supervisors, and were told not to worry, they would not be losing their jobs. After about three weeks of frantic workers' phone calls and visits, the managers finally admitted that a move was planned. The managers held a meeting for the laid-off employees, to explain what was happening. The managers promised that the workers could all transfer, and the workers were relieved that they were only going to be relocated thirty miles away after all. Then, three weeks after that, management sent all the workers a letter inviting them to come to the new plant to fill out an application to work there. As one worker said, "We could go to the place where we had been working for ten and a half years, and apply for a job. It was unbelievable." [23]

Then they learned that the jobs themselves had not survived the move. At the new site all work would be subcontracted, and workers would be hired through a new independent contracting company called Usco Distribution Services, Inc. Still, GE tried to reassure the workers. "We were told that they were contracting our jobs out to a private contractor and we would be given applications and told that the contractor would pay a competitive wage." [24] After a meeting with Usco representatives, the workers found out differently. Although the work itself was no different from before, the pay would be about $6 an hour (about one-half of the wages at the Morristown site), with no benefits. While the workers had paid about $17 monthly for their insurance at GE, at Usco an inferior optional package would cost $150 a month. The

Usco jobs provided no job security or pension benefits—a far cry from the union job protections and wages the workers had once anticipated. Even the optional health benefits were expensive and inadequate, and "the subcontractor urged their employees not to take them." [25] GE did not apologize. The move was part of a national GE corporate strategy. As the GE vice president for employee relations stated that year, "The use of contingent workforces, such as temporary, part-time and contract workers, will grow." [26]

In a typical twist on capital mobility, these jobs were staying within the state and within the region, but they were being downgraded considerably. Morristown's loss was Mascot's economic development miracle. Knox County executive Dwight Kessell commended the county's director of economic development for "the extraordinary work she did in securing this new industry and these new jobs for Knox County." [27]

Despite the workers' shock and dismay, they retained some confidence in GE's management. Wondering if there might be an alternative, a large group of workers met with managers to discuss possible courses of action. "We asked for meetings with some of our Division General Managers, in which we relayed that we were willing to take a freeze in wages or a cut in pay to keep our jobs with our benefits and seniority." [28] Their offers were all refused by management. They attempted to open negotiations to retain their jobs, and were again thwarted. "We sent a petition to the [General Electric] company's President, Jack Welch, asking him to visit Morristown so we could negotiate to keep our jobs. The only result from this was harrassment from the management." [29]

Officially, the company stated that in order to remain competitive in the global market, tough measures were necessary. As one worker said, "Their explanation was 'restructuring.'" [30] The workers were surprised, because they had been told that the Morristown plant had been very profitable, shipping approximately $88 million in goods and earning profits of $26 million a year.[31]

Beyond competitiveness, workers heard various reasons why the move was necessary. One said "their main excuse for laying us off was that they would be closer to the population center of the eastern United States. That was about the lamest thing I ever heard of. Moving thirty miles down to Mascot was centrally located?! It insulted me when I sat there and heard that. I'm from the backwoods, but I know a little better than that."[32]

Temp Work or No Work

The workers realized that they were not going to change management's decision to close the warehouse and subcontract the work. In a last attempt to hold on to their jobs, some workers simply drove down to the Usco plant in Mascot and asked to be hired—as the company had originally suggested. They were desperate enough to accept their old jobs back for half the pay, with no benefits or job security. Ernest Gardiner, who had been earning $10.97 per hour plus benefits when he was laid off, was told the most he could make at Usco was $5.25 an hour with no benefits. Swallowing pride as well as rage, he and many others applied for work. Yet not a single one was hired. The workers believed that they had been asked to fill out applications (at the initial October meeting at which management explained the situation) because the new Usco team had to meet state government regulations to demonstrate that the laid-off workers had been offered the opportunity to apply for jobs before new hires were trained for the positions. As Mary Hutchinson said, "GE told the JTPA [Job Training Partnership Act] office in Knoxville at this time that all GE employees were offered these jobs as GE employees, but that no one wanted them. GE made this claim so they could apply for federal funds in Knoxville."[33] The workers believed that the company had planned from the start to keep out anyone connected with the old regime.

By the end of 1989 most of the workers were looking for new jobs. This was not a purely private experience. The process brought them into contact with an array of governmental agencies responsible for administering programs and assisting unemployed and displaced workers. For many of the GE workers the experience of asking for help from the state—with unemployment insurance, or with new job opportunities—was their first encounter with the government's economic programs. For those who had trusted in government, or assumed it would help them if they were ever in need, the experience was a rude awakening. They began to question the state's role in job creation and economic development.

As in most plant closings, representatives of state agencies encouraged the displaced workers to go back to school, to learn new skills, or to prepare for careers in the supposedly booming "service sector." The workers, however, did not believe that this job training would serve their needs. They did some research, spoke with their friends and neighbors, and discovered that, even for those with training and education, few job opportunities existed in Morristown. As Muller said, "You hear everybody talk about retraining—well, the problem, we ask, is, *for what?* What do you retrain a fifty-six- or fifty-seven-year-old man for? Where does he go?. . . . Because you get out there and look for jobs that pay, there's not enough. Everyone can't be a nurse!"[34] Calvin Brown confirmed this impression: "Recently I was told by an official of the Vocational School that this [job training program] was all in vain, because they could not place any of their graduates—because no jobs exist."[35]

Many workers considered moving away from the area, and some moved to Nashville or Atlanta, which reportedly were "booming." But many had commitments that made it very difficult to leave the area, particularly the women, and particularly the women with families. Alice Rollins recalls, "I thought about maybe going down and working with my brother [in Kentucky]. He works in a plant down there. But my husband, at that time, he was working . . . I thought, I got a husband, my son was still home at the time, I thought, I can't do that. Men can do that, but they frown on women." [36]

Very few workers found new opportunities that were at all comparable to the jobs they had lost. Seeing no jobs available, most decided not to pursue the state-sponsored education and training programs. One exception was Ernest Gardiner, who went to vocational school and studied to become a high-tech machinist. Even with the new skills, however, the only job he could find was far from home, for $8.25 an hour. "The pay is not near what I was used to." [37] Everyone who looked for new jobs found scant openings. [38] Like many of the men laid off from GE, Perkinson found part-time work as a nighttime security guard at the mall, earning less than five dollars an hour. [39] The women were more likely to find work in retail stores or restaurants, the backbone of the new service economy.

The official listings at the Tennessee Department of Employment Security Job Service office offered very few full-time job openings, and hardly any above minimum wage. State officials at the unemployment office were not encouraging. The workers received a glimpse of a government that could not provide them with any concrete assistance when they most needed it. Even worse, they experienced a bureaucracy that repeatedly disrespected them, trivialized their needs, and was unconcerned about the outrages that had landed them in the unemployment line. The Department of Employment Security officially advised the GE workers to contact temporary services and contract-labor agencies. Temporary agencies were no longer confined to the clerical and service sectors—in fact a majority of workers in industrial jobs were hired through temporary services. Unlike traditional employers, these agencies were hiring continuously. Increasingly factories in the Morristown area were contracting out for "temporary" employees rather than hire their own permanent workers.

The GE workers were shocked to learn that permanent, decent-paying jobs like the ones they had lost in Morristown were systematically being replaced by temporary jobs, either through agencies or through in-house temporary labor pools at large companies. Most laid-off workers who were lucky enough to find new jobs could only procure temporary or contingent placements. This seemed grossly unfair, and it awakened the workers to the facts of the changing economy. Alice Rollins remembered that "when I went to work at GE in 1978, I went to work for $4.44 an hour. You don't get paid much more than that right now! The minimum wage is [less than that] right now! It seems like we're going back. . . . I thought the whole ideas was to progress. But as far as jobs is concerned—we're not."[40] The workers were clear that temporary work *per se* was not the problem. "There is a place in society for part-time workers. . . . I'm not against temporary services if it's a good thing. If it's not used so they can get rid of one permanent [worker] and hire two, just so they won't have to pay them full benefits—that's not fair."[41] The shift away from relatively good jobs, toward contingent work and rampant uncertainty, was the problem.

The realization that local and state officials were either unwilling or unable to help them was one step in the political transformation of the GE workers. Over subsequent months, as they went about looking for new work and shared their experiences with one another, their understanding of their situation dramatically broadened. After years of enjoying the relatively sheltered life of GE employees, they entered a very different labor market. The realization that they themselves might be consigned to low wages, no job security, and no benefits—and that thousands like them had been stuck there for some years—changed the GE workers' view of themselves in relation to other workers. Although in 1989 the problem of "contingent work" had not yet become a topic of national debate, this group of workers ascribed the source of their misery to the burgeoning contingent labor market.

Organizing CATS

Outraged to hear that temporary work was their only option, the former GE workers shared with each other their findings about the epidemic of temporary employment in Morristown and its negative consequences. Although no one seems to remember whose idea it was originally, the workers decided to meet as a group. The first meeting was "packed" with over a hundred people. Rollins remembers that "the first meetings were just *chaos,* everybody was just trying to talk." [42] The workers shared their stories, described their experiences, vented their anger. No one had any answers to their situation. Nevertheless the outraged workers, mostly women, began to meet regularly. They were determined to do something to remedy their situation, but if that was impossible, then at least to prevent such injustices from happening to other working people. Early on they decided they needed they needed a president, and a name. Kathy Muller was elected president of the group. [43] One worker, Christine Simms, suggested they call their group Citizens Against Temporary Services, or CATS, and the name stuck.

The choice of a name was important, although no one in the group realized it at the time. It symbolized the workers' early understanding that their problems stemmed not only from GE's meanness or disrespect but from the broader phenomenon of contingent work and lack of decent economic opportunity. This judgment, strengthened throughout their campaign, would ultimately prevent the workers from turning against one another or retreating in bitter defeat after the plant closed. Having decided that their real problem lay beyond the gates of GE, and having discovered a vast group of potential allies among workers whose livelihoods had been destroyed by the system of contingent work, the GE workers found both the energy and the vision that enabled them to move forward in addressing their situation.

In its formation, CATS defined an agenda that was both far-reaching and concrete. Although some members wanted to devote themselves to fighting General Electric itself by whatever means available, the group ultimately rejected this narrow focus. It was not an uncontroversial decision, and several members resigned because of it. As Alice Rollins explained, "The different people that got in our group was in it for different reasons. . . . Some of us was in it for revenge against GE. Simple for revenge. Which, to my way of thinking, that was going to help sink us. Because you can't go out trying to advance with revenge behind it—it doesn't work." [44] Instead, the majority decided, the group would pursue an agenda aimed at economic justice in Morristown. "Most of us was in it because the temporary services was taking so many jobs, and we were in it just trying to get labor laws passed, because we found out there was no labor laws in Tennessee—there's really not—so you could go in and not be fired because somebody don't like the way you wear your hair." [45]

Learning About the Contingent Economy

With a little research the workers quickly discovered that the shift from "permanent" jobs to the instability and inequity of temporary jobs was a national trend. In fact the growth of part-time, seasonal, and other forms of contingent work represented what one analyst called "a sea change in the world of work." [46] In 1989 the National Planning Association estimated that nearly one-third of all jobs were held by contingent workers, and the percentage was growing. [47] Another policy group estimated that between 1983 and 1993, the number of temporary workers increased by over 300 percent. [48] The payroll of temporary employment services—only one part of the contingent-work boom—increased by almost 3,000 percent between 1970 and 1992. [49]

In Morristown itself everyone knew that factories were increasingly hiring from temporary agencies and through labor pools and subcontractors. Stable jobs that paid enough to support a family were becoming scarce in manufacturing industries. When the laid-off GE workers organized, they argued that the trend toward temporary work was an issue of economic injustice and that it posed a threat to the entire community, not only to the workers immediately affected. Bill Troy, the director and the Committee on Religion in Appalachia (CORA) and then the director of the Tennessee Industrial Renewal Network (TIRN), explained, "While this development may have been beneficial to corporations seeking to cut costs and remain competitive in the current economic environment, it has imposed significant hardship on many who experience the phenomenon from the other end." [50]

As CATS members began to learn more about these changes in the economy, they found other groups and individuals similarly concerned with the problems of contingent work and casualization. They talked with workers, both in unions and unorganized, as well as with other community associations, politicians, and unemployed people. Workers from all industries were aware of the problem and were troubled by the trend toward contingent work. But the appropriate course of action was still unclear. On the one hand there was broad concern and support for reform; on the other hand there was very little precedent for change, and it was unclear what could possibly be done. No one had tackled this issue directly before. No state legislature or government agency regulated temporary services or contingent work. CATS found that in Tennessee, temporary service agencies were completely unregulated, so that there was no official route through which to address abuses. Government officials as well as workers were aware of the problem. At a legislative meeting in late 1989, the administrator of Tennessee's Personnel Recruiting Services Board, which licenses only permanent employment placement agencies, said she received about ten official complaints per year about legal violations at permanent employment agencies. By contrast, she heard at least three serious complaints each *week*—nearly

200 a year—about temporary agencies, over which she had no jurisdiction at all.[51]

The shift to contingent work had serious consequences for the workers, their families, and the entire community. First and most obvious was the cut in pay. Temporary jobs did not pay enough to support a family. One national survey in 1989 estimated that while full-time blue-collar manufacturing jobs paid an average of $8.80, similar jobs that were part-time paid only $4.95. Across the country, becoming a contingent worker meant nearly a 50 percent pay cut.[52] In Morristown, Tennessee, most temporary jobs paid the minimum wage, which was $3.35 an hour in 1989. Alice Rollins expressed the views of many when she discussed the exploitation inherent in the temporary work system: "A company will pay a service, say, fifteen dollars for somebody. And the service will pay this person, say, four dollars an hour. And they [the temporary agency] keep the difference. Well, my reasoning is, why don't the people just tell the company, you know, give *me* the fifteen dollars. At least I'll have enough money—I know I don't have any seniority, but at least I'll have enough money, maybe, to buy my own insurance. To me, the temporary services is like a side-saddle on a hog: it's just not necessary!"[53]

Second, and even more important for many, was the lack of health insurance or pension benefits. In 1989, while three-fourths of full-time workers nationwide had company-sponsored health insurance coverage, only one-third of contingent workers enjoyed the same benefit.[54] Not only did most have no insurance, but serious illness also meant losing one's job. As Rollins observed, "We all say we cannot afford to get sick, but [temporary workers] *really* cannot afford to get sick."[55] Similarly, 60 percent of full-time employees were covered under a retirement plan, but only 20 percent of part-time workers were, and hardly any who worked for temporary agencies. Temporary workers also often fell through the cracks in terms of coverage for disability and even for workers' compensation claims.[56] Shelley Edwards described a situation in which the company where she was working requested that all temporary workers sign a release form "stating that if they developed carpal tunnel syndrome, they would not hold the company responsible." The employees "were not given any explanation of what carpal tunnel syndrome is, how you get it, or that it sometimes requires expensive surgery to repair."[57]

Third, many workers had to support families and could not rely on jobs with absolutely no security or stability. Contingent work meant never knowing if the job would be there the next day or the next month. As Edwards said, "When you work for a temporary agency or in a factory as a temporary employee, you have no future. You cannot make any major purchases such as a car or a home, because you don't know if you will be working tomorrow."[58] Workers were vulnerable to seasonal layoffs or simply being fired at will, for no reason at all. Bill Troy generalized from his observations: "The uncertainty of not knowing when or whether they may work is a source of tremendous stress. This stress, of course, translates to their families and can produce serious problems there."[59] As a minister, Troy had seen Appalachian families destroyed because of the repercussions of job loss and instability.

Fourth, contingent employees often received poor treatment in the workplace. The CATS workers learned more about other Morristown workplaces, and found many examples of what they called a "two-tier" or "caste system," which raised concerns about equity and rights violations. As Shelley Edwards said, "As a temporary employee, I had no rights, and I was treated as a second-class citizen."[60] Temporary workers "had to go in through a different door. . . . They weren't allowed to eat in the same room with everybody else."[61] There were material consequences to the caste system also. The workers identified many instances where employees were categorized as temporary—and not granted pay raises, benefits, or job security—but did the same work in the same shop as permanent employees, often for long periods. In some factories the "temporary" employees were laid off at the end of their job assignment, "only to be hired two days later at the same job, in a new temporary assignment." [62] Workers took the jobs hoping to become part of the permanent workforce, but instead were cycled from one temporary position to another. Companies were able to replace permanent workers, at considerable savings. Moreover, companies rarely invested in training temporary workers. Instead they only hired those who had already acquired the appropriate skills. The costs of training and human capital improvement were therefore transferred from firms to the workers themselves. Occupational safety and health often suffered. When problems arose, the plant was usually not liable for the workers' compensation claims that resulted. Alice Rollins discussed a case in her area "where a man got hurt in a plant, and they were going to have to go to court, to have a ruling on who was responsible for him. The plant was saying, 'No, you work for temporary services, they're responsible.' And the service was saying, 'Well, we just provided the body, you provided the job, they got hurt on *your* premises. . . . ' No one's accountable if you get hurt." [63] Managers felt less pressure to maintain decent working conditions when they had an impermanent workforce, and therefore temporary jobs in manufacturing were often unpleasant and even dangerous. Edwards described a job at Morrison Printing Company, where she was sent on assignment by Olsten Temporary Services: "I worked a twelve-hour shift for $3.40 an hour. I was told by Olsten that this was an easy job. It was far from it. By the end of the shift my fingers were cut and swollen from handling the paper. . . . The company had very few permanent employees. Everyone that I talked to was a temporary from Olsten." [64]

Finally, the shift to contingent work had discriminatory consequences. Women and minorities were disproportionately represented within the temporary workforce—nearly double their percentages in the total workforce[65]—and these workers were the first to be let go in times of economic hardship. The Morristown workers realized that women, minorities, and elderly workers were most often compelled to take temporary jobs, mirroring the pattern in the national economy. In 1991 African Americans made up 10.5 percent of the U.S. workforce overall but comprised over 20 percent of the temporary workforce.[66] According to the National Association of Temporary Services, women constituted 72 percent of temporary service employees.[67] The laid-off GE workers were overwhelmingly women and older workers, and they found themselves part of an unwelcome national trend. As one worker explained, even with twenty-three years of seniority, she was "too old" for a permanent job—at the age of forty-two. She ended up with temporary work. "I just like to be treated like a normal person . . . [but] I felt like they felt like they could put you anywhere and do you any way. I'm older, and I know people want to hire younger people. And it makes you feel like you have to take something you really don't want."[68] Workers with the fewest choices in the Morristown labor market—women, minorities, and older people—were relegated to contingent work.

As a beginning, CATS decided to tackle the issue of contingent work, with the goal of stopping the trend toward temporary employment in industrial sectors. Over the course of many meetings and attempts, the group crafted a four-pronged strategy to achieve this goal. Their strategy included the following elements: working through local politics, a legal challenge, community mobilization, and a legislative strategy.

The Political Campaign

Just as in the other communities, the Morristown workers were initially optimistic. They believed that they if they could publicize the facts of what GE had done, public support and governmental assistance would be forthcoming. Accordingly, CATS members began to contact politicians and community leaders to see if anything could be done. To their surprise, they met only apathy at best, and outright hostility at worst. Their elected officials either did not consider the plant closing to be a problem for the community or they said there was nothing they could do. In fact, as the workers found out, the town leaders had known about GE's possible move for nearly a year. Morristown and Hamblen County could not match the incentives Knox County provided—including free space in an industrial park—and therefore had considered the move inevitable. Rather than fighting the inescapable, the public officials had been most concerned with keeping other GE jobs in the county after the distribution center left. The workers were frustrated with the politicians' apparent lack of concern and the secrecy of the government's negotiations with GE. "We contacted our state and federal and our city officials for assistance and found out that GE had been working on the transfer since early 1988. They kept this information from us."[69]

Local officials advised the workers to drop their campaign, and repeatedly urged CATS to disband. As one worker was told, "You're only hurting GE and you're hurting your community by being a part of CATS, because no industry will want to come to Morristown where people want more money and demand so much."[70] The politicians maintained that Morristown's future would be served best by the residents' acceptance of the changing global economy. As chapter 2 explains, political officials were most concerned about preserving Morristown's good "business climate." Protest activity, they believed, would make new industries less likely to locate in Hamblen County. They severely discouraged any demonstrations that could be perceived as anti-business, believing that this would hurt Morristown's ability to attract economic development opportunities in the future.

The leaders of CATS paid a price for their visibility. In a small town like Morristown, with a closely linked political and economic elite, it was in fact dangerous for workers to protest or to be visible in any way. CATS was taking big risks when it decided to confront community leaders, hold community meetings, or march in protest through the center of town. Many had evidence that they were subsequently black-listed and denied jobs for which they were absolutely qualified. After the closing one woman was told by a GE production manager that she had better cease her involvement with CATS. "He told me if I didn't break away and not be a part of this I wouldn't be able to find a job in the Morristown area."[71] Shelley Edwards described looking for jobs at the state employment office and being told nothing was available: "However, later that same day, I learned that Job Service was sending applicants to two different factories in our area. I called Job Service to ask why I was not referred to these companies. [She persisted, and was granted an interview the next day.] I went on the interview. With seventeen years' experience and an excellent work record, I still did not get the job. Why? Was the personnel manager made aware of how I got the interview? Was I labeled a troublemaker because I fought for my rights? I believe so."[72]

Muller also believes she was kept out of jobs, and therefore had to endure a four-year job search, unable to find even a temporary placement. Yount knew of workers who had been harassed at home by GE managers, and even physically threatened. "So I could see why some people are uneasy about speaking up, because this is not a popular issue."[73] None of the core group found permanent full-time work with benefits. As Brenda Green said later, at the legislative hearings, "I speak tonight on behalf of myself, my children, and the people who are afraid to speak, because we have no future if you [the legislature] don't do something for us."[74] It took significant courage to "go public" with one's support for CATS.

The CATS activists were dismayed by the response of their representatives. Ernest Gardiner said, "If we got any support from anybody from

Morristown [government], I don't know who it was . . . They were all oriented to try to cooperate with the businesses, and if the big businesses wanted this or that, then the people in the high positions around town were more than glad to give it to them."[75] The CATS leaders began to question the century-old pattern of economic development in the South, and the understanding they gained was key to their ability to resist. They saw the complicity of their local elite in an economic development system that undermined their interests. No local political leader supported CATS' efforts, and in the end working locally within "the system" proved futile.

The Community Campaign

Having failed to enlist local officials in their cause, CATS members decided to take their issues to the Morristown community, both to generate support and to educate others who were or easily could be in similar situations. The group began to increase its visibility in the community and to publicize its issues in any way possible. At first the workers were their own best advertisement. After organizing in the fall of 1989, CATS members made themselves bright red T-shirts with "Citizens Against Temporary Services" emblazoned across the back, and were visible wearing these around town. They also had hats made, and they began to run off fliers and leaflets to distribute around town, announcing the formation of the group and its purpose.

CATS' first step was to plan a community-wide meeting in Morristown, both to put pressure on GE to reinstate their jobs and to expose the public to their larger concerns about the increasing use and abuse of temporary and contingent workers by large companies. The community meeting was CATS' first attempt to publicize its plight and the issue of temporary jobs. The group had invited local officials as well as community residents. According to Muller, the organizers "thought it was going to be three or four people there, and 350 people showed up!"[76] Workers from all over the area showed up and told their stories. Some described being fired from jobs, only to be replaced by temporary workers. Others told of being laid off and then offered the option of taking their jobs back on a "part-time" basis, for far less pay and with no benefits. Union representatives told of entire union locals being destroyed when managers replaced all of the hourly workers with temporaries. Contingent workers described the unfair treatment they received at the hands of temporary agencies, and the humiliation of being at the bottom of a severely divided, stratified workforce. Several public officials, including state representatives and city officials, realized that there would be a large audience and decided at the last minute to attend. Some of them spoke up after listening to the workers' stories and concerns. Most expressed sympathy, but declared that the situation was out of their hands. One politician told a worker simply that "the state of Tennessee had no laws to protect the working person."[77]

The workers were taken aback. But they determined to change the situation through pressure from the entire community. "We then passed out 5,000 letters to the community to send in to our state representatives to urge some type of laws to help the working person."[78] With phone calls and letter-writing campaigns, CATS members and their friends and neighbors made sure their legislators understood the plight of workers in the new contingent economy.

Shortly thereafter, CATS led a march down the streets of Morristown calling for fair labor laws in Tennessee and an end to the abuse of temporary workers. Hundreds of people attended the parade, which was spirited yet serious in its demands for attention and reform. The march began in downtown Morristown and wound around to the shopping areas on a busy Saturday, and it was a unique event in Hamblen County. One worker recalled it as "the first [protest] I heard of in Morristown."[79] Soon most of the town was aware of CATS' existence, its grievances against General Electric, and its demands for reform. This was only the beginning of a community campaign that would continue. While the political and legal routes were exhausted quickly, with few positive results, the community-based organizing drive grew—albeit in various forms and directions—and became an effective ongoing movement.

These events, and the remarkable turnout they generated, were all the more impressive because the only newspaper published in Morristown refused to carry any stories about CATS. Other papers in the state had carried brief stories on CATS and its activities, but the local paper would not. The owner of the paper, Jack Fishman, had previously been the president of the Hamblen County Chamber of Commerce. His paper, the *Citizen Tribune,* would not recognize CATS as a legitimate news story. Once again the workers were shocked to find that their own local newspaper did not consider them newsworthy. It was an important lesson in the political power relations of their community. As Rollins says, CATS had "pissed off the opposition. Like the paper. He [the owner] is part of our town elite, you know all towns have them, some of them are really worse than others. He [the owner of the paper] is really terrible. . . . He's very cliquey, very clannish. And he rules Morristown. Because everybody does exactly what he wants them to do. The big boys in town. Most of them are just yes-men." [80] Brown said that Fishman "more or less controls the city. Controls the economy." [81] The city and county governments, the chamber of commerce, the local business community and the local media all either actively opposed CATS or dismissed it as irrelevant and backward. They argued that the group's activities were antagonistic to corporate interests and therefore harmful to Hamblen County's widely touted "business climate."

The workers knew that being publicly associated with CATS was frowned upon by powerful local elites, who could make their lives very difficult. Members were reluctant to become public spokespersons for their cause, once it was clear that the town's rulers opposed their activities. Attracting members and supporters became more difficult once CATS was labeled as oppositional rather than simply a group of working people who had been wronged.

After being blacklisted by the town's sole newspaper (there were no local television stations), CATS had to find other strategies to publicize its message and events. The workers used this opportunity to develop their skills in media and public outreach. One solution was for members and their families personally to distribute leaflets advertising events, at supermarkets and other public places. Another was to creatively use whatever media was available. This included radio stations, and CATS members found their way onto many talk shows and news hours. They talked to reporters in nearby towns and even as far away as Knoxville, the nearest big city, but were rarely able to generate news reports. Finally the president of the group had an idea that no organization had used before: to buy space in the *Smoky Mountain Trader,* a small advertising weekly available free in stores all over town. Space was not expensive, and CATS members could use it to write stories or post announcements. In the *Trader,* CATS publicized its meetings and other activities, and even published short articles written by members about the temporary work situation. This proved most effective. The *Trader's* wide local circulation made it a very useful conduit of information.

If CATS' public events did not draw mainstream media, they served another crucial function. They attracted the attention of important potential allies. One of the marchers at the April parade was Bill Troy, from the Committee on Religion in Appalachia (CORA), a coalition of church groups working on economic justice issues. In 1989 Troy was in the process of founding a new organization, the Tennessee Industrial Renewal Network (TIRN), in order to bring together labor, community, and environmental groups to work on economic issues statewide. Having found out about the CATS march through friends at the Highlander Center for Education and Research, another Appalachian institution with a long history of economic-justice work, Troy was inspired. He immediately got in touch with the group, and would remain involved for the next five years. After learning about their experiences, Troy invited CATS representatives to a conference he was organizing in June 1990 in Chattanooga, called "Responding to Plant Closings in Tennessee." CATS members did attend the conference, speaking movingly about their ordeal with the GE warehouse closing and afterward, and learning from other groups that had been through similar crises. This was the beginning of a close alliance between CATS and TIRN, which set up a standing committee to assist CATS' efforts with staff support and resources.

The Chattanooga conference was attended by organizations all over the country that were working on grassroots efforts to improve the local economy or at least to minimize its deleterious effects. The Morristown workers were alerted to the possibility of abuse under the Job Training Partnership Act. "We met all of these people who kept talking about JTPA and how companies would apply for it . . . so we came back from Chattanooga *knowing* that GE was going to use that JTPA money."[82] Even more than the details, the experience of becoming part of a coalition was transformative. Muller remembers: "When we went to Chattanooga, to that plant-closing conference, Bill Troy talked me into getting up and speaking. And I was *so scared!* But once I got started, it all came out. I reckon they said I done okay. It's just—once you believe in what you're doing, and you think, well, if I don't say it. . . . If not me, who? And if not now, when? We've got to do it now!"[83] The workers' bravery paid off. Representatives from the Federation for Industrial Retention and Renewal (FIRR), a national coalition with experience in community organizing and policy advocacy, publicized the CATS effort nationally. CATS received supportive letters and phone calls from across the nation. The CATS story encouraged other groups to consider becoming more involved in advocacy around issues of temporary and contingent work. CATS was about to undergo a transformation, from a local organization responding to a local problem, to a small organization at the forefront of a new movement.

At each stage in their campaign so far, two things had occurred. First, CATS lost at the local level. Local efforts failed to achieve the group's goals. These failures were disappointing, but also led the group to realize that the problem was bigger, and thus to tackle an even larger set of concerns. Then, at each step CATS accumulated more support, new resources, and a set of allies that would help the group persevere.

These early experiences already indicate some clear differences between CATS and the groups discussed in the previous two case studies. First was CATS' choice of an agenda and a target. The decision to take on the issue of the contingent economy and the problem of subcontracting was a choice, and it was a choice that had both costs and benefits. The group lost some members who wanted to focus on the narrower problem of GE itself, but it also gained an array of external allies who were similarly concerned about its issues. The decision was made by a group of leaders who took seriously their responsibility to the community but were also optimistic enough to take the risk of tackling a huge question.

Second, CATS had perhaps even more barriers to overcome than either the Greenbrier or Acme Boot workers. Morristown's local elite was more unified and powerful, and the media were more determined to keep CATS invisible. CATS was fighting one of the largest and most influential transnational corporations in the world, a more serious opponent than Greenbrier Industries or even Acme Boot and Farley Enterprises. Despite these barriers, CATS was able to organize and sustain mobilization even more effectively than the others. Its successful perseverance demonstrates that there is no necessary correlation between the level of obstacles facing an organization and its level of activism. While the barriers may have made it unlikely that CATS would win its bid for political and economic change, the group nonetheless took on the most ambitious and transformative campaign.

Third was the importance of existing organizations with experience and a tradition of community-based organizing. Its allies included historic organizations like the Highlander Center, as well as new organizations like TIRN and FIRR. Because of CATS' choice of themes, all of these groups—which have distinct and diverse missions themselves—were interested in CATS' campaign and became active participants. This influx of support, activists, and resources was invaluable.

Although the group faced the most severe challenges, CATS was able to become the most successful of the three failures analyzed in this book. Its experiences show that one of the most important questions for an organization involved in such a struggle is how to keep going after each failure. Because of the above elements—its target and analysis, its leadership, and its coalition building—CATS was able to do what any marginalized group in the early stages of such a struggle must do: it persevered.

The Legal Campaign

Through Bill Troy and TIRN, the CATS activists learned of a lawyer from Knoxville who had heard of their predicament and was interested in pursuing legal action. CATS members decided to pool whatever savings they had, to hire this attorney and file a lawsuit against GE. They charged breach of contract. GE's benefits package book had given laid-off workers the right to transfer or bid for their jobs before outside workers were hired, if the plant moved within a 250-mile radius. They also charged age discrimination—since older, better paid workers had been disproportionately singled out for layoffs—and fraudulent use of government funds. Using the discovery process to gain access to corporate records, CATS compiled evidence for a case against GE. Although they believed the case was strong, the initial hearings dragged on and the workers were short on the time and money required for a court battle. It became apparent that even in the unlikely event that the workers won the case, the legal route would not further their goals in a timely fashion.

Eventually the workers went to court and lost a summary judgment. Intimidated by GE, their lawyer refused to take the case any farther. CATS could not afford to hire a new lawyer and begin again, so the group was forced to drop the suit without winning anything. "When she finally withdrew, we had something like a week to appeal, and we just didn't have time to get another attorney. . . . We didn't have any other alternative. We just didn't have the money." [84] Most of the workers believe that the lawyer "sold out to GE." [85] "I feel that the company threatened our attorney." [86] The most generous reading is "she got into something with GE over her head, that she couldn't handle, and GE was so powerful that she just *had* to get out of it. It hurt us bad. But that's how big companies eat you alive." [87] Without considerable resources the workers were not likely to benefit from a legal contest with GE.

After the workers lost their case, GE sent each one a bill for over $5,000 in court costs. The attorney had agreed to these fees when the workers lost the summary judgment. But not a single worker could afford that amount of money. Muller decided to fight it. "I got to thinking about it and I thought, 'If I don't do something, these people are going to have to pay this.' And I called [the lawyer], but she said, 'You're going to have to pay it, you might as well agree to it.' And I said, 'No, I'd rather go to jail first.' She said, 'Well, they'll put you there.' " Muller called all the other plaintiffs and told them of her intentions. "I said, 'I'm prepared to go to jail.' I told my family I was prepared to go. I meant it. And my family backed me up. They said that would be fine! I said, 'I am *not* paying them. I will *not.*' " Finally Muller called GE's attorney, and said, "I've read over all of this, and I've come to this conclusion. We are not paying GE any money. We're not! I only have one thing that I can do, and I make you this promise. You come after us for that money, and I will spend *the rest of my life* [fighting you] . . . I'll be on every television show I can; I'll be on every radio show I can; and I will blast GE from every corner of this country, and I will do it for the rest of my life. You know I'm telling the truth. You know that I can do it. . . . How do you think it will look when I take Joe Perkinson and we put him on prime time television, and he says that he's a Korean War and a Vietnam veteran and GE throwed him out and then come after him when he didn't have anything—how do you think that's going to look?"[88]

After an hour of this the GE attorney said he would think about it. Two weeks later Muller got a letter saying that GE would drop the case and would not pursue the fees. "All I had was the truth. But . . . I felt I had won that fight."[89]

The Public Policy Campaign

Having despaired of pursuing change through local institutions and politicians, as well as the courts, and after consulting with other organizations in other states, CATS began to consider statewide legislative strategies. Through their contacts with staff at TIRN and at the Highlander Center, CATS became aware of a grassroots Appalachian community-based organization, Save Our Cumberland Mountains (SOCM). SOCM had worked primarily on environmental justice and land-use problems for many years, but had recently become more involved with economic and jobs issues as well. In fact, the SOCM executive board had recently voted to make the issue of contingent work one of its priorities. Faced with the dilemma of an ambitious program on the one hand, and a severe lack of resources on the other, CATS had to make a decision about its future as an organization. In 1990 CATS voted to become the Hamblen County chapter of SOCM, thereby taking advantage of SOCM's extensive experience in organizing, strategizing, and lobbying skills and resources. SOCM could provide a staff organizer, who would work with CATS on a long-term basis and help develop strategies and campaigns. The alliance with SOCM was adopted as a further means of institutionalizing CATS and ensuring a strong base from which it could continue its work.

This decision was controversial. Although everyone seemed to agree in the end that the affiliation was the only real option if CATS was to achieve its practical goals, many resisted the merger. SOCM had devoted most of its history and resources to environmental issues, and was not experienced in the area of labor law. Some CATS activists were uncertain that SOCM would be sufficiently committed to the issues of contingent work. SOCM was seen as an organization with its own agenda, coming in from outside the Morristown community. As Alice Rollins said, "I liked the idea of what SOCM was all about, I mean, I think what they're doing is wonderful . . . like at the landfills. But that just wasn't my baby at the time. . . . Getting labor laws was my main concern."[90] Others felt that as a grassroots organization with a long history of aggressive community-based organizing, SOCM was an appropriate choice. "They are aggressively working on economic issues too. . . . Wherever they think that something needs to be looked into, or needs to be changed to be worked on, they will get interested and get involved. I think that's good."[91] Eventually Perkinson's arguments prevailed; CATS affiliated with SOCM.

With the help of SOCM staff, CATS designed a strategy to push for state governmental action. SOCM staff suggested that the workers do more research to investigate the state's role in facilitating GE's move. This proved difficult. CATS leaders made hundreds of frustrating phone calls to Nashville and Washington, to every office they could think of. Several members traveled to Nashville and even Memphis (nearly 500 miles each way from Morristown) to ask questions in person. After nine months of research, and repeated outright denials from state officials, the workers finally found out that indeed many tax dollars had been allocated to GE to support its move from Morristown to Mascot. With the assistance of Harold Woods, the head of the Knoxville Labor Council and a member of the Private Industry Council (PIC), whom they had met in Chattanooga, the CATS activists learned that GE had been promised $200,000 in Job Training Partnership Act (JTPA) "on-the-job-training" (OJT) funds to train new workers for the exact jobs from which they had been fired.

CATS argued this use of federal funds was illegal, since JTPA money cannot be used for jobs from which fully capable workers have been laid off. The workers were outraged that their tax dollars were allowing young people to take their jobs. "I don't see any point in training a college student to do warehouse jobs; it's ludicrous. At the same time, the government was subsidizing the JTPA, paying me unemployment, sending me to school. . . . I could have got food stamps, and not only that, I wasn't paying any taxes to amount to anything." [92] It was also illegal. As one worker said, "GE asked for and was awarded JTPA funds to train people for our jobs thirty miles from the closed warehouse. As the law states, no company can receive JTPA funds with people on layoff. In order for GE to have been approved for these funds, they had to lie. This constitutes fraud, in my opinion. I think this should be looked at very seriously by all of our legislators." [93] GE argued that the new factory was operated by Usco (the labor contractor), not GE. State officials supported this argument, finding that GE had closed its plant and gone out of business before Usco opened, so the plants were separate and unrelated. The $200,000 in JTPA funds were distributed to Usco.

CATS members continued their research and carefully documented their claims. Harold Woods, whom they met at the TIRN conference, used his contacts in state government to track down the actual contract that was signed when JTPA funds were allocated to the new warehouse.

He sent copies to the workers, showing that GE representatives—not Usco—signed the contract. Operating plans showed use of "GE checks, insurance forms, equipment, and some management from GE."[94] Although they had no idea how to do it, the workers determined to rectify the situation. The $200,000 was not much from GE's point of view, but the CATS members badly wanted to win the case, to prove that GE could not get away with illegal and unethical activities, and to prove themselves right.

Toward the end of 1989, CATS members asking questions at state agencies in Nashville learned that any group of citizens could ask the legislature to establish a committee to hold public hearings on a policy issue affecting their community. CATS began to press Tennessee's state legislators to set up a study committee to look at the issue of temporary services. It also lobbied for a study committee on fair labor practices in Tennessee. Both committees were set up, and CATS then demanded that these committees hold hearings in Morristown. After much prodding and negotiation, the committees organized three hearings across the state. The first joint hearing was scheduled for October, at Walter State Community College in Morristown, and hearings in Nashville and Memphis were promised to follow.

The Morristown Hearings: Community Mobilization

Having won public hearings for their community, CATS leaders once again began a huge effort to turn out residents to participate and to testify about the issues. CATS members leafleted, wrote articles in the *Trader,* activated their telephone tree, talked to their friends, relatives, churches, and other groups, and contacted other organizations in the area—including labor unions, community groups, churches, and anyone else they could think of. Their efforts paid off more than even they had anticipated, as an unexpected crowd of 750 people showed up to educate the legislators. The workers felt that the law was finally on their side; the legal requirement that the committee accept public input strengthened the group and helped mobilize support.

The members of CATS, TIRN, and other groups wanted to use the hearing as an opportunity to present their experiences and concerns to a body with power. As Bill Troy explained to the committee, "The growth of temporary, part-time, contract and employee leasing activity in our state is causing serious hardship. . . . We are hopeful our remarks will reinforce the need for the state to take steps to protect employees against the abuses involved in this activity." [95] They urged the representatives to "take a broad perspective on the problem. We need more than an attempt just to 'fix' a few things here and there, or to stop abuses by a few renegade temporary service employers." [96] Rather, the workers wanted the state to investigate and regulate the abuse of contingent work, and to seek out and prevent inequities.

Many workers testified about their experiences. Some of the most memorable testimony came from a member of the glassworkers' union from Kingsport, Tennessee, who told the story of his co-worker, Jimmy Weaver. "He worked for this company in Kingsport for twenty years. Then one Friday they told him, 'We don't need you anymore.' They gave him a pink slip. But with the same breath they told him, 'You can come back in Monday morning as a temporary.' Jimmy, with his head held high because he had a family to support, came walking back in Monday morning, clocked in at the same place he had always worked, went to the same machine he had worked at for twenty years, the only difference was he was making half the money with *no* benefits. And Jimmy worked that way for a year, until he died of a heart attack. . . . Tonight I'm speaking for Jimmy Weaver." [97]

One by one, more workers stood up and told similarly heart-wrenching stories. They described the anxiety of contingent work, and they compared temp work to the sweatshop of the early 1900s. "You worry that your family will need medical care that you can't afford because you have no insurance. You worry about what will happen if you get injured on the job. . . . I worked at one small factory that was nothing more than a modern day sweatshop"[98]

Many emphasized the fact that, for most workers, temporary employment was not a choice. It was the only work available. Shelley Edwards, for example, had been a manager at another factory, American Enka, for fourteen years before moving to GE. After being laid off from GE, the Job Service office sent her to a local factory as a temporary employee. "Some weeks later, I found out about the displaced workers program, and since I was laid off and not subject to recall, I thought that I might apply. I called JTPA. . . . They told me that I could not qualify under the job displacement program because I had accepted temporary assignments while I was laid off."[99] Most workers were disappointed that a temporary placement did not lead to a permanent job. "While I didn't mind being a temporary for the first couple of months, seventeen months is a bit ridiculous."[100]

The workers deplored the unfairness of the caste system, which privileged full-time employees above the casual workers who did the same job. "I work just as hard and do just as good work—so I've been told—as any permanent person employed there. What is the reward I get? Lower pay, no benefits, and treated like 'just a temporary.' . . . I had a terrible time trying to get a loan for my home because I was termed 'temporary.' "[101] The workers described the invisibility and the powerlessness of temp work. Bobbie Hoxit, an SOCM member from Farragut, Tennessee, condemned the divisions between part-time and full-time workers, and the competition that inevitably erupted among temporary workers trying to become permanent: "How is it possible in our country to have American against American? How is it possible in our state to have East Tennessean against East Tennessean? How is it possible in our factories and workplaces to have fellow workers against fellow workers? *How is all this possible?*"[102]

As the workers were gradually learning, the problems of temporary employees extended beyond the psychic and material tolls of downward mobility. Organizing a union was nearly impossible for temporary workers because the labor law required recognition from both the temporary agency and the actual employer. At the legislative hearing, Fran Ansley, a professor of law at the University of Tennessee, raised issues of accountability and liability. She pointed out that it remained unclear who was responsible for unemployment insurance, workers' compensation, and disability for contingent workers. The problem of deciding if the contractor or the temporary agency was the "employer" under the law was only the first dilemma, Ansley said. If a worker was diagnosed with employment-related cancer, for example, after working at a number of jobs with a number of contracting services, who was responsible for the workers' compensation claims to which he had a legal right? Ansley noted that by shifting to contingent work, U.S. employers were abandoning the hard-won standards that had made America great. Instead, they were mimicking the practices of nations like Indonesia or Mexico. Moving toward an employment system in which workers were disposable and underpaid would only intensify the "race to the bottom."[103]

Workers testified that the shift to contingent work was having deleterious effects on "permanent" jobs in the region as well. One Morristown worker testified that when her company had taken on temporary services, the permanent staff took pay cuts. In one year she went from earning $260 for a forty-hour week to earning $256 for a fifty-two-hour week—twelve hours of mandatory overtime were uncompensated.[104] The permanent employees accepted their fate, because full-time employment was still far preferable to a temporary job without benefits. Thus the availability of a large pool of casual workers allowed employers to wrest concessions from longtime employees and to lower the expectations of the entire workforce.

Beyond telling their individual stories, the workers argued to legislators that the shift to temporary employment had grave results for American business. The temporary employment patterns TIRN had uncovered were not only unfair but inefficient. They were being instituted "with scant attention being paid . . . to the long-term consequences for the success of American enterprise." [105] In the long run, firms would suffer from a decrease in morale, dedication, quality, and employee loyalty—and society would suffer from a reduced investment in human capital, diminished demand, and a declining standard of living. "We hear so much about low productivity in America. It is unreasonable to expect a person working temporary to be concerned about producing quality work if they do not have a promise of a job tomorrow." [106] The workers' argument was corroborated by many management experts. The shift toward "downsizing" permanent workers is often harmful to a firm—including its bottom line—unless there is careful planning and an exceptionally good reason to make the change. Otherwise the decreases in production and productivity often exceed the savings. Ernest Gardiner remembered making this argument to GE managers.

"It was about the motivation of the people. . . . They should have seen that, and said, 'We have a crew here that will do anything we want. [Kathy] will stand in traffic, [Ernest] will juggle three oranges and whistle Dixie—why, we've got it made!' . . . I told the plant manager, 'Look, rather than have these closed-door sessions with management, deciding this and deciding that, right here on this line you've got hundreds of years of experience right here inside these walls.' I said, 'Come out here and ask somebody, somebody out there will know.' But they would have never done that then." [107] The company did not want to concede any control over production.

Many testified about questionable corporate accounting practices. One worker explained that she had worked at the same job as a temporary for a year and a half, but was laid off every month or so for a few days. As many temps testified, periodic layoffs allowed managers to keep them on the books as temporary workers, with a "new" job every time they reappeared. But the use of casuals served another function for managers eager to compete in a tighter market. Just before monthly reports had to be made, "the plant manager lays off all his temporaries for two to three days so that he doesn't have to report their production, and therefore he turns it all in as output done by permanent employees." The contingent workers were like ghosts; their production was attributed to others. "Sure it makes him look fantastic and he receives rewards for what appears to be a job well done. It's not well done when you are the one being laid off every few months at closing when head count is done." [108]

The workers pleaded with the legislators to change the system. "People with children, who are divorced, etc., have no means of security with a temporary job. Please help do something about those of us who are willing to work, but are sick of being used." [109] Echoing other witnesses, Calvin Brown called upon the representatives to reconsider their role in the regional economy. "My final question: Why should such companies as GE with profit in the billions be allowed to use either JTPA funds or temporary services with so many of the people that made them what they are today: *rich!* . . . Where is our government leaders when they are needed?" [110] One anonymous temporary worker wrote out her testimony for the hearing. It began: "To Whom It May Concern: Not that it seems to have concerned anyone so far." [111]

By contrast with the politicians' lack of concern, CATS members were surprised and heartened by the outpouring of support for them and their issues, from all over East Tennessee. They heard horrible stories similar to their own, from friends and allies they never knew they had. Everyone seemed to agree that the situation for factory workers was dire and was only becoming worse, and that it was the government's responsibility to take action. The witnesses proposed many concrete legislative remedies. Some of these were technical, such as the inclusion of temporary service agencies, contracted business services, and employee leasing companies in existing regulations governing other employment agencies. (Temporary agencies were exempt from these regulations and licensing requirements.) Others were more global, such as the idea that all companies be required to adhere to minimum standards ensuring fair treatment for all workers. Bill Troy pointed out that government—the taxpayers—would end up bearing the burden of increased contingent work, in one way or another. It was important that businesses be held responsible for a share of these costs. "Some would point to the social service system as the appropriate vehicle for preventing large numbers of contingent workers from falling through the cracks, as they are today. We would suggest that the first place to look is to the employer, first to the company who offers temporary services . . . and then to the company who uses those services."[112] Workers discussed issues including portable health insurance and pensions, and even national health care. It had become clear to them that these issues of national social policy were inseparable from the practices of economic development—job destruction and creation—played out at the local level.

The many hours and thousands of pages of testimony submitted by CATS members and their allies across the state demonstrated an impressive level of political consciousness and a sophisticated analysis of the political economy going into the 1990s. Nearly a decade before the rise of contingent work or the sweatshop economy became topics of national political debate, workers in Morristown were investigating the issue of contingent work in their local economy. Even more important, they were considering the political ramifications of the phenomenon. They offered a precise analysis of the shifting patterns in the economy. They presented copious evidence to support their argument. They proposed a positive policy agenda to minimize the negative impact of the shifting employment structure on working families and citizens.

The CATS workers' sophistication and even their outrage represented a far distance from where they had begun. Their ability to think about the problem of contingent work in collective economic terms—rather than blaming temporary workers for stealing away their jobs—was a leap forward. Their analysis of potential political solutions was creative and innovative, especially because no state or locality in the country had ever passed legislation regulating temporary employment. The CATS workers were able to take on this impressive task because they had prepared thoroughly for their meetings with political officials and for the hearings. The hearings themselves came about because of leadership, the support of allies with strong ties to the community and a grassroots base, and political analysis. CATS members had been encouraged to understand their dilemma in broad political and economic terms, and to take on an ambitious fight.

Throughout the hearings the committee members listened dutifully, and at times seemed impressed and moved by the testimony of the people of Morristown. For months afterward, CATS members and their new allies from the region waited hopefully to hear back from the committee about new proposals for reform. They never heard a word. The committee fulfilled its responsibility as an ad-hoc body commissioned to study the problem of contingent work in Tennessee, by holding public hearings in three counties. The state, however, never even issued a written report on its findings. Despite pressure from CATS, the legislature decided not to act on the issue. None of their work was translated into policy recommendations or legislation.

A Victory at Last

Many of the workers had testified at the hearings about the unfairness of JTPA funds—their own tax dollars—being used to support GE's "training" of new workers for their old jobs. They argued that JTPA should be revised or regulated so that this type of abuse would be impossible. Some argued that contract labor—including temporary services and labor pools—should be explicitly disqualified from JTPA funds. Others stated the importance of governmental regulation of the distribution of funds, to monitor and enforce the requirements that workers be trained for permanent jobs. Counties and towns, they argued, should be held accountable for the JTPA money they distribute, and the companies as well as the local governments should be audited regularly and penalized harshly for misuse of funds. Mel Summers presented the legislators with a copy of Public Law 97-300, the legislation enacting JTPA, and a copy of GE's contract with the state. "GE received JTPA funds," he said, "which are federal funds monitored by the state and by signing this contract GE was trying to use public funds in violation of Public Law 97-300. I call this an unfair labor practice. . . . I ask this committee to contact the Tennessee State Attorney General's office and the National Labor Relations Board in Atlanta to determine if laid-off GE employees are eligible for compensation under the law." [113]

Since GE's defense had been to argue that Usco was a different, independent company—and that GE itself had hired no new workers—many workers challenged that claim directly. Linda Yount compiled twenty-seven different pieces of evidence supplied by herself and other GE workers, proving that the Usco plant was really GE under a different name, with merely a different payroll system. She noted that the legislators had said "that you could not penalize Usco because GE closed its warehouses and went out of business, and yet I have the [JTPA] contract with the GE representative signature instead of Usco." She added other examples of proof that GE and Usco were the same entity. "When you call up the Distribution Center [in Mascot] a Usco employee answers the phone, 'General Electric Distribution Center.' " [114] Mary Hutchinson added her observation that "when we received our cut-back slips, these slips did not state lay-off or cut-back due to lack of work, but a warehouse *transfer*—and we were told from the beginning that it would be treated as a usual lay-off." This proved that GE considered the move to be a work transfer to another location rather than a true plant closing. Nonetheless, the state had treated it as a plant closing and a new business in Mascot. Hutchinson continued, "If this is not a GE facility in [Mascot], why is GE supplying all funds, GE equipment, GE management, GE checks, insurance forms, and a contract with JTPA for funds?"[115]

CATS' arguments were finally heard. The group was able to sustain pressure on Tennessee economic development officials, Knox County, and officials at the state and federal Departments of Labor, to enforce the law. Eventually CATS was able to prove to the state's satisfaction that GE was directly responsible for the Usco warehouse, and that the fully capable laid-off Morristown workers had not been offered the new jobs in which they were well trained. CATS finally persuaded the Department of Labor to declare the GE/Usco warehouse in Mascot ineligible for JTPA funding. The DOL withdrew the $200,000 GE had been awarded. CATS had won the battle over JTPA.

This victory may have been a small one in some respects, but it was a major turning point for the CATS participants. For the first time, they felt powerful. "The commissioner [of Labor] said that GE would not get a dime, and they did not get a dime. That's several hundred thousand dollars that the taxpayers did not have to put out!"[116] They had established connections with others across the state, and these connections had unexpectedly provided them with the ammunition to change the behavior of the government itself. They experienced themselves as not just marginalized, oppressed workers, but as part of a collective that could actually wield power. After being lied to and turned away by not one but several government agencies, the satisfaction of having their instincts proven correct was tremendous. At the highest level, the state had sided with CATS, against both the transnational company and their local officials.

The workers felt emboldened to question other policies that those state and local officials had told them were impossible to change. After denying GE the taxpayers' money, CATS members wanted everyone to know what their government was doing. "You can't get JTPA funds to train people if you've got people already laid off that's trained in that field. It's illegal. *But* it happens every day! If people don't say anything about it, the state gives it to them; they go right ahead and do it. It's just that we raised such a ruckus, they *couldn't*."[117] The workers began to consider it their responsibility to continue making that "ruckus" if that was what it would take to keep officials accountable to the people.

The small reform they had won inspired CATS to do more. As political scientist Michael McCann predicts, even relatively minor and non-transformative gains can lay the groundwork for further organizing efforts and thus strengthen social-movement organizations. He points out that these "struggles can be expansionist . . . in that they not only achieve short-term benefits but also generate significant new resources, opportunities, and aspirations for continued counterhegemonic struggle. In short, such reform efforts can create the potential at least to sustain the momentum for change, and at best to snowball into ever more comprehensive demands and conflicts."[118] CATS was pleased but not satisfied with its victory. It had cost GE/Usco $200,000 but had not really changed anything in east Tennessee. CATS finally decided that if fair labor laws were to exist in Tennessee, the people would have to create them themselves and convince the legislature to adopt them. CATS resolved to change the law.

The Legislative Campaign

In 1990, with the help of SOCM and TIRN staff, the members of CATS wrote legislation that would regulate the use and abuse of contingent employees. In order to come up with the particulars for the legislation, the SOCM leadership took CATS through a democratic and participatory process that SOCM had perfected in other struggles. The members devised the legislation themselves, over the course of several meetings. They began by brainstorming, setting out all the features they would ideally like to see in a bill, and the facilitator encouraged participation while writing all of their suggestions on a large flip-chart. When all their most ambitious goals were enumerated, the workers were then led through the second step: narrowing down the list. When they had fully discussed the issues and come up with their most urgent priorities, they then began thinking about how they could codify their suggestions into specific laws. In an orderly and inclusive process, all the members present helped to design a legislative proposal that would go straight to the Tennessee state legislature.

This process provides a striking contrast to the ones that took place with the Greenbrier workers and the Acme Boot workers. Under SOCM's guidance, the CATS members were asked to use their own knowledge and ideas in order to generate the group's proposal and course of action. They would then be responsible for carrying it out, by lobbying for their bill. With the Greenbrier Workers' Committee, by contrast, the experts had presented proposals and the workers acquiesced. The Acme workers were educated about some issues, but not really given leadership roles in their union's struggle. The CATS process was not only more democratic, it demanded much more of participants, and was ultimately more empowering to the workers involved. The members became more invested in the legislative process, and more cohesive. Leadership (from SOCM and TIRN staff organizers, in this case) was no less active or involved, but it served a different role. Leaders specifically attempted to pull forward individual CATS members, to think through their ideas and to assume positions of leadership themselves. This is the most important role of leaders working with marginalized groups. In the case of CATS, leaders were able to persuade workers to take charge of their own struggle. This was not always easy;

the workers did not believe they were capable, and often resisted the organizers' suggestions. The leaders' perseverance, however, overcame the
workers' hesitation and provided them with the skills and confidence to
pursue political strategies.

The bill they ultimately agreed upon contained several provisions.
First, "temporary" workers who stayed on beyond ninety days had to be
given the same benefits as permanent workers. Contingent workers
doing the same work as permanent employees, for the same hours, over
a period of time, could not be defined as "temporary." Second, permanent workers could not be replaced with temporary workers. Third, the
bill would regulate temporary agencies. It required all temporary services to be licensed and regulated by a state board, subject to all the re-
porting and inspection demanded of other employers. Fourth, the state
would have to collect a range of information about temporary employment. And fifth, temporary agencies would have to give notice to workers of their rights to workers' compensation, overtime pay, and coverage
under other employment-related legal provisions. Any one of these
clauses would have represented precedent-setting legislation, since there
was no state or local legislation anywhere in the country prohibiting
abuse of temporary workers or regulating temporary employment services. The provisions designed by the GE workers comprised an ambitious agenda for change. The bill was also a testament to the workers'
farsightedness. The issues of subcontracting and temporary work were
only beginning to be apparent to groups across the country.

With help from TIRN and SOCM, CATS members pressed for
their bill to be introduced in the 1990 legislative session. SOCM especially had a broad membership base, and extensive experience with lobbying and advocacy. With pressure from their districts, House members
on three relevant committees agreed to sponsor the bill, and the Commerce Committee took up the proposal and began drafting a bill. As the
vote approached, CATS organized a delegation of about fifty members

and citizens to drive the four hours to Nashville to lobby for the vote. Although CATs and SOCM had done extensive lobbying ahead of time—and believed they had strong support within the legislature—when the members actually arrived in Nashville, they found themselves outnumbered and outmobilized by opponents. Federal Express, Eastman Kodak, and other major Tennessee employers were pushing hard against the CATS bill. In addition, the National Association of Manufacturers and the powerful National Association of Temporary Services (NATS) and its Tennessee affiliate were lobbying against it. For the second time, the Morristown workers had brought upon themselves the wrath of the business community. This time they faced not only General Electric but a united front comprising some of the most powerful transnational corporations in the United States.

Still, CATS lobbied actively for its proposals and, against the odds, succeeded in winning new legislation. But the members were disappointed with the result. In the end the legislature passed only a very weak provision, requiring temporary service agencies to register with the state. Although CATS had received promises from a majority of committee members, at the last minute several decided not to show up for the vote, and their version of the bill never made it out of committee. Rollins remembered being lied to by her own representatives: "You can tell that the people that you're talking to—the representatives and senators—that they are just talking through their butt, and they don't care if you know it or not. Some of them try to be really slick about it, and they try to lie without letting you know they're really lying. . . . We needed seven votes to get [our bill] through the Senate, and this one lady [senator] said, 'Let me go home, and let me pray on this.' And so Kathy said, 'We got her, I believe we got her!' I said, 'Kathy, you gotta be kidding. This lady ain't gonna go home and pray about this, because there's no way G-d is gonna tell her to vote *against* it!' So the next day she didn't show up, and we lost."

Rollins believes that CATS could not have beaten such powerful opponents. "The temporary people [lobbyists from NATS and the corporations] said right up front, 'We've got the money, we can fight this. You don't have it.' They knew right up front they were going to win, and they did."[119] Calvin Brown listened to a corporate executive in Nashville "make a statement that he was paying to defeat our bills to the tune of like $10 million, that he would spend to beat any regulations to regulate the temporary services."[120]

The final version of the bill, House Bill 1777, included only a minimal requirement that contained no provisions for regulation or enforcement. It included new definitions of "contract labor firms," "employee leasing services," and "temporary help services," and required all of these to register with the Personnel Recruiting Services Board of the Department of Commerce and Insurance.[121] In cases of complaints filed by workers against any such organization, HB 1777 permitted the Department of Commerce to investigate and "in a lawful proceeding assess a civil penalty of not more than five hundred dollars ($500) for each violation of a statute, rule or order enforceable by the department."[122]

The workers were disappointed but not deterred. The following year CATS returned with a more streamlined, less ambitious bill. Instead of presenting their proposals as labor-related reforms, CATS leaders decided to frame the issue as a human rights violation—another move that would prefigure the anti-sweatshop and living-wage movements that exploded years later. The 1991 proposal focused on prohibiting discrimination on the basis of employment status (temporary or permanent). After ninety days on the job, all workers would be considered "regular workers"—whether classified as temporary, permanent, contracted, or part-time—and as such would have the right to be treated equally. This bill would amend Title IV of the Tennessee Human Rights Act.

A key section of CATS' bill made it illegal for employers to: "limit, segregate, or classify an employee, relative to other employees in similar positions in any way which would deprive or tend to deprive an employee of wages or benefits based on his or her categorical status. . . . Any employer may not discriminate against employees who work in similar positions, in terms and conditions of employment, including the provision of wages and benefits based on his or her categorical status." To mitigate the concerns of employers, the proposed act also included provisions that "nothing in this section shall prohibit wage differentials based on a seniority system," and "nothing in this act shall affect an employer's right to designate the categorical status of an employee."[123] The bill amended the state's human rights code so that the definition of "discriminatory practice" included discrimination against contingent workers.

CATS members once again did extensive lobbying, with even more preparation than before. Every Tuesday a group of about fifty members of CATS and SOCM made the trip to Nashville to meet with and lobby their representatives. They believed they had a good chance of winning. Because of CATS' alliance with SOCM and TIRN, both statewide organizations, the little group from Morristown had important help in its campaign. The groups enlisted individuals and organizations to lobby their elected representatives all across the state. SOCM brought its members from Murfreesboro, Lebanon, Chattanooga, McMinnville, Knoxville, and Memphis to lobbying days in Nashville. From all of these places and more, from Upper East Tennessee all the way to the Mississippi River, CATS generated hundreds of phone calls and letters to legislators.[124]

On the other hand, some powerful allies did not help with TIRN's campaign. The president of the statewide AFL-CIO, Jim Neeley, refused to support the new bill or to lobby on its behalf. He considered the proposal utopian, impractical, and overly divisive. Neeley explained to SOCM that in order to get the Temporary Services Registration Bill passed the previous year, he had promised several legislators that he would never work on passing a more ambitious bill in the future. Neeley said he supported the bill in principle, but at a meeting with SOCM and CATS representatives he "stressed again and again that it is not winnable."[125]

In the Tennessee House of Representatives, SOCM members asked Matt Kisber of Jackson to sponsor the bill, and he agreed. The CATS activists were surprised and pleased to get his endorsement, for Kisber was a well-respected legislator and a hard worker. Because Kisber was from West Tennessee, members of SOCM—as well as another West Tennessee community-based organization, JONAH (Just Organized Neighborhoods Area Headquarters), which had often worked in coalition with SOCM—in his district had urged him to support the bill. Similarly, in the state senate, SOCM and TIRN members lobbied Senator Ward Crutchfield of Chattanooga. After much reluctance, Crutchfield also agreed to sponsor the temporary work bill. SOCM staff member Sean McCullough worked closely with the legislative campaign. He believed that when CATS and SOCM began their lobbying effort, "we were getting decent response. It didn't seem like the other side was lobbying very hard."[126] Soon, however, CATS' opponents heard about the bill, and legislators began to have qualms. SOCM staff decided the bill had a better chance of passing in the House, so they began the campaign there.

Kisber was a member of the House Consumer and Employees Affairs Committee, and was well placed to introduce the bill. But Kisber became nervous about the original CATS proposal, and began insisting on changes. He spoke with the grassroots group—composed of representatives of SOCM, TIRN, and CATS—about possible amendments. CATS agreed to some, and wrote up amendments that seemed like a reasonable compromise. They exempted workers filling in for other workers who were expected to return to work. They also explicitly made the bill not apply directly to part-time workers but only to full-time "temporary" workers. These compromises were not enough, and Kisber finally added his own amendments, extending the 90 days to 180 days (before achieving status as a "regular" worker) and excluding companies with less than fifty workers. As McCullough said, "Our emergency decision-making team decided we did not like these amendments but were willing to negotiate." [127] Meanwhile the top priority was to get the bill on the calendar for the last House subcommittee meeting, so that the full committee could consider it before adjourning for the year. When the bill was proposed to the full committee for inclusion in the agenda, Committee Chair Representative Dick Clark of Nashville decided that the bill "didn't have a chance of passing this year" and declined to include it on the committee's calendar.[128] The bill was dead.

After two years of legislative work and intensive lobbying, CATS' only tangible results were to rescind JTPA funding for GE, and a bill requiring temporary services to register. CATS had succeeded in building support, mobilizing the community, providing information, and pressuring politicians. But the concrete results envisioned by CATS' founders had eluded them entirely. The workers are frank about this: "In the end, the result was nothing. We didn't get anything accomplished." [129]

After Failure

CATS' members may have been disappointed, but in retrospect their accomplishments were most impressive, both personally and politically. The individuals involved in the organizing detailed the positive and lasting impact of their experiences. Alice Rollins said, "It was one of the most fascinating things I've ever done." [130] Muller said it even more strongly: "It took a lot of pain, it took a lot of heartaches, it took a lot of crying . . . but I'm grateful. My life turned upside down. [But] I don't want to go back to where I was. I don't want to be that person any-more."[131] Many others echoed this, referring to CATS' work as a political and educational transformation, and the beginning of an important fight. CATS members' continuing interest and involvement in political issues, and the continuing struggles that resulted, are the hallmark of what I call a "successful failure."

In CATS' case, a succession of failures did not lead to resignation, but produced in members a determination to directly challenge political and economic power in the United States. Having begun by blithely resolving to reverse the shift toward contingent work, after a few campaigns the group had learned exactly what it was up against: multibillion-dollar transnational corporations determined to oppose oversight or regulation of any kind, at any cost. This knowledge led to some critical decisions. The group realized that the only way to achieve its goals would be to build coalitions with other organizations—statewide and nationally—with broader bases, more experience, and re-sources. Once they understood this imperative, CATS' leaders were on their way to building a nascent social movement. In the years that fol-lowed, the group would not only put the issue of contingent work on the map, it would also go on to work on a range of political issues, cre-ating the foundation for continued local mobilization, as well as influ-encing national political debates and events.

After the second legislative defeat, CATS—now officially the Ham-blen County Chapter of SOCM—considered its options for future leg-islative work.[132] The group got together and listed both the pros and the cons. Under "pros" they listed, for instance:

- We keep the issue on people's minds.
- We had much positive response last year—we can build on that if we keep moving.

- We don't want to back down, or appear to have backed down.
- If we don't do a legislative campaign, will we really be able to work on this issue in another way? Will we actually do the other campaigns or strategies we identify?

Under "cons" they had a long list also. It included:

- Doesn't seem winnable right now.
- We haven't figured out how to go against the powers in Nashville on this one; need to develop new ideas and strategies to be more effective.
- There are better ways to use our resources to push ahead on this issue.
- If we use a year to really build power, knowledge, and resources on the local level, we can be more effective next year.[133]

The group considered its strategy honestly and openly, with the advice and leadership of the organizing staff, and decided not to pursue another legislative campaign. Instead CATS members, together with SOCM's committee on temporary work, came up with a list of goals for 1992 and 1993. They decided to focus on building organizational capacity in order to take on a more ambitious campaign at a later date. Their goals for the year included: informational pickets at targeted temporary agencies in three areas to inform workers about the abuse of temps and the loss of permanent jobs; visits and presentations to SOCM chapters in different counties; meetings with ten key legislators; presentations to Democratic Party groups in Tennessee's big cities; visits to labor unions to gain their sympathy and support on the issue; and media and research work to build public support and lay the groundwork for a later campaign.[134]

They focused on long-term objectives, reflecting the core group's philosophy that the immediate strategy had not achieved its desired outcomes, and that it was more important to prepare for a long struggle. Some in the original group became discouraged at the prospect of years of building strength. They believed that CATS had lost, first its campaign and then its focus, and they slowly stopped participating. CATS' legislative and political efforts had been unsuccessful. They had not changed the law substantially, and they had not won jobs for any of their members in Morristown. This failure hurt the group's morale and attendance. Yet the CATS members did not give up on politics. They were disappointed, but they did not see failure as a sign of their own weakness—they saw it rather as a result of the economically and politically powerful global opponents they faced. They realized they needed to figure out how to amass more resources and more strength if they were to prevail in the future. As Joe Perkinson said, "You organize the best you can, and still, with the best job you can do . . . the bigger the picture, the harder it is to win." [135]

Political Action After Failure

A surprising number of the former GE workers became involved in political and economic organizing through other organizations. In very different ways, they continued to broaden and apply the lessons they had learned through CATS. For example, a year after CATS' legislative defeat, organizers from the United Electrical, Radio, and Machineworkers of America (UE) contacted the Morristown workers. That union was in the midst of a difficult organizing campaign at a GE Plastics plant in Parkersburg, West Virginia. The staff members had heard about the CATS fight, and wondered if some of the participants would assist their drive. Calvin Brown and Kathy Muller agreed to go to Parkersburg, to discuss their experiences with the GE workers there and to help union supporters organize their co-workers. Working with the UE in Parkersburg, the Morristown workers learned that their predicament had not been unique. GE had been steadily downsizing its Woodmar factory. In three years the workforce had shrunk from 1,700 to 1,200 workers, while GE's use of temporary services and subcontracting had increased.[136] As it had done in Mascot, Tennessee, GE created a new business in Parkersburg—known as Information Alliance—and transferred clerical and administrative work, data processing, and mail room positions. The new jobs were lower-paying and unprotected.[137] The workers were attempting to unionize, primarily to halt the trend toward contingent work.

Brown and Muller proved invaluable to the UE, which had already lost one election in Parkersburg. The CATS members quickly saw that GE was using the same union-busting strategy that had worked so well in Morristown. Muller got out the video GE had made in 1988, "where they said we were family," and showed it to the Parkersburg workers. "We got out and went door to door. It upset GE awful. . . . You know, I would have *never* done that before. I would never have believed that GE wasn't the greatest company. Now I know they're just a *money* machine, that's all. They don't care about people. Nobody means anything to them at all." [138]

The CATS members also broadened the struggle, informing the West Virginia workers about the nationwide boycott against GE because of its involvement with nuclear weapons. CATS had received "a lot of mail from California and other places where they told me about GE testing stuff, and working in chemical plants where people died, and they lied, and the government backed them up. You know, it was really something," Muller recalled. "We got involved in the nuclear boycott. And it was *great* when they sent me that thing, and said that GE had agreed to stop making nuclear weapons. So people *do* make a difference. Every day." [139]

In November 1992, representatives of CATS made a trip to Washington, D.C., to attend a conference. The Highlander Center helped with the workers' expenses, making the trip affordable to participants. After the conference, the workers stayed and set up visits with groups and legislators who were potentially sympathetic. They urged their representatives to take a proactive role in regulating the abuse of contingent workers across the country.

Back in Morristown, the workers continued to struggle around a variety of issues. As the Hamblen County chapter of SOCM, CATS became involved in local and statewide issues of environmental justice. Muller and others became active in a new campaign, to get city drinking water for people in a neighborhood near a polluted landfill. Not all of the original CATS members wanted to get involved in environmental issues, however. As one said, "It wasn't my baby, and I didn't want to rock it. I wanted to take care of mine, which was getting labor laws." [140] The workers who agreed with her were able to get involved with other campaigns. Rollins and others became members of TIRN and continued to think about ways to improve the situation for working and unemployed people in Tennessee.

Other CATS members—including several who were previously virulently anti-union—led and worked in union campaigns at their new workplaces. Ernest Gardiner, for example, says that at the time of the Morristown plant closing he was against unions. "I didn't think we needed it. We had all these great benefits. What more could we want?" Later he changed his mind. "It couldn't have hurt. . . . At least we'd have had an option anyway, except to sit there and listen." [141] Brown agrees, in retrospect: "I feel that had a union been voted in [at GE], the majority of the people would still be at work today. With the contract, at least you have something in writing, and you have a leg to stand on. Without a contract, you have nothing." [142] Perkinson says "Honestly, I'd always felt that we didn't need a union. But when this happened, you'd better believe that I said, 'Hey, I really blew it!' " [143] As a part-time security guard, he did not have an opportunity to participate in other union drives, but he remained involved with SOCM on issues of economic justice.

Fighting "Smokestack Chasing"

Within the Morristown community the CATS activists launched a campaign pressuring local officials to change the way the county pursued and evaluated economic development. Having learned about GE's subsidies, the workers became aware of the entire system of "smokestack chasing" that was taking place in Morristown and across Tennessee. Muller recalls her realization that Morristown was part of a much larger political economy. "One day when we were having a meeting, I said, 'When GE moved to Morristown, where do you think they came from? Do you think they just decided one day they were just going to build a plant in Morristown? Or do you think that plant came from someplace else, and somebody else suffered when it left? That's what we have learned—we would never have thought of that.' "[144]

Armed with this understanding, they decided to confront local politicians. The GE workers began to challenge a century-long practice of economic development in their region. CATS was the first group of workers in the area to identify the endemic pattern of capital flight and economic blackmail, and to demand that their representatives be accountable to the people instead of the corporations. "I asked the chamber of commerce, 'Are we *sure* we want that plant? If they're coming to Morristown from Canada, then what's to prevent them from going to Mexico from Morristown?' Because I think companies that play these jump-and-hop games, that's what they're going to do. . . . So now, when the mayor says we might be getting a new factory, I say, 'Well, *why* is it coming? *Why* is it moving?' "[145] These questions had a direct impact on the jobs that were created for the Morristown community. If the reason to spend public funds on private corporations was to provide work for local residents, the local residents wanted to know what kind of work would be created. Brown suspected that "the founding fathers of Morristown will not allow decent-sized industries to come in. . . .

Many of them own little sweatshops, and if decent-paying jobs come in, they'll lose their employees to better paying jobs. They won't allow that."[146]

CATS members found out that the mayor and the economic development officials were sending representatives and publicity materials all over the United States and Canada, promising that Morristown workers were non-union and would work for low wages. They also promised generous incentives and industrial parks where environmental regulations would be looser for start-up companies. "You know, we went to the chamber of commerce and *raised Cain* because they were using low wages and lax environmental laws to get companies to come to Hamblen County. We pitched a fit about it! Because, see, they were using a film that said that we had low wages. In Canada they ran it. It got on TV up there. . . . To me, that's unfair. Those people had worked *hard* for what they got. And for us to say, well, if you'll move down here, we'll work for $4.00 cheaper—it doesn't help either of us! It took a long time to see that that type of economics is not going to work. You're going to hurt somebody all the time. Or everybody. Because they'll stay here for a while, but eventually they're going to be moving on down the road."[147]

From the Mountains to the *Maquiladoras*

One of the most important experiences that outside organizations created with CATS was a trip to the *maquiladora* (free trade) zone in Mexico, sponsored by TIRN, in 1992. TIRN knew that displaced workers were particularly susceptible to antiforeign ideologies and other right-wing propaganda, which were popular in East Tennessee. Therefore they designed the trip to allow the workers to see for themselves what the real problem was. TIRN's leaders understood their role as one of educating workers by providing them with new experiences, broadening their awareness, and building their leadership skills. TIRN staff encouraged CATS members to carefully examine not only their own preconceptions but also the series of public policies and private decisions that had contributed to the crisis facing their own community.

Two CATS leaders, Kathy Muller and Christine Simms, participated in the trip, along with seven other women workers from other factories in East Tennessee. TIRN had established a connection with the American Friends Service Committee's Border Project and the *Comite Des Fronterizas Obreras,* the Committee of Border Working Women (CFO). Before the trip the CFO sent two organizers, Teresa Hernandez and Olga Jimenez, to visit East Tennessee, where they had spoken at union halls, met community people, and presented information at public forums. In exchange, women from Tennessee would visit their homes and workplaces in Mexico. The workers participating in the exchange knew that they would be expected to help plan and lead follow-up activities, for the purpose of the trip was not only to satisfy the U.S. workers' curiosity about Mexican workers who had "stolen our jobs" [148] but also to "build bridges that lead to more effective grassroots organizing when everyone has returned home." [149]

The Tennessee women boarded a van and headed to the border area of Matamoros, Mexico. They visited a brand-new GE plant in Mexico, among other factories, and were horrified by the impoverished living and working conditions provided by American corporations. They learned to make the connections between their own experiences and those of Mexican women working in the *maquiladoras* for very low wages and with no job security or organizing rights. [150] They learned that their plant closing was not just an isolated event precipitated by a union drive or by GE's meanness. Rather it was part of a global political economy that facilitated capital mobility and took advantage of existing systems of racial, gender, and economic discrimination.

The Morristown workers visited GE plants in the *maquiladoras* and saw for themselves the results of the North American Free Trade Agreement (NAFTA) celebrated by government and corporate leaders in Tennessee. As another participant, Mavis Young, said, "We are not against increased trade with Mexico. And we are certainly not against Mexican workers having jobs. But we are against blackmail. We are against any kind of system that pits workers against each other on the basis of which one can be forced to take the lowest wage. . . . A visit to the *maquiladoras* will show you what [corporate] freedoms without responsibility can mean." [151]

The activists were again figuring out global political and economic issues that most of the country would take years to understand. They discussed the situation in Mexico and compared it to their own. The poverty among workers at American-owned plants was shocking. As one participant said, "The whole thing shocked me to death. I had seen pictures, I had seen it on TV, but I never ever dreamed what I saw with my own eyes. . . . I think my heart sunk to my stomach. I thought, 'This is not for real. They don't treat human beings like this. People don't do this.' But they do. . . . It's something you'll never forget. . . . It changed something inside me. We got to talk to some of the workers [in Mexico], and it made me realize, too, that we've got some of the same problems here that they have there." [152] Alice Rollins had been surprised to hear from her friends who went to Mexico that the workers there were working hard, just like those in Tennessee. She could not forget the photographs and slides they brought back: "There was this one little shack, it would break your heart. It was like eight by ten [feet] and in back was this little stack of [cinder]blocks, just blocks. . . . They could only buy one block at a time, one block, and they were going to build a house when they got enough blocks. And they was buying them one at a time. And that broke my heart. . . . These people that they were working for was people like GE and other places, and the pictures was of big, beautiful plants. And the grass was green. And then the poor little shacks outside the fences. I thought, how can these people [the GE owners]—these are supposed to be American people; we're supposed to be among the best people in the world. And it made me ashamed of them." [153] Muller echoed her: "They should have a big billboard there that reads, 'Welcome to the *maquiladoras*. Made in the USA.' We created that. . . . We've gotten to where we're a society that thinks that money and power is where it's at." [154]

The women returned to Tennessee and prepared a slide show and presentation about their trip. Among their goals was to teach others in their community to resist the racist message of companies like GE, which told U.S. workers that Mexican women were stealing their jobs. One of the participants in the exchange explained that she "wanted to see if it was really true what they said about the Mexican people. . . . A lot of us went down there with the understanding the same as a lot of people here today: *they're taking our jobs.*" Now, she says, "I don't blame them; I blame our government. . . . I don't believe in slavery." [155] Mavis Young explained how her thinking changed: "I blamed the corporations—that was my first instinct. And then after I had sense enough to figure it out, [I thought] the government's letting these corporations do it. And to think that they thought that those people weren't human beings and could live in those deplorable conditions—it was beyond me." [156] The workers from East Tennessee began to think in terms of a political economy. They began to connect economic exploitation and injustice with political decisions and government action. They developed an analysis that placed large corporations alongside the U.S. government in a regime that created and perpetuated great poverty and great wealth. This understanding was more grounded and sophisticated than almost any popular or intellectual analysis of the global economy in the early 1990s.

Workers who did not participate in the trip heard about it from those who did. The participants showed their slide show and presentation on the situation in Mexico and the realities of "free trade" to groups like SOCM and TIRN, church groups, community organizations, union meetings, and anywhere else they could get access. As a result, the CATS members became well informed about issues like NAFTA, trade policy, and fast-track authority, even before the subjects were debated prominently in national politics.

The Tennessee women befriended and empathized with their "sisters" in Mexico, and in the process learned the importance of solidarity across racial and national boundaries. This was remarkable, especially considering the racist rhetoric of companies, politicians, and radio talk show hosts at this time. Many have documented racism within the U.S. working class, especially in predominantly white workforces like East Tennessee's.[157] And yet this group of women, when provided with the structure, leadership, and guidance of local organizations, overcame some very deep prejudices, surprising even themselves. As Muller says of the trip, "It left an impression on me that I'll never forget. . . . People live in dream worlds. When I hear people now say, 'Well, Mexicans won't work,' and all that—that's not like how it is at all! The Mexican people are probably the hardest-working people there is. . . . I grew up *real* poor, so I think that I was more prepared for it than some of them was."[158]

Joe Perkinson began to think about the migrant workers from Mexico who arrived in the Morristown area every spring to work on tomato farms and other types of agriculture. The workers were subject to discrimination, and Perkinson, like his neighbors, had always considered them unwelcome. But after his own experience, and after hearing about his co-workers' experiences in Mexico, he began to think differently. "We have workers from Mexico come and do a lot of farm work, maintenance and all that, and they come here and eagerly do these jobs, hard physical work . . . where our people won't even accept that kind of work. They're gonna die young."[159] The workers' actions and experiences transformed their political consciousness. Racism and xenophobia, fostered by their families, community, and culture, slowly abated.

The workers learned to be critical of the experts'—economists' and politicians'—pronouncements on the economy. They saw that the unbounded optimism of political leaders about a "global society" and the rise of a high-technology "information age" was not shared by communities directly affected by economic change. They had experienced this in Morristown, and in Mexico they saw that a very different community was affected in a similar way. A new form of capitalism was developing, one characterized by capital mobility, contingent labor, impoverished workers, and sweatshops. The workers contrasted the realities in Morristown and Matamoros with the images GE had presented in its films and promotional materials on the "GE family." The global economy was, for low-income communities, a "bandit economy," extracting wealth from the poor to benefit the corporations and their shareholders.

To the workers, it was neither inevitable nor progressive for the United States to condone this behavior. "I'm so sick of hearing about the 'global market.' We'll do *anything* to compete in the global market! Anything. That's why we lost our jobs—they told us they had to do that in order to compete in the global market. I think they did it because of *greed*. I *still* think that it's important to treat people with dignity, and I think you can still compete."[160] Brown echoed her: "In 1980, GE had a net worth of $12 billion, which took in excess of a hundred years to accumulate. In 1992, the company had a net worth of $72 billion—an increase of $60 *billion*—but yet they were using the excuse that they had to eliminate people to stay competitive. To me that's not staying competitive. It's greed. Corporate greed and nothing more."[161]

The workers began to imagine positive steps they could take to address the problems. Some of the answers were local—for example, ques-

tioning Hamblen County's or Tennessee's industrial recruitment strategies. Some were global—"I think the only way we can survive is if we
work together as one—Canada, the United States, and Mexico—to
help *all* the people. . . . [Then] I think free trade *could* work."[162] This
analysis and sense of potential distinguishes the CATS group from other
displaced workers. Their experiences laid the groundwork for them to
participate in future campaigns, around local economic issues, but also
around international issues such as NAFTA, and GATT, and the WTO.

New Perspectives

Scholars who study social movements have complained, for the last fifteen years or so, that while the field has burgeoned, there has been very
little literature investigating the transformations in people's lives as a result of activism. Doug McAdam reviewed the literature and concluded
that very little attention has been paid to "biographical or life-course
consequences that have been empirically tied to movement activity."[163]

The story of CATS makes it clear that during a period of intense activism—what I would call a proto-social movement—participants un-
derwent a significant political education and transformation. Their
understanding of themselves and their role in politics and the economy
changed dramatically. In interviews it is striking that every CATS member could tell a story of personal and political development over the
years of activism following the plant closing. This is not true of either
the Greenbrier or the Acme Boot workers. In the Greenbrier case, since
there was little or no political activity, the workers' worldviews and political attitudes were largely unchanged. In the Acme case, workers were
well educated on several important features of the political economy,
and they participated in political campaigns. The majority, however, did
not make connections between the set of issues around which they had
mobilized—tax policy, free trade, Puerto Rico's status as a territory, and

government incentives for economic development—and a broader political agenda. They were ambivalent about organized labor as a political force. They were disparaging of welfare recipients, and characterized welfare abuse and crime as some of the biggest problems in American politics. The CATS members provide a remarkable contrast. Following their struggle the GE workers held fresh attitudes about both the United States and the global economy in the 1990s.

Kathy Muller, for example, had for many years looked down upon "those little people" who had inferior jobs or no jobs at all and therefore depended upon food stamps and welfare. When she heard GE was closing, she had initially blamed the workers who "stole" her job—the poor and undiscriminating workers who took temporary jobs or accepted public assistance. Over time her attitudes changed dramatically. Muller says, "I must have been a shallow person. Because, see, I was in my own world. I got up every day, and I went to work, and I made good money. . . . I think I was a snob. . . . Now I'm grateful that I'm able to look and see and have compassion for people, because they're having a hard time. I really think if you give people the incentive, they'll work." [164] Alice Rollins used to look down on temp workers: "I used to think I wouldn't work for a temporary service. That is so easy to say. Words are so easy to form and let them trip off your tongue, but they are so hard to take back. And when I think now how foolish that was, to even think such a thing. Because people who work for these services are *just like me,* they're just trying to make a living, they're just trying to get by, and that's all you got. I'm sure, when the time comes, I'll have to do it, I won't have a choice. And so I have a little more empathy for people. . . . Seems like it used to be, we would help people when they were down. When did we change our policy? When did we go to: 'When they're down, kick them'?!" [165]

Ernest Gardiner grew up hearing "People are poor because they choose to be," but he now disagrees. "There's a lot of hardworking people out there that have had a lot of bad luck, whether it be sickness, their house burned down, they couldn't afford insurance, couldn't get a good job. . . . Could be that they lost a good-paying job to temporary workers, I don't know. Life can take a lot of strange turns. You just can't tell what's happened to somebody, why they're poor." [166] Brown had an even more structural explanation, explaining that the causes of poverty were directly "due to the big corporations. The elimination of jobs. . . . The wages have gone down, and there's no doubt that the benefits that people have had have deteriorated. People have started to take lower-paying jobs; many of them have to work through temporary services, which they have no benefits whatsoever. You can't support yourself! . . . I don't blame the people. I blame the top. . . . The corporate people are getting filthy rich." Brown saw these trends as a broader indictment of American democracy. "I think *democracy* is fair treatment of all people. Treating people with dignity and respect. Allowing people to have a chance to earn a good living without being threatened. Having benefits when they become old. . . . I don't think that [the U.S.] is a true democracy anymore." [167]

The process of beginning to ask questions and doubt long-held beliefs and trust in authority was extremely difficult for many. Joe Perkinson, a veteran of Korea and Vietnam who was fifty years old when he was laid off, seriously contemplated suicide and other types of violence. He threatened to bring in a gun and force GE managers to give him his job back, at whatever wage. Others in the group convinced him to use more peaceful means. He took a minimum-wage, temporary job as a security guard at the Morristown mall. Having survived a nadir of desperation and disillusionment, he says he understands why the crime rate is so high in areas where there are no good jobs. [168] Ernest Gardiner agrees: "[Temporary work] creates an atmosphere of apathy over a period of time. They talk about the crime rate is going up, and I'm not saying temporary people are criminals, but a man keeps getting beat down and beat down, and pretty soon something snaps, you know. Whereas if this particular person had a regular job, he might go to that job instead of knocking over a liquor store." [169]

GE officials, like most managers, had often invoked the metaphor of "family." In good times most workers believed that they were part of a cohesive workplace, and accepted their place in the implied hierarchy. But the idea of the factory as one big family could not hold up after the workers' experiences with CATS. They had sued their employer, marched against it, and waged a public war with GE. They were not merely rebellious children. Because they had found a new political analysis of their predicament, the workers had moved beyond blaming GE, and focused on their own power to transform their community—and public policy.

As a result, unlike the Greenbrier workers or even the Acme Boot workers, CATS members refused management's attempt to label them one big family. This was not because they had cared about their co-workers any less; in fact, they had felt very close to one another. It was because of GE's actions, as well as their own. Muller provides an interesting analysis of GE's change away from familylike caring: "Maybe the company doesn't want it to be like that. They don't like that closeness. They want to get away from that family. It threatened them. Because if something happened to one, it happened to all. They don't want that. They can't deal with that." [170] Muller has appropriated the metaphor of family for herself. Her analysis reveals not only a sense of community and a collective identity with the other workers but a real understanding of the power workers have if they actually behave as a "family." It is remarkable that she retains the positive implication of the metaphor—a family loves and takes care of one another—while strongly critiquing the employer's manipulative use of the term. In their trip to West Virginia, Brown and Muller were able to warn those GE workers that GE did not want them to be part of a "family." The collective, the union, or the community organization came to represent more of a true family than the hierarchical workplace ever had.

The workers carried this knowledge with them to their new jobs. When Muller began working at Lowe's, they showed an orientation film welcoming the workers to the "Lowe's family" and promising to take good care of the workers. Muller remembers, "I knew it was brainwashing. I had to turn it off and just think about something else. . . . I told [my co-workers] that I've heard that one time before, you know, and I've learned that they hire professionals to make those tapes—to brainwash people. It's good to know those things. . . . They told these young kids that if they go to work for Lowe's and they work there fifteen years, they'll be millionaires. And I say, 'Well, I wouldn't put all my money in the bank if I were y'all.' So now those same kids, if they're going to make a decision, they come to me and talk it over. In my own way I've taught them: Don't believe everything this company tells you." [171]

Some of the workers changed their political affiliations because of the CATS struggle. Alice Rollins said that her family had always voted Republican and that her husband was still a staunch Republican. But now, she said, "We don't agree on politics at all. . . . I say what worked for your daddy when he was twenty-five years old don't work now." Before the CATS struggle, she says, "I voted for Bush. I did. But now this time [1992], I voted for Clinton. [The Democratic Party] is more for the people. [But] I don't vote for a party, especially not the Republicans. I will never vote straight for one party. I'm for me. I'm for my family. If you're for me and mine, I'm for you." [172] Gardiner similarly began wondering which representatives were actually looking out for his interests: "I defended my country, I volunteered for service during that old Vietnam War. Now how about somebody defending me? Who will do it?" [173]

While voting based on economic issues may not seem remarkable, it represents a significant change from the past. Rollins and many others in East Tennessee had consistently voted Republican. They had two reasons: first, tradition; and second, values. Their families had been Republican; furthermore, the Republican Party stood for freedoms (such as gun ownership) and values (religious and antiabortion) important to them. To place economic and class-based issues instead at the forefront of one's political behavior represented a clear departure from tradition and an assertion of a new political identity as a worker, or a woman, or a member of a community that demanded activism and change from the government. Rollins says that her husband advised her to ignore candidates' platforms, because "they get in office and really, he can't do jacknothing." She rejected his cynicism. " 'But at least,' I said, 'Clinton has a plan, at least he's talking like he's on my side.' . . . If you don't vote, you may as well vote for the other man. That's how I look at it."[174]

As Rollins's struggle with her husband suggests, workers' personal lives were changed by the experience. Many told stories of their husbands, wives, or families seeing them in a different light after they became activists and troublemakers in the town. Established roles and relationships were upset. As in other plant closings, the divorce rate among displaced workers was high. Ernest Gardiner had spent months applying for jobs, receiving no interviews, and simultaneously watching his marriage fall apart. "The psychological effect of it is devastating. And I guess if a person gets pretty hard to live with, and the other person responds by becoming pretty hard to live with, then the first thing you know. . . ."[175]

Some of the changes, however, were more positive, as the workers' new roles at work and in CATS bled into their personal lives. As Kathy Muller said, "The one thing I made my mind up was, people won't intimidate me. They can send me out the door! But they can't intimidate me. I've done been through all that. In four years I had all the intimidation, all the put-downs. . . . I've been through hell and half of Georgia, and I don't have any room for any more intimidation. . . . If I'm in a group of people, and somebody says, 'Well, this is the way it is,' I'm not afraid to say, 'Well, I don't believe that.' It doesn't bother me anymore to say that. I feel comfortable with saying, 'I don't go along with this!' or, 'I feel different.' And I'm comfortable with being the only one to say it. . . . It takes a long time to get to that. I'll never be intimidated again. And that's good for me." [176]

Some of the CATS members became unofficial consultants, at-large union stewards to others in town who needed an advocate. They helped people investigate hazardous substances that were making them sick at the workplace. They helped fired workers file charges with the National Labor Relations Board. They also learned to challenge authority. Linda Yount remembered that during the unionization drive one of the managers from the North had spoken disparagingly of the workers, saying, "All you have to do to get along with the people here in Tennessee is to look at pictures of their children and tell them what pretty tomatoes they have." At the time, Yount had laughed and accepted his assessment, and voted against the union to show her loyalty and confidence in the company. A year later her attitude had changed dramatically. "If you feel as strongly as I do about this, it's going to take a hell of a lot more than bragging on my young'uns and 'maters, to settle this issue!" [177] While the Greenbrier workers claimed they only wanted an apology and the respect of the managers they had once considered family, the CATS participants wanted to see justice done.

The CATS participants believed strongly in the power of collective action. After their failure to persuade their elected representatives, the courts, the media, or their own managers, the GE workers realized that they had to depend on one another. Many of the workers—including those who had rejected the idea of a union at GE—became more sympathetic to labor unions and unionization drives in the area. At the same time they were not optimistic about the ability of unions—or any other organization—to stop the economic changes they saw, without the intervention of legislation. Political solutions were necessary. Alice Rollins, for example, now supported unions in general because she saw them as "mostly set up to protect the workers." But she said about the GE situation, "I honestly don't see how a union could have helped what they did, because it wasn't against the law. The only way I see it could have helped was if it had been against our union contract for them to move it. But, on the other hand, there was a plant in Morristown a few years back, they had a union. They shut the doors, honey, and then they hired everybody back at lower wages, and broke the union. So unions don't have that much power." [178] Public policy was essential. The role of the state, in their view, was to regulate corporate actions that directly destroyed jobs or lowered living standards. This analysis was crucial in taking workers away from self-blame and scapegoating, toward more global analysis. It also reminded the activists that they did have some power—potential if not realized—and that it was up to them to get to work.

CATS' Ongoing Legacy: The Roots of Social Change

The GE workers became involved in a serious political campaign as they organized CATS. Not one member had ever been to the state capitol in Nashville, and very few had ever so much as written a letter to a public official. As Muller says, "When I worked at GE, I would've never asked my government a question. I would've never challenged them on anything. Now I challenge them on *everything*. I mean, I wouldn't take their word for nothing. . . . I can see beyond what they say. [Before the CATS campaign] I had all these ideas that there was justice in the Labor Department. Even when I lost my job, I thought, 'Well, not to worry, I'll go out and find another job.' And then when reality started setting in, I thought, 'Well, our government won't let GE do this.' And when you realize they *will* let 'em do it, they're doing it every day, then I began to ask questions." [179]

None of the CATS members had ever fought for something like this before. They had followed the rules and done well. This made their ordeal even more devastating. Ernest Gardiner, who had had perfect attendance at GE for five years in a row, testified to this: "The emotional impact of something like that is just beyond belief. . . . You determine in your mind that you're going to do a good job, keep your nose clean, retire, and the ol' American way of life is just right there for you, and then all of a sudden the rug's yanked out from under you, and you're forty-two, forty-three years old, and all of a sudden you're saying, 'What's going to happen next?' " [180] Muller said, "I was the type of person, I guess that if they [GE] had told me to go out in a lake and jump in, I would've went on, because I thought they knew what was best for me. . . . I had been brought up to think that if you got a job, you did the very best you could, you worked as hard as you could, you did what they said, because they were boss—and you'd be okay! When I realized that didn't work, it was hard, it was really hard." [181] Rollins explained how she came to identify with other oppressed people rather than with the better-off. Being one-eighth Cherokee, she began to think about Native Americans: "I can imagine how they feel, when they moved out and thought, 'This was mine and you took it.' You know, when you think about it, that's exactly how we are. This was ours, and they took it, and they gave it to somebody else." [182]

These hard-learned lessons stuck. More than most participants involved in typical plant-closing struggles, the members of CATS continued to participate in political activities. Many of the workers became involved in the struggle to amend or defeat NAFTA when it came up for a vote in Congress in 1993. The issue of corporate mobility was very close to their hearts, and the workers who had been to Mexico were especially aware of the consequences of unregulated "free trade." Far more than the workers from Greenbrier or Acme, the CATS workers understood what was at stake with NAFTA. "They all [Congress and the president] took the side of big business and they turned their back on the working people of this country. . . . It wasn't that people were against free trade. It was just that they wanted *fair trade*."[183] When TIRN learned that hearings were scheduled to take place on the possibility of a North American Free Trade Agreement, Muller and another participant from the *maquiladora* exchange made the trip to Atlanta to testify. Muller told the story of GE and CATS, and then she said, "It may sound like a long way from the unemployment line in Hamblen County, Tennessee, to the Office of the U.S. Trade Representative. But really it's not. In fact, I have come to believe that trade policy and unemployment are all tied up together. . . . The multi-national corporations bear much responsibility for what is happening. But it is not just the corporations I blame. I blame the government too. Our government should be insisting on corporate accountability. . . . We must learn from the failures of the *maquiladora* program and develop a free trade agreement with Mexico that will not repeat the same patterns. We need decent jobs at decent wages for workers on both sides of the border."[184]

CATS members met with Representative Jim Cooper, the congressman from Morristown, and proposed amending NAFTA to make it fairer to the people of all three countries. For example, "Why couldn't we have an agreement that said that a company that moves to Mexico will have to pay *our* minimum wage? Which would bring their standard of living up, and nobody would lose." Cooper had responded, "We can't do that." But as Muller said, "We *could* do that. Can you imagine those people [in Mexico] making four dollars and a quarter an hour? They'd think they'd died and went to heaven. I mean, to me that would be the answer."[185]

These transformations created democratic citizens and political actors out of individuals. The change in participants' understanding of their identity, as well as their behavior, is remarkable. Testimony by members proves the truth behind Tocqueville's description of community-based organizations as classrooms of democracy. Some of the lessons learned in the CATS classroom were very difficult ones—including the truth about workers' own powerlessness and their betrayal by political elites. Nevertheless, the skills and experience of participation in strong collective action created in them valuable principles of democratic citizenship.

CATS also transformed Morristown. Anyone in Morristown who had a problem in the workplace knew how to contact a CATS leader. Moreover, public officials in Morristown remembered CATS. The country executive and chamber of commerce officials referred to CATS as the strongest protest about jobs and the economy that Hamblen County had ever seen. Although CATS lost the immediate battle, its legacy was clear in the ongoing decisions by local officials who had known their power and would anticipate their reactions before choosing a course of action. Although the impact was impossible to quantify, interviews with officials suggested that CATS had a significant effect on Morristown economic development policy.

Seeds of a Social Movement

The most significant fact about CATS is that, although it was born in the hills of Appalachian Tennessee, it had an influence on a wide array of organizations and institutions. There are many indications that CATS was the beginning of a regional and even a national social movement around the issues of contingent work in the political economy. In the end, this may be the GE workers' most enduring legacy. Because of CATS, a number of nonprofit, political, and educational organizations have become involved in the issue of casualization and temporary work, and the circle of interest continues to grow.

CATS has transformed the institutional landscape of Eastern Tennessee. CATS' struggle inspired the newly forming TIRN to decide to focus on contingent work as one of its three issue areas. TIRN has continued to bring together workers and activists from all over the state to discuss the problem and to strategize about organizing temporary workers and addressing economic injustices through legislative or political strategies.

The Highlander Center also took on the issue as a result of CATS' activism, incorporating exercises and materials on the problems of temporary work into its workshops on the global economy and on community organizing in Appalachia and the South. In July 1991, the Highlander Center held a three-day workshop on "Part-time, Temporary, and Contract Workers: Issues of the Disposable Contingent Work Force," with participants from CATS and other community-based and workplace-based groups from across the South. Thus the issue of contingent work became part of Highlander's ongoing "economy schools" program. The workshops trained participants in how to broaden the coalition to work with other groups, how to plan specific events, and how to build political influence in their region.[186] Groups that attended the workshop left with specific plans to fight the shift to contingent work in their own communities.

Because the issue of temporary work was becoming increasingly prominent across the southeastern United States, but also because CATS had framed the issue and waged a legislative battle around it, other groups began to make it a priority. Two regional organizations, Southerners for Economic Justice (SEJ) and the newer southeastern Regional Economic Justice Network (REJN) also began to look at questions of contingent work in late 1990. At its September 1990 gathering in Atlanta, SEJ and REJN (with active participation from TIRN and Highlander staff) held a workshop on "Temporary Services, Labor Pools, and Contracting Out." The workshop was a first step in bringing those groups together, networking, and planning the next steps in a regional effort.

REJN held a similar meeting in Atlanta in September 1991, including representatives of CATS, TIRN, SOCM, Nine-to-Five, and other regional and national advocacy and grassroots organizations. Susan Faludi, a Pulitzer Prize–winning reporter with the *Wall Street Journal*, participated in the meeting and interviewed members of CATS and other organizations, in preparation for a long article on the trend toward contingent work.[187] The REJN group came up with several concrete plans for future work on the issue. The goal of the organizations who participated was to devise a joint campaign, "where we could fight on this problem in our different states at the same time."[188] The campaign against contingent work was becoming a movement. At least at the regional level, CATS had sparked numerous and diverse groups to mobilize their memberships around temporary work, and more broadly around the changing political economy and the quest for economic justice. This was a huge achievement, and more than a small local organization could have hoped for. CATS had started a social movement.

The organizations had a multipronged strategy, discussed at length at a series of meetings. First, they would develop together a Bill of Rights for contingent workers, that could be used in various campaigns. Durham, North Carolina, was the site of the first such effort among temporary and part-time employees. Second, they would begin local campaigns in several cities, counties, and states around the region, pressuring governments and legislatures to regulate the abuse of contingent workers. Third, they decided to do some research into the issue of temporary work, including information on the National Association of Temporary Services, information on trends in other countries, and strategies for regulating contingent work. Once the research was completed, the group wanted to release a report with a press release, to get some publicity on the issue. Fourth, the group that was represented at the meeting agreed to share information and strategies with one another as the work proceeded. "We continue to want to work toward a joint legislative campaign," they said.[189] To that end, the group agreed to reconvene in Greenville, South Carolina, in March 1992. Finally, the REJN group concluded, "We think it is important to continue organizing locally on these issues and to encourage other groups to organize." [190]

Within a few years many more organizations had taken on the issue. One of these, the Carolina Alliance for Fair Employment (CAFE), sponsored the March 1992 regional coalition meeting on temporary work. The planning committee—with representatives of Highlander, TIRN, CAFE, SOCM, the Southern Rainbow Project, and Up and Out of Poverty—emphasized the importance of including other groups in the South "who might be interested in working on the issue of the loss of permanent, stable jobs and the abuses to workers in the contingent work force." [191] That gathering included representatives of some new groups, including the Atlanta Coalition for Labor Pool Reform, Coalition on Jobs and the Environment from Southwest Virginia, the Atlanta Central Labor Council, AFSCME Local 1194, and Partnership for Democracy's Appalachian Region. That group expanded on the ideas developed in earlier meetings, including concrete plans for regional-action days—coordinated events where several organizations would plan actions aimed at appropriate targets in different areas on the same day—and media exposure "as a way to build this issue toward 'critical mass' in the public mind by 1995." [192] The ultimate goal would be joint legislative campaigns in 1995, in South and North Carolina, Tennessee, Georgia, Arkansas and Florida—the states with the most active grassroots support. Having won the support of the Industrial Union Department of the AFL-CIO and the National Committee on Pay Equity, the group began to make concrete plans for joint fundraising, media and education, and building a local, regional, and eventually national coalition. Even more organizations were brought into the coalition, and emphasis was placed on the importance of including unions, churches, civil rights groups, and other groups with mass constituencies and resources. In June 1992, TIRN met with staff members of the Federation for Industrial Retention and Renewal (FIRR), a national coalition based in Chicago, and the Piedmont Peace Project, a community-based coalition in the Carolinas, and enlisted their support.

After these major regional gatherings and workshops, the groups reconvened periodically to follow up with each other and plan coordinated events, but the different groups also began to address contingent-work issues as part of their own work. CAFE went on to pursue the issue of contingent work on its own, finding tremendous support among its constituency in North and South Carolina. CAFE received a grant from the Poverty and Race Research and Action Council, and held a "temp school" in 1994, inviting long-term temporary workers to come from all over South Carolina for a week of discussions. CAFE paid the workers $7 an hour for their forty hours, and held the school in donated space. The contingent workers, mostly women, half of them African American and half of them white, participated in workshops, teaching the organizers about their situation and prospects. By the end of the week they had come up with ambitious plans: a newsletter and a telephone hotline for mistreated workers; principles of fair conduct for temporary agencies; a program of undercover testing for temporary workers to rate agencies according to how fairly they treated their employees; and a network of temp workers to share information and support, and to plan future campaigns in the Carolinas.[193]

The movement spread all across the South. In Charleston, South Carolina, and Atlanta, Georgia, groups discovered that the local government was complicit in the shift from full-time to temporary work. Both cities had made deals with temporary and contract service agencies to provide municipal services. Part-time and temporary employees were hired at 10 percent less pay than permanent full-time workers, with the agencies receiving kickbacks on a portion of the cities' savings. CAFE and the Atlanta Coalition for Labor Pool Reform, together with the Central Labor Council and Up and Out of Poverty, worked on campaigns to repeal these laws and to ensure equal pay for publicly employed temps and part-timers. In Durham, Southerners for Economic Justice campaigned for the city council to pass a Workers' Bill of Rights. The REJN group worked on a "Contingent Workers Bill of Rights."[194] All these efforts are part of the legacy of the fight waged by CATS.

REJN has also continued to address the problem of contingent work as one of the centerpieces of its campaign on economic justice. And, with grant support from Oxfam America and other organizations, TIRN hired a full-time organizer in Nashville to work exclusively on contingent-work issues. With the example of the early activists from CATS, other groups and networks have taken up the effort and will continue fighting for economic justice for displaced and temporary workers.

In 1995 and 1996 the issue of contingent work became much more visible nationally. Major organizations began to make it a priority. Kathy Muller was invited to be a panelist at a conference convened at the Department of Labor on issues facing working women. The Institute for Women and Policy announced funding for organizations studying contingent work, and invited TIRN staff to a national academic conference on the topic. International labor unions began to consider organizing temporary workers and discussing the issue publicly for the first time. The Service Employees International Union (SEIU) and Nine-to-Five, the National Association of Working Women, began a campaign called "Flexible But Fair," seeking to organize contingent workers to achieve wage parity with full-time permanent workers, coverage under the NLRA, and a requirement that employers offer—and subsidize if possible—benefits for contingent workers. Flexible But Fair began—with direct input from the CATS organizers and from TIRN and CAFE—with a survey of its members on temp issues. The group col-

lected stories from contingent workers for publication, and drafted a
statement of principles for employers to sign that could become the
basis for future legislation. Organizers from Nine-to-Five and SEIU believed that the process they began in 1995 was a long-term campaign
whose time had come, and they compared it to the successful multiyear
campaign that led to the passage of the Family and Medical Leave Act in
1993.[195]

Finally, the National Labor Relations Board in 1996, chaired by
Clinton appointee William B. Gould IV, began considering changing
legal procedures to make it easier for temporary workers to join labor
unions, which is virtually impossible under current rules. Business
groups warned that they would fight any changes that could have a
deleterious impact on corporations. "Clearly it's going to discourage
the use of temporary workers," said one business lobbyist.[196] Political
pressures increased the salience of the issue of contingent work and
pushed the NLRB to reconsider it. If these initiatives by groups all over
the country indeed lead to important legislation, it will not be directly
attributable to the work of CATS. But the group that formed in Morristown, Tennessee, served as a critical early step in a process that resulted in important national political debates and policy changes.

Beyond contingent work, the efforts of CATS, SOCM, TIRN, and
the other coalitions with whom they organized had ripple effects in
other arenas. TIRN produced a video based on the workers' exchange
in Mexico, called *From the Mountains to the* Maquiladoras, and circulated
it to community-based organizations and labor unions all over the
country. Only a few years later literally hundreds of worker exchanges
had been organized between American and Mexican workers, and both
scholars and labor leaders were promoting worker exchanges as the best
strategy for creating a truly internationalist labor movement in the
global economy.[197]

The AFL-CIO changed its position on globalization dramatically in the 1990s. Its office of international relations changed its name to Solidarity Center, and adopted a vision based on global solidarity between workers. According to its director, Barbara Shailor, the new department established in 1997 "is designed to assist unions in the developing world in building their capacity to become strong partners," working with community-based organizations and NGOs rather than enforcing the foreign policy objectives of the U.S. government and the economic agendas of American business.[198] Shailor discussed cross-border exchanges like TIRN's as central to the mission of the AFL-CIO's international program. "American workers increasingly understand that their fate is intimately connected to the fate of workers the world over."[199] Independent, progressive workers' organizations in countries from Mexico to Romania to Indonesia for the first time found strong institutional support from the American labor movement.

CATS instigated organizing on other issues too. In 1997, TIRN initiated a living-wage campaign in the city of Knoxville—based on the idea that all working people, contingent or otherwise, deserved a wage that could support them and their families. TIRN developed an interactive workshop that members presented to various constituency groups, and they built a coalition including religious groups, labor unions, community organizations, and student activists. Two years later activists in Nashville used TIRN's model to launch their own living-wage campaign. TIRN was in the forefront of a national movement that saw over seventy-five living-wage ordinances passed in the late 1990s and early 2000s. The national AFL-CIO embraced the growing movement and called on its affiliates and labor councils to help pass local living-wage laws in the cities and counties.[200]

Inspired by TIRN and CATS before them, students at the University of Tennessee in Knoxville organized a Labor Teach-In, involving 350 participants, including members of TIRN and SOCM and their coalition partners. Local and national labor leaders and rank-and-file activists told their stories and discussed their visions for the future of worker struggles for economic justice. In 2001 a group called the UTK Council for a Living Wage and Worker Justice was created, inspired by the living-wage campaign, to work with TIRN and other organizations on a range of economic justice issues. The council published a study of the wage structure and labor policies at the University of Tennessee, perhaps planning for university-wide campaigns of its own. For the first time, an organized university-based group was joining the coalition and lending its energy and expertise to the struggle in Tennessee.

CATS had been on an amazing journey. Since 1989, when GE closed its Morristown warehouse, the group had organized, protested, lobbied, testified, written legislation, and moved beyond Hamblen County to do these things in other parts of the country and in Mexico. The displaced workers had gone from attracting no attention at all (shut out of the Morristown press) to achieving recognition throughout the South and then all over the United States. The group's political trajectory is equally impressive. CATS had begun with local protests, first against GE and then attempting to enlist the support of local political leaders. When that failed, the group had turned to the state legislature, initiating hearings and attempting to pass legislation regulating the temporary-services industry. When that failed, the workers continued to foster alliances with other organizations, and to persuade these groups to take on the issue of contingent work.

A string of failures paved the path from a living room in Morristown to the Labor Department in Washington, D.C., to Matamoros, Mexico, to Seattle and back to Tennessee. CATS had shown that intense collective activity over time could transform a local group's protest into an emerging social movement. The story of CATS shows that although local organizing cannot compete with the forces shaping national and global economic policy, the process of transforming local politics, organizations, and institutions, leading others to take up the cause, had tremendous results. CATS helped to build a movement that made a dif-ference—and this is the greatest hope for low-income communities in the twenty-first century. As Kathy Muller says, "Instead of getting de-pressed, and going home, I came out fighting. And basically I've been fighting ever since."[201]

6

Conclusion:
Local Democracy in a Global Economy

While a half-dozen activists from Tennessee traveled to Seattle for the 1999 demonstrations, TIRN organized rallies to support them in Knoxville and Nashville, sponsored by unions, the Catholic Diocese, Amnesty International, EarthFirst!, and other groups. TIRN had been building its labor-community coalition around global economic justice issues since 1989, when CATS first faced the impact of the new economy—making it one of the oldest organizations involved. TIRN's moment had finally come: Seattle would be a huge boost for coalition building in Tennessee and elsewhere. Cheryl Brown, a new leader of TIRN, observed, "There's a real upswing in interest from enviros and labor now, plus student groups that we haven't seen before. . . . The internationalist message is really out there. Folks are genuinely concerned about the fate of workers in other countries."[1]

The activists from Tennessee were no longer alone. In Bangor, Maine, a new Global Action Network united loggers and environmentalists protesting the Irving Corporation's use of low-wage bonded labor. In Prescott, Arizona, activists organized trips to sweatshops across the border in Nogales—much like the trip that CATS members participated in a decade before—showing videos and leading workshops. In San Francisco students of color returned from Seattle and began an organization linking prison labor and privatization to the WTO and free trade regimes, "where capital has all the freedom of movement and people have none."[2] What all of these groups had in common was a commitment to a coalition building, between labor organizations and other activists—and a commitment to direct action. They had learned that the processes of education and relationship building that are so essential to grassroots coalition politics were best achieved in the midst of struggle. Dan Solnit from the Direct Action Network observed, "There was more alliance-building the day of November 30 [in Seattle] than in the 15 years of clever strategies before."[3] In the heat of militant protest, confrontation, and an ambitious vision of economic justice, people from all over the world came together, educated each other, and made a commitment to join forces for a new kind of globalization.

Local Democracy in a Global Economy

What happened in Seattle—and in the years before—challenges theories of democracy and power. In political theory as well as in practice, the United States has always been considered the ultimate localist state. Local community activism and civil society are celebrated as solutions to a diverse set of problems, including alienation and anomie, voter resentment, low rates of political participation, and the decline of family values. At the same time, many analysts argue that the new "global economy" has made localist politics—and even national politics—obsolete. Everything is determined in the international marketplace, they say, and there is nothing that local communities, states, or even sovereign nations can do to avoid its imperatives. Localism may be our only hope for salvaging community and American values, but it cannot compete with new forms of economic and political power. Community-based groups can fight for better schools or more stop signs, but they cannot challenge the global economy. In some ways these cynics are clearly right. The failure of nearly all communities that protest plant closings or other injustices to influence economic outcomes reveals the grim prospects for local democracy in a political system committed to a particular type of global economy. The most devastating economic changes in low-income communities are resulting not from inevitable processes of an optimizing free market but from political decisions by national, state, and local policymakers, and the institutions and imperatives that structure those decisions. The barriers to change are high.

The workplace and community-based organizing efforts in Tennessee provide examples of exactly what President Lyndon Johnson would have lauded during the War on Poverty as "long-range plans for the attack on poverty in their own local communities . . . based on the fact that local citizens best understand their own problems and know best how to deal with those problems."[4] But because these groups are fighting for structural economic change, they have met with extreme resistance at the legislative level. Wealthy and powerful forces arrayed against them have been impossible to defeat in the short term. For the long term, however, community-based organizing efforts provide examples of the most ambitious and potentially successful types of economic development. The very process entails democratizing the political system and guaranteeing access to those who have been excluded.

In a democratic system citizens have the right and the responsibility to fight for policies that serve their interests, and against those that threaten them. As Browning, Marshall, and Tabb point out, Tocqueville was mistaken when he wrote about American politics: "The gradual development of the equality of conditions is therefore a providential fact . . . it is universal, it is durable, it constantly eludes all human interference, and all events as well as all men contribute to its progress."[5] In fact, in the United States the strongest pressures are in the opposite direction. Equality of conditions improves only with strenuous effort and sustained political mobilization. Communities that organize effectively can shape their own economic future. They can democratize the process of economic policy making, and they can also influence economic outcomes in a positive way. Grassroots organizing remains the only alternative to an antidemocratic and ultimately economically destructive politics of business development.

Economic changes in the twenty-first century affect not only the traditional membership base of trade unions but new constituencies and entire communities. Entire communities are affected when tax funds are spent on poor or transient jobs, when plants close, when workers have less purchasing power, or when good jobs are converted to unpredictable jobs with poverty-level wages. This reality brings new organizing challenges. Rather than relying on conventional labor-based strategies, organizations are beginning to consider ways to be more effective, by pursuing strategies that focus on outreach to other groups and that build on community organizations. Community-based organizing approaches can work to bring new groups together to fight for change. Labor-community coalitions are essential in building this new political movement.

Citizens have many options in devising campaigns around economic development issues. They can demand benefits to the community in return for tax incentives and other corporate "welfare" provisions, or they can join with labor unions to promote participatory decision making about local economic development and employment. These types of coalitions have the potential to include a more diverse constituency and a wider cross section of a community. Contingent workers, for example—largely low-income, women, older workers, and racial minorities—are likely to be more receptive to approaches that originate in their community or church rather than a traditional union structure. Struggles around economic justice issues, beginning in the 1990s and continuing today, are finding new political forms. Unions are bridging the gap with community organizations, receiving support for cam-

paigns and appealing to new constituencies. These unions realize that
their survival depends increasingly on the economic survival of low-
income communities, and vice versa. Both groups are considering possibilities for collectively developing new agendas for political action.

This book has examined the political impact of economic change,
focusing on the crises created by plant closings in three communities.
Plant closings may seem to be the antithesis of economic development
and progress; after all, no public official wants a plant closing in his or
her jurisdiction. And yet the connections are obvious. Traditional economic development practices bring in industries without ties to the
community, companies that are more likely to move on. The emphasis
on capital accumulation shapes the local political climate and acceptable
range of political behaviors. And economic development strategies that
satisfy employers at the expense of employees and taxpayers prove detri-
mental in the long run.

Plant closings are political, because plant openings are political. If the
state takes credit for new jobs, then should public officials not be held
accountable for lost jobs? If public resources are used to initiate and sustain industry, then is that industry accountable to the public? Can the
state address problems such as poverty, social policy, and welfare reform
without addressing systems of economic development and job creation
and retention? What becomes clear is that these are political questions
that demand political solutions. Banfield and Wilson put it well:

> To the extent that social evils like crime, racial hatred, and poverty are
> problems susceptible to solution, the obstacles in the way of their solu-
> tion are mostly political. It is not for lack of information that the prob-
> lems remain unsolved. Nor is it because organizational arrangements are
> defective. Rather it is because people have differing opinions and inter-
> ests, and therefore opposing ideas about what should be done . . . The
> impediments to such solutions are a result of disagreement, not lack of
> knowledge.[6]

Political action against plant closings can have far-reaching repercussions. It is possible for political mobilization to transform participants, communities, regions, and ultimately national political debates. The nature of this qualitative change depends upon the organizing process itself—its approach, leadership, and political goals—and thus affects each community in a different way. Mobilization is not an inevitable outcome of economic or political events, but instead the product of hard choices and hard work. Communities face abundant crises, some of which stimulate popular mobilization and some of which reinforce existing patterns of hierarchy, power relations, and quiescence. The emergence of organized protest, its institutionalization, and its consequences depend upon both indigenous and external constraints and opportunities.

Two conclusions become clear. First, working people have enormous potential to take on complicated global issues, educate themselves, fight for what they deserve, and transcend narrow and localist convictions to join together with others in a common project. The organizing process, when effective, leads to dramatic transformations in political education, consciousness, interests, and behavior. These small-scale and individual changes are vitally important in creating the possibility for a new kind of political engagement, a new kind of social capital, and a new kind of global social movement.[7] In the case of CATS, the mobilization of a small group of laid-off workers in Morristown, Tennessee, led to an emerging social movement encompassing issues of economic justice, international solidarity, global trade, and development policy. Given effective leadership and opportunity, workers in small communities, with little formal education or political sophistication, learned to analyze the economies of their own neighborhoods and towns in a framework of globalization and coporate power. Through their action they were educated in the art of organizing, gaining the ability to take on, and eventually to win, similar struggles in the future.

Second, grassroots mobilization sets the stage for a much larger political struggle around issues of political economy. Although the groups I studied had very little actual power to shape national and global economic policy, in the long run they accomplished more than anyone would have predicted. Local organizing grew into larger struggles that eventually shaped national political debate and policy. Local protests and efforts to achieve a voice for marginalized groups created a base on which further efforts could build. What started out as a group of workers wanting to protect the status quo and keep their imperfect jobs became a movement challenging the largest global imperatives. As Michael McCann aptly observes, "Counterhegemonic movements most often evolve incrementally through a series of more limited local struggles over quite concrete, often trivial ends . . . Small-scale acts of quiet resistance or simple demands for reform . . . often provide rehearsals of opposition that prepare the way for bolder challenges in more propitious moments."[8]

The cases of Acme Boot and CATS show that workplace and community-based organizing have the potential to create the structures, leadership, institutions, and the political analysis necessary to launch a larger coalition or social movement. This is not just a progressive ideal; it is a practical necessity if communities are to protect their own interests. In order to achieve the leverage necessary to meet their local needs, communities will require greater numbers and greater resources than they possess as a community; they will need something more like a social movement. Eventually local groups must form coalitions with other such movements across the country and in other parts of the world. This is the task that the workers at Acme Boot and in CATS began, perhaps unknowingly. By standing up for their local interests—and *at the same time* placing those concerns into a larger political framework—they laid the institutional groundwork for building a true progressive coalition to fight for economic justice.

Successful Failures

The story of these three Appalachian communities also creates a new framework for understanding failure in American politics and social movements. Given the proper conditions, collective community-based political movements—even those that fail—may become what I call "successful failures." Evaluations of success must take into account more than a group's ability to achieve its concrete, articulated end goal. Failures—rather than resulting in humiliation and depression—can create the context for social change and pivotal political movements. Successful failures do not always transform the economy, or the social or political landscape, but they can accomplish crucial outcomes.

First, the organizing efforts that I call successful failures demonstrate to marginalized groups that resistance is possible, even against powerful forces of oppression. Second, they create structures and networks of people that are essential to any mobilization attempt—for even if they decline, they always have the potential to be rebuilt. Third, struggle itself trains people in the skills of political action and democratic citizenship. Fourth, small victories along the way teach marginalized communities the strength and power of collective action, and thus make them more likely to stand up for their goals in the future. And finally, failures in particular teach communities the strength and power of their opposition—essential knowledge for any political effort. The efforts of these communities demonstrate that successful failures are able to accomplish these five goals, and therefore to lay the groundwork for progress and social change.

The very idea that organizing failures can have positive effects is counterintuitive. My argument that failure is a necessary (although not sufficient) prerequisite for success is directly contradicted by much of the academic literature on power and social movements, as well as by the beliefs of organizers and activists themselves. And the traditional analysis of failure is sometimes correct. Failure does not always teach people the power of collective action or lay the foundation for future success. Failure certainly has the potential to demoralize and demobilize already marginalized communities, leading to bitterness and cynicism, especially in the short term. When this happens, as it did at Greenbrier Industries, described in chapter 2, I call it a "failed failure."

But failure need not teach quiescence, and in many cases it has not. External events themselves do not determine whether a failure will be a successful failure or a failed failure. Indigenous resources, leadership, local history, organization, structure, political analysis, allies—all of these are crucial factors that make long-term victories possible. This book shows that failed organizing efforts have the capacity to become positive, productive, and even transformative for the communities willing to risk mobilizing in the first place—and for the world beyond.

Successful failures—communities that organize effectively to challenge political and economic circumstances—are possible only if certain criteria are met. First, and perhaps most important, a movement or community organization must have effective leadership. Leaders must take seriously participants' ideas, energy, and time commitment, and must be chosen democratically. The most effective leaders work closely with people to help develop an analysis of their situation and a method for achieving their goals.

Second, mobilization requires organization and structure. Spontaneous rebellions may occasionally arise, but political and social change in the United States of the twenty-first century requires sustained efforts and organized activity. Organization and leadership provide focus for protest activity, ensure that participants are coordinated and working toward a unified goal, and create the motivation and structure that allow groups to continue organizing after defeats.

Third, good leaders and organizations develop both a political analysis and a vision of possibilities for change. Analysis must situate the present crisis in the context of power relations more broadly. It must provide participants with an understanding of what has caused the immediate crisis, and it must correctly identify the specific agents who profit or benefit from it. An effective framework reveals the political structures that make the current situation possible, and the policies that have the potential to transform the underlying problem in a fundamental structural way. An analysis helps participants interpret failure as a product not of their own failures or weaknesses, but of powerful political forces. This ability to place immediate struggles in a longer-term context is essential to any progressive social movement.

Fourth, a struggle is strengthened if it can build on a local history or tradition of community-based organizing. This history can provide a community with the cultural background that enables protest to emerge and endure. A history of mobilization means that a community has individuals and groups that can transmit tangible skills and ideas that facilitate future mobilization. Change does not seem quite as impossible if it has been attempted before.

Fifth, sustained mobilization is most effective if allies are present. Other organizations can provide a fledgling group with essential support—moral, financial, and political. The case studies in this book show that the ability to attract allies and to form coalitions can be a crucial determinant of a group's ability to survive after losing battles.

Sixth, a minimal level of indigenous resources is essential to the long-term prospects of an effective mobilization campaign. Aldon Morris has shown that the civil rights movement required sophisticated preexisting formal and informal communication networks, local leadership, and strong institutions—including community-based organizations, educational institutions, legal-defense groups, and religious institutions.[9] The stories in this book demonstrate that those types of indigenous resources are invaluable to any grassroots effort. Given appropriate leadership, organization, resources, a history of organizing, allies, and a political analysis, failed struggles can lead to increased resolve and dedication, and can have impressive immediate and long-term effects, reaching even beyond national borders.

The Global Economy Revisited

Economists and political scientists argue about the extent to which global forces are constraining policy decisions in the United States. Some argue that certain decisions—joining free-trade agreements such as NAFTA or GATT, for example—are now inevitable, dictated by the logic of market forces. Some celebrate the development, arguing that the results will benefit both rich and poor nations alike. Others condemn it, arguing that the resulting economic and policy shifts are creating inequality and instability, and undermining democracy and national autonomy.

The cases in this book suggest that global economic forces—especially transnational capital flight and what economists call "global factor price equalization"[10]—do influence local economies. It is not a coincidence that the international economy is characterized by the same trends occurring locally. Firms have increasing power to negotiate profitable deals and wrest concessions from the public sector. Low-income areas are competing for investment based on their poverty and desperation, with devastating results in the long run. Businesses have never been particularly loyal to their home communities, but companies that invest some of their profits back into their hometowns or home countries are rarer than ever before. While profits and corporate salaries have risen, the communities that supply the education, workforce, and infrastructure have become more impoverished. All of this has occurred at the international level as well as in local communities within the United States.

On the other hand, these changes are not the product of an autonomous global economy. This research shows that they are politically shaped and institutionally bounded. Many of these political influences are not global at all, but purely domestic. An analysis of the political economy in East Tennessee reveals that while the global context forms an important backdrop to local events, American political institutions share a large portion of the responsibility for events at home. As Paul Krugman says, "reports of the death of national autonomy are greatly exaggerated . . . [there is] an odd sort of tacit agreement between the left and the right to pretend that exotic global forces are at work even when the real action is prosaically domestic."[11] The plant-closing stories from Tennessee support his argument: "Many observers seem determined to blame global markets for a host of economic and social ills in their countries, even when the facts point unmistakably to mainly domestic—and usually political—causes."[12] These political causes include the privileged position of business in local and national politics; a dominant ideology that supports traditional forms of economic development policy despite vast evidence of their long-term failure; and the lack of political will to enact mechanisms to limit the erosion of job stability, environmental protection, working conditions, and living standards. A range of political considerations, coupled with increasing disparities in resources and power, comprise the most important factors behind the worsening inequality and disempowerment facing low-income communities in the U.S. As Krugman concludes,

> None of the important constraints on American economic and social policy come from abroad. We have the resources to take far better care of our poor and unlucky than we do; if our policies have become increasingly mean-spirited, that is a political choice, not something imposed on us by anonymous forces. We cannot evade responsibility for our actions by claiming that global markets made us do it.[13]

Whatever the economic reality, the global market remains an extraordinarily influential idea politically. This book shows that arguments about "international competitiveness" and global imperatives are proving effective in legitimating corporate restructuring and downsizing. Economic development policies are formulated under the assumption that all localities, in all countries, must compete for business investment. Politicians, including many local officials in East Tennessee, support cutting social programs and reject solutions that increase Americans' standard of living, on the grounds that we must tighten our belts in order to compete with workers in developing countries. Firms travel the globe in search of low wages and less regulation, suffering no negative social, economic, or political consequences for doing so. Perhaps most important, inequality within the U.S. has risen to all-time high levels—and yet political leaders refuse to accept responsibility for promoting fairer systems of economic distribution. Local economies—outside of a few sites of booming investment—are more unstable and subject to upheaval, and Americans are increasingly mistrustful of government and alienated from politics.

Power and Civil Society

In this context, the challenge facing local organizations is daunting. Political decisions may be shaping the global economy, but those political decisions are surely beyond the influence of local communities, especially rural, low-income, or otherwise marginalized groups. Yet the analysis presented here makes it clear that the only hope for influencing what are otherwise devastating political and economic trends is a mass political mobilization among the people most seriously affected: working and unemployed families. The question is how this mobilization will begin, and what structures and actions are necessary to sustain it. I argue that the movement for economic justice in the global economy will most likely begin in a series of failures. These failures, including those discussed in this book, have the best chance of creating the structures and opportunities that will eventually form the foundation of a coalition that can influence policies and politics at a much larger level.

Tocqueville's interpretation of community organizations suggested that local groups could only teach the value of good citizenship if they succeeded in achieving participants' goals, thereby legitimating the peaceful resolution of local concerns. Similarly, Harry Boyte's assertion that such groups enable ordinary citizens to wield power depends on the assumption that collective action achieves its members' desired aims. This book refutes these traditional theories of localism. CATS did not win back jobs or improve the economy of Morristown—at least not in any observable, immediate way. The group did not succeed in its mission. And yet it was not only a "classroom of democracy," it also created the possibility of a larger social movement with the potential to challenge an important element of the political economy of the 1990s.

The CATS story proves that the success or failure of community-based, grassroots mobilizing efforts must be evaluated in a new way. Unlike service-delivery enterprises or other public organizations, grassroots political groups may be extremely successful even when they fail to achieve the immediate goals they had articulated. The stories of both CATS and Acme Boot show how the experience of self-organization and political mobilization can lead to changes not only in individual participants but also in their communities and eventually in larger political debates as well.

The skills that workers from Acme and from GE learned in Tennessee are precisely the skills of a democratic citizen; their new understandings of power and authority at the local, national, and international levels comprise an essential component of democracy in the global economy. Departing from scholarship celebrating small-scale citizen resistance, however, this book argues that these local battles are only a beginning of a much larger struggle. Although small rural communities may draw on very traditional values and ideas of community and political life, the context of mobilization must not be limited to traditional neighborhood issues. The Tennessee workers proved to be more than capable of seeing their struggles in a national and even international context, and of learning to analyze even the economy of their own town in this framework. Once they understood it in this light, they could strategize and form alliances necessary to influence its direction. It is this transformation—from the personal and local to the global—that remains the test of successful organizing in the global economy. Mass mobilization is essential if a movement for economic justice is to be launched—and only this movement has a chance of influencing the decisions that are shaping the economic future of low-income people around the world. Small, disadvantaged communities will always have difficulty mobilizing around economic issues, yet if they do not do so, they will be excluded from the decisions that most affect their lives. The question of how excluded groups can achieve a voice in these decisions—the study of successful failures—is central to questions of democracy and power in America.

Appendix:
Research Methodology

Selection of Case Studies

Much of this book is based on field research in Tennessee conducted over a period of nearly three years between 1992 and 1995. In beginning the project, the first question I faced was the selection of three community-level case studies. My primary goal was to examine communities' political response to economic crisis and change, in order to study both the causes and the consequences of grassroots mobilization. I wanted to analyze the effect of organizing and leadership—as opposed to demographics, ethnic or racial background, or class position—on the level and type of mobilization. This required holding constant as many variables as possible in order to pinpoint more accurately the impact of organizing. Thus all of the cases are in one area of the United States, in small- to medium-size towns in otherwise rural areas, with similar demographic composition and socioeconomic status. All of the plant closings were in low-wage, low-skilled manufacturing industries of the type that are facing intensified international competitive pressures. All of the closings took place within a single five-year period in the beginning of the 1990s. The similarity of the three plants and the three communities allowed the research to focus more precisely on the differences in political activity.

I selected Tennessee as the location for several reasons. First, I was looking for a region that had experienced many plant closings, and where there had been sustained political activity around at least some of them. Tennessee offered several good examples of plant-closing struggles, allowing me to choose the three that provided the best opportunity for comparison. Second, because the book focuses on political change, I was interested in labor–community coalitions rather than purely workplace struggles. Only a handful of such coalitions in the country are active around plant closings. The Tennessee Industrial Renewal Network (TIRN), based in Knoxville, was a practical choice. It was a relatively new organization, which meant that I could analyze its organizational history and interview all the participants responsible for forming the group. TIRN was kind enough to allow me access to its archives, meetings, and members. Finally, Tennessee was an area rarely studied by social scientists or labor scholars. Most studies of deindustrialization have taken place in the midwestern Rust Belt cities or in the urban centers of the Northeast. As chapter 2 explains, Tennessee is at the intersection of the booming Sun Belt and the deteriorating rural Appalachian region. The bulk of manufacturing in the United States takes place in relatively rural communities, and this area therefore represents an important frontier for research on political responses to economic change.

The number of Tennessee communities with labor–community mobilizations around plant closings was obviously limited. The three presented here were the only ones that fulfilled the criteria of being similar in many ways, but having different levels and types of political activity. They provided an excellent opportunity for an in-depth analysis of political mobilization and the early stages of a social movement.

Data

Several sources of data were crucial to the analysis in the three case studies. First, I examined the archives of the organizations themselves. Most important were TIRN, in Knoxville, Tennessee, and the Highlander Research and Education Center, in New Market, Tennessee. I read histories of the area, and reviewed firsthand accounts of previous organizing efforts. I also studied many collections of documents pertaining to the mobilization efforts. The participants shared with me hundreds of original documents, including memoranda, minutes from meetings, letters, organizational histories, mission statements, fliers, leaflets, and other forms of communication within organizations, between different organizations, and between organizations and the public. These sources provided invaluable information about the conversations and debates that occurred within the organizations before I arrived, as well as the dynamics of organization and mobilization itself.

A second source of data was participant-observation research. Over the course of three years in Tennessee I attended hundreds of meetings, protests, demonstrations, and other events in each community. During the period of my research, each mobilization was at a different stage. The last plant closing was Greenbrier Industries in Clinton, Tennessee. That group was still having regular meetings, as well as group lunches, picket lines, and protests, and I attended every one. The workers at Acme Boot had just concluded the bulk of their campaign, but were continuing to meet socially and to have union meetings, which I attended. The CATS workers had dispersed, but many of the participants were active in other political activity, including SOCM, the campaign against NAFTA, union drives, and other economic justice work through TIRN. I attended meetings and events along with the participants. All of these events provided important data about the current activities, perspectives, and interactions among participants.

Third, I investigated all published materials related to the plant closings and ensuing political events. These included newspaper accounts, television reports, transcripts of legislative hearings and legislative proposals, and published accounts of previous organizing efforts in East Tennessee. These sources provided historical background and a sense of the community's response to the events, which was important as I planned the interview phase of the research.

Finally, and perhaps most important, were the interviews with participants in the organizing efforts. Detailed, open-ended interviews were conducted with more than seventy individuals, over the course of three years. These interviews provided several types of information. They allowed me to fill in gaps in the available archival materials. Whenever the facts or timetable about a campaign were unclear, the participants were asked to reconstruct the chain of events. The interviews furnished insights into the organizing efforts, and indicated new avenues of investigation and theoretical frameworks for this project. Besides providing factual information and recollections, the men and women I interviewed discussed the changes in their personal and political lives during and after the plant closings. By allowing the participants to elaborate on their own ideas and experiences, the interviews revealed the political consciousness and activities of the participants themselves. This set of interviews provided important data for evaluating the impact of organizing around plant closings. Because I carried out so many interviews—and because I included two studies of "successful failures" rather than one—the data overlapped. This allowed independent verification of the narrative and analysis.

Methods

In terms of the first three data sources—archives, meetings, and news accounts—my methodology was straightforward. As far as I know, I examined every available document, read or watched every media report, and attended every meeting related to the three communities during the period of field research. I participated in the groups' activities and took copious field notes detailing my observations. All of these sources formed the basic framework for the case studies. This research was theoretically informed, and I attempted to evaluate local events in light of dominant approaches to collective action and social movements. I was especially sensitive to data that could illuminate some of the key debates in the scholarly literature. For example, was mobilization spontaneous or carefully planned? Where did the groups find the necessary money, skills, and leadership? Were the participants able to gain sympathy and support from their community and outside groups? How did their economic and education levels affect their ability to mobilize? Did the efforts succeed or fail at achieving the participants' originally stated goals? The archival and participant-observation research enabled me to formulate some working hypotheses about these questions before beginning the interviews. This was important in order to make the interviews as productive and focused as possible. It also enhanced my credibility with the workers, for I had done my homework and could sound knowledgeable about their experiences.

The interview process was necessarily more complex than other methods of collecting data. Certain questions could only be answered by interviewing the participants themselves. What motivated them to participate in collective action? Why did they decide it was worth the inherent costs and risks? What was their subjective experience as part of the mobilization? How had their lives and political behavior changed as a result? Did they believe they had succeeded or failed in the end?

In order to evaluate these questions, before beginning the interview phase of the research, I designed an outline for a semistructured, open-ended interview. I began each interview with a standard set of questions, and covered all of these during the course of the conversation, but participants were also encouraged to pursue tangential ideas that arose. Some of the workers deviated from the original questions more than others. Their digressions often led to interesting points, which were then incorporated into later interviews. In this way the research was able to reflect the experiences and thoughts of the participants rather than adhering strictly to the researcher's preconceived notions. In the same way, participants were encouraged to recommend other co-workers for future interviews, and other avenues of inquiry. This "snowballing" process was important to the sampling process, for it led to new interviewees and allowed me to corroborate or challenge the perspectives of the original group. The research design remained flexible in order to capture unanticipated aspects of mobilization and political change.

Participants were selected for interviews based on several criteria. First, in each case study, I attempted to survey a cross section of participants, representing as accurately as possible the group as a whole. For example, I tried to match the racial, age, and gender makeup of the group, and to find workers who lived in different areas.[1] Second, I asked activists from outside organizations (TIRN, the Highlander Center, SOCM, and several labor unions) to identify individuals who had been involved in local activities and who were well connected to the community, who were central to a group of their peers, or who would have an interesting perspective on the events. I contacted all the men and women they suggested. Third, because one of the major theoretical issues motivating the project was the question of leadership in political mobilization, I made a special effort to identify and interview all the leaders of each effort. I did not define leadership in advance, but asked the activists and workers to name the individuals they considered to have played a key role. I spoke with all the identified leaders. Through these three methods, I compiled a list of participants to be interviewed.

Participants were contacted by phone, and all interviews took place in person, at a location of the individual's choosing. The workers who agreed to participate were assured that their real names would be changed before publication, in order to encourage openness and honesty. As in any research design, nonresponse was a concern, but in this case the response rate was relatively high. Of approximately sixty-eight workers contacted, fifty-five agreed to be interviewed, for a response rate of about 81 percent.[2] Of the public officials, every one contacted agreed to be interviewed—a response rate of 100 percent. In the end, I interviewed fifty-four workers and activists, and twenty officials or heads of organizations.[3] The interviews lasted on average two hours, ranging from one to three hours. All interviews were taped and transcribed for future analysis. The interview process continued until a wide range of views had been recorded, and until the answers and ideas were becoming repetitive. At this "saturation" point, the original set of questions and the expanded set had been answered, and the interview process was concluded.

All interview processes are subjective, and therefore subject to bias. It is possible that the participants had faulty memories of events, or that things seemed different in retrospect, or that they rewrote the narrative to suit their purposes. It is possible that participants provided the answers they believed the interviewer wanted to hear, and withheld critical responses or negative analyses. These possibilities would be of greater concern, however, if interviews alone had informed the research project. Instead, the research design attempted to minimize these dangers by including archival research, published materials, and participant-observation research—and three entire case studies. The material in the organizations' files and my observations at meetings, protests, and events corroborated the respondents' responses in interviews. There was little dissonance between the information offered by these different data sources, suggesting that the data were as accurate and complete as possible. Where there were discrepancies, I have tried to account for them in my analysis.

Notes

CHAPTER 1: THE ORGANIZING MOMENT

1. John J. Sweeney, Address to the Italian Trade Union Delegates, Genoa, Italy, July 19, 2001 (http://www.aflcio.org/publ/speech2001/sp0719a.htm).
2. Naomi Klein, *No Logo* (New York: Picador USA, 2002), p. 447.
3. See, for example, Naomi Klein, "The Vision Thing," *Nation* (July 10, 2000); Janet Thomas, *The Battle in Seattle: The Story Behind and Beyond the WTO Demonstrations* (New York: Fulcrum, 2000); Alexander Cockburn, Jeffrey St. Clair, and Allan Sekula, *Five Days That Shook the World: The Battle for Seattle and Beyond* (New York: Verso, 2001).
4. John J. Sweeney, Remarks to World Economic Forum, Davos, Switz., January 28, 2001.
5. Alice Rollins, interview with author, Morristown, Tenn., December 9, 1993.
6. See, for example, Marco Giugni, "Introduction," in *How Social Movements Matter,* ed. Marco Giugni, Doug McAdam, and Charles Tilly (Minneapolis: University of Minnesota Press, 1999); Doug McAdam, John D. McCarthy, and Mayer N. Zald, "Social Movements," in *Handbook of Sociology,* ed. Neil J. Smelser (Beverly Hills: Sage Publications, 1988), pp. 695–737.
7. See, for example, Bill Bamberger and Cathy N. Davidson, *Closing: The Life and Death of an American Factory* (New York: W.W. Norton, 1998); Carolyn C. Perrucci et al., *Plant Closings: International Context and Social Costs* (New York: Aldine De Gruyter, 1988); Allison Zippay, *From Middle Income to Poor: Downward Mobility Among Displaced Steelworkers* (New York: Praeger, 1991); Gilda Haas, *Plant Closures: Myths, Realities and Re-*

sponses (Boston: South End Press, 1985); Staughton Lynd, *The Fight Against Shutdowns* (San Pedro: Singlejack Books, 1982).

8. Robert D. Putnam, *Bowling Alone: The Collapse and Revival of American Community* (New York: Simon & Schuster, 2000). See also Theda Skocpol and Morris P. Fiorina, eds., *Civic Engagement in American Democracy* (Washington, D.C.: The Brookings Institution Press, 1999).

9. Theda Skocpol, *The Missing Middle: Working Families and the Future of American Social Policy* (New York: W.W. Norton, 2000), p. 170.

10. William Greider, *Who Will Tell the People: The Betrayal of American Democracy* (New York: Simon and Schuster, 1992), p. 319. See also William Greider, *One World, Ready or Not: The Manic Logic of Global Capitalism* (New York: Simon and Schuster, 1998).

11. John Gaventa, *Power and Powerlessness: Quiescence and Rebellion in an Appalachian Valley* (Urbana, Ill.: University of Illinois Press, 1980), p. 42.

12. Lawrence Goodwyn, *The Populist Moment: A Short History of the Agrarian Revolt in America* (New York: Oxford University Press, 1978), p. 332.

13. Greider, *One World, Ready or Not,* p. 11.

CHAPTER 2: SELLING POVERTY

1. General Electric was not unusual. In the many documented cases of firms moving jobs to and from Appalachian Tennessee, every move has involved a reduction in wage rates, benefits, and/or employment status. Bill Troy, interview with author, Knoxville, Tenn., January 25, 1994; Bob Becker, interview with author, Knoxville, Tenn., July 14, 1995.

2. For an excellent example of one company's odyssey, see Jefferson Cowie, *Capital Moves: RCA's Seventy-Year Quest for Cheap Labor* (Ithaca, N.Y.: Cornell University Press, 1999).

3. Dennis R. Judd and Todd Swanstrom, "Business and Cities: The Enduring Tension," *Urban Resources* 5 (1988): 3–8, 44–6.

4. This dichotomy has been noted by Peter K. Eisinger, *The Rise of the Entrepreneurial State* (Madison, Wis.: University of Wisconsin Press, 1988); Pierre Clavel and Carol Kleniewski, "Space for Progressive Local Policy: Examples from the U.S. and the U.K.," in *Beyond the City Limits,* ed. John Logan and Todd Swanstrom (Philadelphia: Temple University Press, 1990); Norman Krumholz and John Forester, *Making Equity Planning Work* (Philadelphia: Temple University Press, 1990).

5. David L. Imbroscio, "Alternative Strategies for Local Economic Development: Exploring Five Models," paper presented at American Political Science Association Annual Meeting, Chicago, September 1995, p. 2.

6. Ibid., pp. 3–4.

7. Quoted in Alan Wolfe, *America's Impasse: The Rise and Fall of the Politics of Growth* (New York: Pantheon, 1981), p. 67.

8. Paul E. Peterson, *City Limits* (Chicago: University of Chicago Press, 1981), p. 41. Emphasis in the original.

9. Charles M. Tiebout, "A Pure Theory of Local Expenditures," *Journal of Political Economy* 64 (1956): 416–24.

10. Peterson, *City Limits,* p. 132.

11. Edward C. Banfield and James Q. Wilson, *City Politics* (Cambridge, Mass.: Harvard University Press, 1963), p. 1.

12. See, for example, Charles E. Lindblom, *Politics and Markets* (New York: Basic Books, 1977). Lindblom led the way in this type of analysis. He looked at the problem from the national level and showed that the "privileged position of business," created out of the state's necessity for economic success and growth, clashed with democratic needs and processes. Local studies followed Lindblom's example, rejecting Peterson's claim that economic development is an uncontroverted boon, benefiting the entire polity. They have found no "unitary interest" among local residents; rather, economic development policy has been a source of intense conflict since at least the 1960s. Local public officials' efforts to create and sustain vital local economies have consistently undermined their popular legitimacy. The need for economic performance is often in profound tension with popular demands and democratic institutions. See, for example, Stephen L. Elkin, *City and Regime in the American Republic* (Chicago: University of Chicago Press, 1987); Clarence N. Stone, *Regime Politics* (Lawrence, Kans.: University Press of Kansas, 1989); Clarence N. Stone and Heywood T. Sanders, *The Politics of Urban Development* (Lawrence, Kans.: University Press of Kansas, 1987); Susan S. Fainstein and Norman I. Fainstein, "Regime Strategies, Communal Resistance, and Economic Forces," in *Restructuring the City: The Political Economy of Urban Redevelopment,* ed. Susan S. Fainstein et al. (New York: Longman, 1986), pp. 245–82.

13. Judd and Swanstrom, "Business and Cities" pp. 3–8, 44–6. See also, Martin Shefter, *Political Crisis/Fiscal Crisis* (New York: Basic Books, 1985). Peterson, in fact, acknowledged the persisting "trade-off between equality and productivity" at the local level. The pursuit of business investment and productive capacity often compromised polit-

ical and economic equality, thereby undermining the democratic legitimacy of a local regime. Peterson, *City Limits*, p. 222.

14. Banfield and Wilson, *City Politics*, p. 258.

15. David Osborne, *Laboratories of Democracy* (Boston: Harvard Business School Press, 1988).

16. As C. Vann Woodward has observed, the New South envisioned by this generation required a type of top-down planning and control not very different from that of plantation owners in the Old South. New South elites knew they could only attract Yankee investments if they could promise stable political institutions, which meant crushing challenges from disenfranchised whites and blacks alike, and granting blacks' constitutional rights while quietly preventing their exercise. C. Vann Woodward, *Origins of the New South, 1877–1913* (Baton Rouge: Louisiana State University Press, 1951), pp. 107–74.

17. Michael J. McDonald and William Bruce Wheeler, *Knoxville, Tennessee: Continuity and Change in an Appalachian City* (Knoxville: University of Tennessee Press, 1983), pp. 10–12.

18. Ibid., p. 11.

19. James C. Cobb, *The Selling of the South: The Southern Crusade for Industrial Development 1936–1990* (Urbana, Ill.: University of Illinois Press, 1993), pp. 2–4; McDonald and Wheeler, *Knoxville, Tennessee*, pp. 20–22. Cobb has published the most thorough and sophisticated historical research on economic development in the South in the early twentieth century, and this section draws heavily on his work.

20. Cobb, *The Selling of the South*, p. 1.

21. There was always opposition to the imperatives of business development strategies. As early as the 1920s, groups like the Nashville Agrarians were arguing against this "progressive" model, warning that the best elements of the region's rural, agricultural way of life would be destroyed by ugly, crowded cities, polluting manufacturing plants, and the dehumanizing regimen of the factory. Ibid., pp. 1–2.

22. Since the mid-nineteenth century, many states added provisions banning state subsidization of private industry to their constitutions, largely in response to early nineteenth-century experiences that had proven this type of policy to be a disaster. See, for example, Lawrence M. Friedman, *History of American Law* (New York: Simon and Schuster, 1985).

23. Cobb, *The Selling of the South*, pp. 5–6.

24. Some of these bills blatantly lied, claiming that the bond issue would fund "the erection of municipal buildings for public purposes," while others stated their true intent to provide sites for buildings for new industry. Ibid., p. 6.

25. Ibid., pp. 6–7.

26. Into the 1990s, many of these companies still employed thousands of workers, and represented the backbone of the local economy.

27. McDonald and Wheeler, *Knoxville, Tennessee,* pp. 70–75.

28. Although Mississippi's BAWI is better known, Tennessee's completely unconstitutional industrial-bond program between 1935 and 1945 actually involved three times the amount of money as BAWI. After 1945 the Tennessee State Planning Commission decided that subsidization was here to stay and might as well be legalized, and the constitution was changed. By 1968 all the Southern states except North Carolina, and nearly all Northern states as well, had followed suit and instituted industrial-bonding programs. Cobb, *The Selling of the South,* pp. 35–36.

29. Ibid., pp. 12–23.

30. Ibid., p. 12. These statements foreshadow precisely the message and even the language used by economic development officials in the South in the 1990s, as I discuss below.

31. Michael V. Miller, "East Tennessee: America's Leader in Quality and Technology," *Financial World* (March 15, 1994), p. 53.

32. Ibid., pp. 54–62.

33. It does not mention that the state sales tax on most goods, including food and clothing, is one of the nation's highest. Since so many other taxes are waived, the state depends heavily on a regressive sales tax for its revenue.

34. "Tennessee," flier (Nashville: Tennessee Department of Economic and Community Development, 1994).

35. "Mountains of Business Opportunity," brochure (Oak Ridge: Tennessee's Resource Valley, 1994), p. 15.

36. Ibid., pp. 6–7. In 1994 the region's union density was below 10 percent.

37. "Occupational Wages and Benefits: State of Tennessee/East Region" (Nashville: Tennessee Department of Economic and Community Development, June 1992), p. 2.

38. "Tennessee Tax Incentives," brochure (Nashville: Tennessee Department of Economic and Community Development, 1994).

39. "Tennessee: The Ticket to Tomorrow," brochure (Nashville: Tennessee Department of Economic and Community Development, 1994).

40. "Tennessee: The Ticket to Tomorrow."

41. The economic developers noted that competition is much worse when the national economy is perceived as slow. Incentives are increased in a desperate attempt to win some of the limited new jobs and investment created each year. Douglas J. Watson, *The New Civil War: Government Competition for Economic Development* (Westport, Conn.: Praeger, 1995), pp. 62–63.

42. Greg LeRoy, "It's Time for a Federal Remedy to Stop the State-Eat-State Civil War Over New Jobs," *FIRR News* 5 (Winter 1993): p. 2.

43. Greg LeRoy, "Terrible Ten 'Candy Store' Deals of 1994," press release (Washington, D.C.: Grassroots Policy Project, January 23, 1995). In its applications for economic development assistance, Exxon told the state that it would use the tax abatements to hire non-union, out-of-state contractors. The Louisiana Coalition for Tax Justice documented the fact that Louisiana gained hardly any tax revenues from this deal, but incurred new costs for schools, roads, and crime control. Almost 75 percent of the state's business-property tax exemptions went to projects that created no new permanent jobs. The lack of property taxes cost the Louisiana school system $941 million in the 1980s.

44. Watson, *The New Civil War*, p. 63.

45. Quoted in ibid., p. 68.

46. Ibid., pp. 60–68.

47. Ibid., pp. 67–71.

48. Lawrence Young, interview with author, Oak Ridge, Tenn., January 14, 1994.

49. Watson, *The New Civil War*, p. 71.

50. Ibid., pp. 72–3.

51. Ibid.

52. Lawrence Young interview.

53. Watson, *The New Civil War*, p. 77.

54. Quoted in ibid., p. 72.

55. Quoted in ibid., pp. 70ff.

56. Lawrence Young interview.

57. "Mercedes Wiggled Off the Hook," folder (Oak Ridge, Tenn. Oak Ridge Chamber of Commerce, 1994).

58. As Stephen Elkin says, echoing an idea of Fred Block's, "Public officials do not have to be told to worry about economic performance or to facilitate it; they understand that,

if they are to . . . stay in office and pursue their ambitions, then owners and managers of productive assets must do *their* job." Elkin, *City and Regime in the American Republic,* pp. 135–6; Fred L. Block, "The Ruling-Class Does Not Rule: Notes on the Marxist Theory of the State," *Socialist Revolution* 7 (1977): 6–28. Politicians and economic development officials I interviewed expressed their determination to support the interests of business above almost everything else.

59. Dwight Kessell, interview with author, Knoxville, Tenn., February 3, 1994.

60. These sorts of deals have been popular since the early 1900s. Recall the earlier example of Lewisburg, Tennessee, which held one meeting in its newly constructed "town hall" before turning it over to a shoe manufacturer.

61. Kessell interview.

62. Paul Peterson highlights this strategy: "The consensual politics of development is illustrated by the frequency with which responsibility for developmental policy is granted to groups outside the mainstream of local politics. In smaller communities, the Chamber of Commerce is as likely to direct developmental programs as is an agency of local government." Indeed, the chamber often provides "more leadership than the city council." Peterson, *City Limits,* p. 133.

63. Bill Niemeyer, interview with author, Knoxville, Tenn., February 3, 1994.

64. Kessell interview.

65. Ibid.

66. Niemeyer interview.

67. Lawrence Young interview. In exchange for the $160,000, the chamber had certain performance criteria it was obligated to meet. For example, Young's department was expected to provide a net increase of 250 jobs each year. In 1994, Young said, "I don't believe we'll meet those. We certainly have lost quite a few jobs." Much of the job loss was due to downsizing in the defense budget, for military production was the major industry in Oak Ridge. As Young commented, "Don't you just *hate* peace?"

68. Ibid.

69. Ibid.

70. Marc Sudheimer, interview with author, Morristown, Tenn., January 25, 1994.

71. Ibid.

72. Jim Henry, interview with author, Oak Ridge, Tenn., January 24, 1994.

73. Ibid.

74. Kessell interview.

75. Henry interview.

76. Sudheimer interview.

77. Ibid.

78. Of course, most economists would agree that workers who take the new jobs will be better off. If a business can find workers willing to accept its wages and working conditions, microeconomic theory says that those workers must be better off working there than they were before the opportunity arose—otherwise they would have stayed where they were. In the 1990s this logic was also used to explain why sweatshops in developing countries were a good thing for those workers and communities. It ignores the fact that desperate workers will accept many types of undesirable and even exploitative employment. For this reason the role of the state has often been to protect vulnerable workers from abuse—and to raise standards for the entire community as much as possible.

79. Sudheimer interview.

80. Henry interview.

81. Ibid.

82. Kessell interview.

83. Ibid.

84. Henry interview.

85. Jack Hammontree, interview with author, Knoxville, Tenn., February 2, 1994.

86. Ibid.

87. Henry interview.

88. Sudheimer interview.

89. Henry interview.

90. Kessell interview.

91. Henry interview.

92. Sudheimer interview.

93. Niemeyer interview.

94. Steve Queener, interview with author, Clinton, Tenn., January 13, 1994.

95. Sudheimer interview. Although several officials referred to economic development as a marriage, the metaphor was clearly limited. As long as the firm agreed to wed, no further demands were placed on it. When one partner abruptly ended the relationship—in the case of a plant closing—no reparations were requested, and no obligation to the other partner—the community or the state—remained. This is a most one-sided marriage.

96. Queener interview.

97. Queener interview. Sewers are not irrelevant, of course. As Dwight Kessell says, "Development will follow sewers." In other words, companies will locate where the infrastructure can support their demands. Queener's comment, however, reveals the extent to which the immediate needs of industry have supplanted the needs of the citizens as the public official's primary concern. Kessell interview.

98. Henry interview. The largest recent plant closing in Henry's territory had been at Greenbrier Industries. The company had shut the doors, and most of the employees who succeeded in finding work had gone to other "cut-and-sew" factories—some driving up to fifty miles away to do that kind of work.

99. Sudheimer interview.

100. Lawrence Young interview.

101. Ibid.

102. Sudheimer interview. The business community, of course—and therefore the officials who work with them—are much more concerned with inflated wages than with unfairly depressed wages.

103. Lawrence Young interview.

104. Sudheimer interview.

105. Niemeyer interview.

106. Sudheimer interview.

107. Lawrence Young interview.

108. Ibid.

109. Henry interview.

110. Ibid. On the other hand, of course, Henry has very different standards for himself. In discussing why he left the Tennessee state legislature, he says, "There's no money in it. . . . You can't survive on $16,000 they pay in the legislature. . . . I owned a real estate business and it was getting too busy to go back and forth. [Now] I have an easy job. . . . The easiest job!"

111. Robert Dahl, *Who Governs?* (New Haven: Yale University Press, 1961), p. 293.

112. Queener interview.

113. Ibid.

114. Ibid.

115. Kessell interview.

116. Niemeyer interview.

117. Hammontree interview.

118. Lawrence Young interview.

119. Ibid.

120. Kessell interview.

121. Ibid.

122. Ibid. Kessell does not mean to sound un-American. He believes our system is democratic, for everyone has input at one crucial moment, in the voting booth. "The voters still have a choice—picking the leaders to make the choices. And that's important."

123. Lawrence Young interview.

124. Ibid.

125. Banfield and Wilson, *City Politics,* p. 21.

126. Fainstein and Fainstein, "Regime Strategies, Communal Resistance, and Economic Forces," p. 248.

127. Kessell interview.

128. Alan H. Peters, "Clawbacks and the Administration of Economic Development Policy in the Midwest," *Economic Development Quarterly* 7 (1993): 328–40.

129. See Eisinger, *Rise of the Entrepreneural State,* and John Portz, *The Politics of Plant Closings* (Lawrence, Kans.: University Press of Kansas, 1990).

CHAPTER 3: YOU CAN'T FIGHT CITY HALL

1. Ed Damiano, interview with author, LaFollette, Tenn., December 9, 1993. Damiano continued defensively, "I mean, it wasn't like everyone down there was making $4.25 an hour. Because they weren't." Supervisors earned about $5.50 an hour. As Damiano says, "They paid their supervisors good." In fact, he says with pride, "I know one lady was making $8.00."

2. Series of in-depth interviews with author, November 1993 through February 1994. The ideology of "family" at Greenbrier is discussed below.

3. Tom Schlesinger, John Gaventa, and Juliet Merrifield, *Our Own Worst Enemy: The Impact of Military Production on the Upper South* (New Market, Tenn.: Highlander Research and Education Center, 1983), p. 56.

4. Ibid., pp. 56–7.

5. Ibid., p. 56. By comparison, this was three times more per capita income than that received by traditional military-dominated towns like Newport News, Virginia, and 15 percent more than the Lockheed Corporation's hometown of Marietta, Georgia.

6. In 1981 Huntsville's per capita military contracts exceeded its per capita income—$5,191 per person—by 450 percent. Ibid., p. 55

7. In many ways the Thiers' operations were representative of most military contracting in Tennessee and throughout the Upper South. In 1981 about 550 companies received all of the state's 2,734 DOD contracts worth more than $10,000. Of those 2,734, only 21 contracts cost DOD more than $5 million—the large military contracts commonly assumed to be the norm. More typical in Tennessee were the small awards to textile or apparel firms, or even smaller contracts, such as the $12,000 to the Picket County sheriff's department for "surveillance services" or $362,000 to Buring Foods for meat and fish. *Military Prime Contracts by State, City and Contractor,* Tennessee, FY 1981 (Washington, D.C.: Department of Defense, Directorate for Information, Operations and Reports, 1982).

8. Schlesinger et al., *Our Own Worst Enemy,* p. 57. Other state agencies also contributed to the Thiers' steady income. In the late 1970s the federal government and the state of Tennessee gave the Thiers at least $80,000 in CETA funds to train workers for minimum-wage production jobs. Besides getting the state to pay their wages, the plants procured raw goods at no cost. In 1981 they received $2.62 million in Government Furnished Material (GFM) subsidy programs, via nine separate contracts. There is little accounting for GFM, especially useful in the military garment industry, where raw material accounts for 65 to 85 percent of the total contract cost.

9. Damiano interview.

10. Schlesinger et al., *Our Own Worst Enemy,* p. 57.

11. "They used to cut material here and send it to Israel." Bruce Mackrey, interview with author, Clinton, Tenn., December 7, 1993.

12. Mackrey interview.

13. "Greenbrier Industries to Move Production to Czestochowa," *BBC Summary of World Broadcasts,* part 2, Eastern Europe, March 24, 1993.

14. Bob Walker, interview with author, Clinton, Tenn., December 6, 1993.

15. Schlesinger et al., *Our Own Worst Enemy,* p. 29

16. Bobbie Bishop, interview with author, Clinton, Tenn., December 6, 1993.

17. Ibid.

18. Mackrey interview.

19. Health-Tex had been bought out by Cheeseborough-Ponds Corporation, and then by Vanity Fair, the largest clothing manufacturer in America. According to the assistant

plant manager, the Tennessee plant, "was operating $1 cheaper an hour than any of their other plants [in the U.S.]. Labor was cheaper. . . . Our retirement was lower and I'm sure our insurance was too. And we just had a very efficient plant, period." The company told the workers it was closing "because of the high cost of workers' comp insurance. Especially carpal tunnel." Damiano believed that Vanity Fair had closed the plant because it did not want to deal with the existing union. Within the garment industry, Vanity Fair was notorious for union-avoidance strategies.

20. Joanne James, interview with author, Clinton, Tenn., December 7, 1993.

21. Ann Ritter, interview with author, Clinton, Tenn., December 10, 1993.

22. Walker interview.

23. Ritter interview.

24. Ibid.

25. Ibid.

26. Mackrey interview.

27. Ritter interview.

28. Damiano interview.

29. Greenbrier looked generous in retrospect. Ritter recalled, "You know, a lot of people didn't see that, but now I've been job hunting and I know. . . . These companies don't do half of what Greenbrier did for their people. At Greenbrier, everyone was given a two-week paid vacation. Where I'm at now, there's no paid vacation. They have no health insurance where I'm at now. [At Greenbrier] they were good to us. We had a big company picnic every year, they paid for everything, had it all catered and everything. . . . We were given a Christmas stocking with $15 gift certificate for the Kmart in it. Companies don't do that, and they did it every year." Ritter interview.

30. James interview.

31. See, for example, Bruce Nissen, *Fighting for Jobs* (Albany: State University of New York Press, 1994); *Taking Charge: A Hands-On Guide to Dealing with the Threat of Plant Closings and Supporting Laid-Off Workers* (Knoxville: Tennessee Industrial Renewal Network, 1991).

32. Bishop interview.

33. This is also a crucial strength of plant-closing struggles. Where there is no boss to threaten or fire activists, the potential costs to workers of getting involved in protests and speaking their minds about work-related injustices fall dramatically.

34. Ritter interview.

35. Ibid.

36. It is important to note that supervisors worked alongside workers in this campaign. Unlike a union organizing drive, a plant-closing struggle often includes a range of employees with no distinction among ranks. In the case of Greenbrier, several of the assembly-line workers who showed strong leadership skills had been promoted to supervisory positions, and they became leaders in the plant-closing protest as well.

37. See, for example, John McCarthy and Mayer Zald, "Resource Mobilization and Social Movements: A Partial Theory," *American Journal of Sociology* 82 (May 1977): 1212–41; Charles Tilly, *From Mobilization to Revolution* (Reading, Mass.: Addison-Wesley, 1978); Mayer N. Zald, "Looking Backward to Look Forward: Reflections on the Past and Future of the Resource Mobilization Research Program," in *Frontiers in Social Movement Theory,* ed. Aldon D. Morris and Carol McClurg Mueller (New Haven: Yale University Press, 1992).

38. This is more typical of an "advocacy" organization than an "organizing" or social-movement organization. In the former model, technical experts, social workers, or consultants act on behalf of a disadvantaged group. They may offer advice or they may find solutions to benefit the group. In an organizing model, by contrast, the organizer or leader helps the group define and achieve their desired goals themselves. The organizer may help the group procure resources, set agendas, discuss options, and evaluate priorities and strategies—but all of these decisions are made by the group itself, based upon its own issues and capacities. The consequences of this distinction will be explored further in later chapters.

39. James interview.

40. Bishop interview.

41. Notes from meeting of Greenbrier Workers Committee, January 27, 1994.

42. Bishop interview.

43. Following Tocqueville, many scholars would not see this as a problem; they assume that community groups spring up to address needs, and then disband when they are no longer necessary. Carl Milofsky argues that community-based organizations are born and die in a natural evolutionary process, in the "free market" of a society. When organizations fail, it is because they are victims of their own inefficiency or redundancy, and society is better off. Carl Milofsky, "Neighborhood-Based Organizations: A Market Analogy," in *The Nonprofit Sector: A Research Handbook,* ed. Walter W. Powell (New Haven: Yale University Press, 1987).

44. Figures on injury rates are impossible to obtain. Most work-related injuries were not submitted as workers' compensation claims, since the management actively discouraged these. Every worker I interviewed had stories of injuries, including both routine repetitive-motion disorders, cuts and scrapes, and more serious equipment-related injuries. The personnel manager confirmed that the rates of injury had been unusually high, especially with carpal tunnel syndrome. Damiano interview.

45. Ritter interview. Many of the women echoed this sentiment. Since these jobs are frequently categorized as "unskilled," blue-collar jobs, it is particularly striking how many of the sewing machine operators discussed the learning inherent in their work, and glowed with pride as they described the speed and precision of their craft.

46. The role of gender relationships in industrial workplaces, especially in textile and apparel mills, has been well documented. See Jacquelyn Dowd Hall et al., *Like a Family: The Making of a Southern Cotton Mill World* (New York: W. W. Norton, 1987); Ruth Milkman, ed., *Women, Work and Protest: A Century of U.S. Women's Labor History* (Boston: Routledge and Kegan Paul, 1985); and essays by Ann Bookman, Ida Susser, and Louise Lamphere in *Women and the Politics of Empowerment,* ed. Ann Bookman and Sandra Morgen (Philadelphia: Temple University Press, 1988).

47. Bishop interview.

48. Margaret Jones, interview with author, Clinton, Tenn. December 8, 1993.

49. Louise Gessing and Lois Palmer, interviews with author, Clinton, Tenn., December 10, 1993.

50. Bishop interview.

51. Ibid. This is interesting, considering the evidence to the contrary. Everyone had heard rumors about corruption, and many had hard evidence themselves. Bishop herself had "heard on TV" that the Thiers had committed fraud, and she knew that Greenbrier's owner, Abe Silvershatz, was using questionable management techniques, but she resisted the obvious conclusions: "I don't see how they could do much, really, with all those government people there, the inspectors and all." Even after the plant closed, Bishop continued to defend the plant manager, Bob Hetzel. "He was probably like me, he knew something was going to happen, he didn't know when, or the extent of it probably. I think he was innocent—well, now I won't say innocent, I won't go that far, but I don't have any hard feelings for Bob. He was always good to me." Bishop interview.

52. Ibid.

53. Ritter interview.
54. Walker interview.
55. Mackrey interview.
56. Bishop interview.
57. James interview.
58. Ritter interview.
59. Bishop interview.
60. Mackrey interview.
61. James interview.
62. Mackrey interview.
63. Ibid.
64. Bishop interview.
65. Ibid.
66. Ibid. She noted that machine operators who had once made $8 or $9 an hour (on piecework) had recently found their wages decreased to $4.50, but she did not connect this fact to the increase in turnover.
67. Bishop explained: "Every once in a while somebody would sew their finger, put a snap through their finger, or something like that. Most of it would be that carpal tunnel syndrome, that got real bad. That happened to a lot of people. We had a lot of back injuries, too, from bending, lifting, carrying things. Shoulder problems, tendonitis." Damiano corroborated: "There were an awful lot of injuries. . . . You could cut your finger off. Or sew your finger with a needle. . . . We had back injuries. But carpal tunnel was the biggest, because there's a lot of repetitive motion in sewing and all." Damiano interview.
68. Ibid.
69. Bishop interview.
70. The personnel manager agrees with the workers: "Oh yeah, we had a drug problem." Asked for specifics, he admits that a random testing program disclosed very few positive results. "Maybe three of them tested positive. . . . I fired two." The one example he can remember in detail happens to be "a black guy" who worked on tents, the most physically demanding job, with the highest injury rates. This individual was acting strangely, Damiano says, and he eventually found out why. "He'd act like he was hurting and he'd go to the doctor and he'd just prescribe him different painkillers and muscle relaxants." Damiano interview.

71. He added, "I'm talking about blacks because you know I didn't have any problem with females, because 90 percent of the plant was female—*at least* 90 percent."

72. He had more reasons that so few people of color worked in the plant: "We had another black guy that we promoted to the cutting department. . . . Next thing I know about him, he's in jail." Given this experience, Damiano is proud of his affirmative action record. "When the plant closed, there was probably eight or ten blacks. I had hired fifteen, I'd say, from January to July." Out of over 400 hires, minorities were 3 percent. Damiano interview.

73. Bishop interview.

74. James interview.

75. This is not to say that the men faced great possibilities for new employment, but their job opportunities were different. Some of the men found minimum-wage work as security guards or maintenance workers, at shopping centers or factories, but others were able to find work as cutters, or in shipping and receiving. These jobs "pay good in all the factories." Bishop interview.

76. Mackrey interview.

77. Bishop interview.

78. David Roediger, *The Wages of Whiteness: Race and the Making of the American Working Class* (New York: Verso, 1991), p. 14.

79. Bishop interview.

80. Others have documented the scapegoating of minority workers in a time of economic crisis. See, for example, Katherine S. Newman, *Falling from Grace: The Experience of Downward Mobility in the American Middle Class* (New York: Vintage Books, 1988).

81. Mackrey interview.

82. Bishop interview.

83. As chapter 5 will show, this particular language and argument are often used in opposing unionization. The ideology of a workplace as a family, appropriately ruled by family values such as compassion, generosity, and sacrifice—rather than universal principles of equality, rights, and justice—is very powerful, and often succeeds at defeating unions.

84. Bishop interview.

85. Ibid.

86. James interview.

87. Despite her experience of distrust and lies, Ritter says the same thing: "I know a union

has good points and bad points, but I've never had a desire for a union, because I feel if I work for you and I have a problem, you know, let's sit down and talk about it. I don't need no middleman taking care of my business for me. That's the way I've always felt about stuff." Although Ritter said her managers had been dishonest and betrayed her, she remained attached to the belief that she could have resolved the problem individually. Ritter interview.

88. Bishop interview.
89. As Margaret Jones said, why bother even having an opinion on NAFTA? "I felt it really wouldn't make any difference, because I felt they would have passed it regardless of whether anybody was for it or not." Jones interview.
90. Mackrey interview.
91. Bishop interview.
92. Jones interview.
93. James interview.
94. Mackrey interview.
95. Jones interview.
96. Ritter interview.
97. See, for example, Roediger, *The Wages of Whiteness;* John F. Keller, *Power in America: The Southern Question and the Control of Labor* (Chicago: Vanguard Books, 1983); Robert Emil Botsch, *We Shall Not Overcome: Populism and Southern Blue-Collar Workers* (Chapel Hill: University of North Carolina Press, 1980).
98. Roediger, *The Wages of Whiteness,* p. 13.

CHAPTER 4: RESISTING THE GREAT SUCKING SOUND

1. Bonnie Baber, "Give 'Em Ad-itude: A Visual Feast of Footwear's Finest and Funniest Marketing Moments," *Footwear News* (August 14, 1995), p. 16.
2. Jean E. Palmieri, "Badovinus Gave Retirement the Boot," *Daily News Record* (February 20, 1995), p. 56.
3. "For the Record: Farley Industries," *Advertising Age* (April 15, 1985), p. 81.
4. Bill Hobbs, "Despite Acme, Boot Makers Like Outlook," *Nashville Business Journal* (June 1, 1992), p. 5. At the time the plant closed in 1992, the Clarksville factory employed about 600.
5. John Sisk, letter to Acme Boot workers, June 10, 1993, p. 4.

6. Barry Bluestone and Bennett Harrison, *The Deindustrialization of America* (New York: Basic Books, 1982), pp. 7–8.

7. Jimmy Settle, "Acme Halts Production Here," (Clarksville, Tenn.) *Leaf-Chronicle* (October 17, 1992), p. A1.

8. Ibid.

9. Hobbs, "Despite Acme, Boot Makers Like Outlook," p. 5.

10. By the time of the plant closing in 1993, years of downsizing had taken their toll. Acme was the second-largest employer in Montgomery County. The largest was the Trane Company, which employed a thousand people manufacturing commercial air-conditioning and heating units. Brochure on Montgomery County (Clarksville, Tenn.: Montgomery County Chamber of Commerce, January 1993).

11. Jane Hutchins, interview with author, Clarksville, Tenn., September 3, 1993; Jane Pryor, interview with author, Clarksville, Tenn., September 3, 1993.

12. Alan Buckner, interview with author, Clarksville, Tenn., December 14, 1993.

13. The URW's official title in 1993 was the United Rubber, Cork, Linoleum and Plastic Workers of America, AFL-CIO. In 1995 the URW merged with the United Steelworkers.

14. Buckner interview.

15. Wilma Mittendorf, interview with author, Clarksville, Tenn., December 14, 1993. In other words, in the late 1980s the pay system changed. Rather than pay workers for "production," on a piece rate, Acme began to pay wages based on "time." This evened out differences between workers, but also brought wages down for most employees.

16. Edna Luttrell, interview with author, Clarksville, Tenn., December 15, 1993.

17. Betty Schmidt, interview with author, Clarksville, Tenn., December 13, 1993.

18. Mittendorf interview.

19. Betty Schmidt interview.

20. Luttrell interview.

21. Ibid. The long hours at Acme Boot were between fifty and sixty hours per week, while at Greenbrier Industries, workers were putting in sixteen- or twenty-four-hour shifts. The protections of a union contract did not eliminate hard work and long hours, but they did eliminate the round-the-clock work that ruined Greenbrier workers' health and increased injuries on the job.

22. Mittendorf interview.

23. Luttrell interview.

24. Ibid.

25. See, for example, interviews with Luttrell, Buckner, Mittendorf, Hutchins, Pryor, Betty Schmidt, and Charles Schmidt.

26. Mittendorf interview.

27. Luttrell interview.

28. Sally Kellam, interview with author, Clarksville, Tenn., December 15, 1993.

29. A "mergers and acquisitions" specialist, Farley had worked for the investment bank Lehman Brothers before going out on his own. In 1984 he used debt to buy Condec, a defense and electrical equipment company. When Condec fell apart, Drexel Burnham Lambert bailed him out with $150 million in junk bonds, but Farley still owed interest of $38 million. Michael O'Neal and Dean Foust, "Bill Farley's $500 Million Needs a Home—Fast," *Business Week* (June 27, 1988), p. 35.

30. Greg LeRoy, "Background and Chronology on William Farley, Farley Inc., and Acme Boot," report (Chicago, January 4, 1993), p. 1.

31. Judith Crown, "Meet Bill Farley," *Crain's Chicago Business* (April 5, 1992), p. 1. Farley was for a time considered a potential political candidate, and he entered the presidential campaign in Iowa in the fall of 1987. But his candidacy seemed doomed after it was revealed he had been married and divorced three times and had an illegitimate daughter. In addition, the media reported his belief in reincarnation, with previous lives as a high priest in ancient Egypt and as one of Christ's twelve apostles. LeRoy, "Background and Chronology on William Farley," p. 1.

32. Ibid.

33. Ibid.

34. "Farley Note Holders File Bankruptcy Suit," *Footwear News* (July 29, 1991), p. 67.

35. Hobbs, "Despite Acme, Boot Makers Like Outlook," p. 5.

36. Ibid.

37. Prominent examples include Nike, which produces no shoes in the U.S., and Timberland, which closed its last U.S. plants (in Tennessee and North Carolina) in 1995. See Richard J. Barnet and John Cavanagh, *Global Dreams: Imperial Corporations and the New World Order* (New York: Simon and Schuster, 1994).

38. "Acme Boot Co. Declines Tax Exemptions for Puerto Rico Operation," press release (Clarksville, Tenn.: Acme Boot Company), May 6, 1993.

39. Bill Hobbs, "Acme Pumps Up Ad Budget While Mulling Closure," *Nashville Business Journal* (June 8, 1992), p. 5.

40. Bluestone and Harrison, *The Deindustrialization of America*, p. 6.

41. Kellam interview.

42. "Stetson Boots May Open at Acme Site," (Nashville, Tenn.) *Tennessean* (May 29, 1992), p. E1.

43. Luttrell interview.

44. Mittendorf interview.

45. Buckner interview.

46. Kellam interview.

47. Luttrell interview.

48. Gary Coffey, "Acme Boot Makes Revisions to Streamline Manufacturing," *Nashville Business Journal* (May 13, 1991), p. 37.

49. Ibid.

50. Luttrell interview.

51. Buckner interview.   •

52. Kellam interview.

53. Buckner interview.

54. Kellam interview.

55. Louis Uchitelle and N. R. Kleinfield, "On the Battlefields of Business, Millions of Casualties," *New York Times* (March 3, 1996), pp. A1, 26–29. For more on this subject, see N. R. Kleinfield, "The Company as Family, No More," *New York Times* (March 4, 1996), p. A1.

56. "United Rubber Workers Boycott Acme Boot for Runaway Plant," press release (Washington, D.C.: United Rubber Workers International, April 29, 1993).

57. Mittendorf interview.

58. Douglas Ray, "Acme Plans Boot Plant in Puerto Rico," (Clarksville, Tenn.) *Leaf-Chronicle* (December 27, 1992), p. A1.

59. LeRoy, "Background and Chronology on William Farley," pp. 2–4.

60. O'Neal and Foust, "Bill Farley's $500 Million Needs a Home," p. 35.

61. Stephen Franklin, "Union Wants Puerto Rico to Boot Acme," *Chicago Tribune* (February 1, 1993), p. 1. The El Paso plants employed over 700 employees, a similar number to those fired from the three other Tennessee plants recently closed. The company would not reveal the wages of workers in El Paso or Mexico.

62. Acme Boot was not unique; Farley was moving production abroad in his other manufacturing operations as well. In 1992 his flagship company, Fruit of the Loom, had reached record levels of both sales and profits. In fact, he told shareholders, "We're

maxed out in terms of capacity—we're not able to fill all the orders we get." Earnings had leaped by 31 percent in a year, to $111 million. Farley expected sales to grow by $1 billion over the next four years. As with Acme Boot, Farley was moving much Fruit of the Loom production overseas. By 1992, Fruit of the Loom was the second largest employer in the Republic of Ireland. David Dishneau, "Farley Unit Defaults on Pepperell Buyout Loan," Associated Press (April 3, 1990).

63. Ray, "Acme Plans Boot Plant in Puerto Rico," p. A1.

64. The 1990s saw a great surge in the popularity of western boots, especially among women, young people, and urban residents. One reason was the rising popularity of country music. "The boot industry should get up every morning and kiss Garth Brooks' picture," said one executive. Hobbs, "Acme Pumps Up Ad Budget While Mulling Closure," p. 5.

65. Pablo J. Trinidad, "Acme Boot to Produce Footwear in Toa Alta," *Carribean Business* (December 10, 1992), p. 1.

66. Luttrell interview.

67. Kellam interview.

68. Luttrell interview.

69. Ibid.

70. Kellam interview.

71. Ibid.

72. Ibid.

73. Letter to President Bill Clinton, signed by Acme Boot workers, February 10, 1993.

74. Franklin, "Union Wants Puerto Rico to Boot Acme," p. 1.

75. Mittendorf interview.

76. Special tax provisions for U.S. corporations operating in U.S. possessions have been on the books since the Revenue Act of 1921, primarily to help U.S. firms compete with foreign firms in the Philippines, which was then a U.S. possession. "Tax Policy: Puerto Rico and the Section 936 Tax Credit," Report GAO/GGD-93-109 (Washington, D.C.: United States General Accounting Office, June 8, 1993), p. 2.

77. Ibid.

78. Ray, "Acme Plans Boot Plant in Puerto Rico," p. A1.

It is interesting to note that Vogel later denied having said this. After Acme's use of tax incentives became controversial, Vogel declared, "Neither the tax exemption nor the benefits offered by filing as a 936 corporation were ever determining factors in our decision to open this facility or to close our plant in Clarksville." "Acme Boot Co. Declines Tax Exemptions for Puerto Rico Operation," press release.

79. Richard W. Leonard, Statement Before the U.S. Senate Committee on Finance Concerning President Clinton's Economic Plan and Section 936 of the Internal Revenue Code (Washington, D.C., April 27, 1993), p. 1.

80. Katherine Isaac, "Losing Jobs to 936," *Multinational Monitor* (August 1993), p. 5.

81. The Puerto Rican government estimated that 300,000 jobs on the island existed because of U.S. corporations with 936 exemptions. Leonard, Statement Before the U.S. Senate; Doreen Hemlock, "Industry Gets Behind 936 March," *San Juan Star* (March 5, 1993), p. 19.

82. Before the trip, Local 330 had met with local congressman Republican Don Sundquist, a member of the Ways and Means Committee. (Sundquist subsequently became governor of Tennessee.) After meeting with Acme workers, Sundquist made a public statement against Section 936: "My attitude is that the tax law has outlived its useful purpose. The law is no longer needed and I'll vote to end it." "Congressman Sundquist Denounces 936; Union Leaders Take Case to Congress," press release (Clarksville, Tenn.: URW Local 330, February 2, 1993).

83. Harry Turner, "Congress Urged to Eliminate 936," *San Juan Star* (May 15, 1992), p. 1.

84. Doreen Hemlock, "Analysts: Drug Firms Will Bolt," *San Juan Star* (February 26, 1993), p. 17.

85. "Puerto Rico Is in Danger!" leaflet (San Juan, P.R. Puerto Ricans Organized for Section 936, June 1993).

86. Beatriz De La Torre, "936 Companies Turn Up Lobbying Heat," *Caribbean Business* (June 17, 1993), p. 6.

87. "Proposed Amendments to Section 936: Resolution," press release (San Juan, P.R.: Puerto Rico Federation of Labor, AFL–CIO, May 7, 1993).

88. William Greider, *Who Will Tell the People? The Betrayal of American Democracy* (New York: Simon and Schuster, 1992), pp. 35ff.

89. Ibid., pp. 35–9. Greider shows that new corporate lobbying techniques are borrowed from the opposition, from community-based "public interest" organizations. Corporate lobbies are now able to build "coalitions," assembling dozens of civic organizations and interest groups in behalf of clients' goals. The pro-936 campaign is a perfect example of a pseudo-grassroots lobbying effort.

90. De la Torre, "936 Companies Turn Up Lobbying Heat," pp. 6, 49.

91. Congressman Jose Serrano of New York later said that, between the community fo-

rums, phone banks, and ads on Spanish-language radio and TV stations, the coalition was very successful in getting its message out. Primarily, he said, "They sowed fear." Rick Wartzman and Jackie Calmes, "Potent Medicine: How Drug Firms Saved Puerto Rico Tax Break After Clinton Attack," *Wall Street Journal* December 21, 1993, p. A14.

92. Pablo J. Trinidad, "Acme Boot's Tax Exemption Goes to Hearings," *San Juan Star* (March 11, 1993), p. 13.

93. "Puerto Rico Official Wants Acme Boot Investigation; Union Leaders Press Case to Congress and Clinton," press release (Clarksville, Tenn.: United Rubber Workers Local 330, February 9, 1993).

94. Robert Friedman, "Rosselló Urged to Deny Factory Tax Benefits," *San Juan Star* (January 12, 1993), p. 1.

95. Trinidad, "Acme Boot's Tax Exemption Goes to Hearings," p. 13.

96. Greg LeRoy, letter to Mitch Tucker, December 3, 1992.

97. LeRoy, "Background and Chronology on William Farley," p. 4.

98. Mittendorf interview.

99. Greg LeRoy, memo to Judy Pfeifer, January 27, 1993.

100. Terry Batey, "Acme Boot Workers, Union Vow to Fight Closing to Bitter End," (Nashville) *Tennessean* (January 15, 1993), p. 1.

101. Robert Kerr, "Faces of Hope: Soul of America En Route to Inaugural," (Memphis) *Commercial Appeal* (January 15, 1993), p. A1.

102. "Unionists Rally in Tennessee, Demanding Halt to Puerto Rico–Bound Runaway Shop," press release (United Rubber Workers Local 330, January 13, 1993).

103. Robert Friedman, "Acme Boot Company: A Runaway Plant?" *San Juan Star* (January 10, 1993), p. 20.

104. Ibid.

105. Kenneth L. Coss, quoted in "United Rubber Workers Boycott Acme Boot for Runaway Plant," press release (Washington, D.C.: United Rubber Workers International, April 29, 1993).

106. Ibid.

107. Mittendorf interview.

108. Buckner interview.

109. "Acme Boot Co. Declines Tax Exemptions for Puerto Rico Operation," press release (Clarksville, Tenn.: Acme Boot Company, May 6, 1993).

110. "Acme Boot Withdraws 936 Application," *San Juan Star* (May 7, 1993).

111. Jimmy Settle, "Will Newest Stitch Come in Time for Acme Workers?" (Clarksville, Tenn.) *Leaf-Chronicle* (May 18, 1993), p. A1.

112. Wartzman and Calmes, "Potent Medicine," p. 1.

113. Pablo J. Trinidad, "Rallying the Forces: The Story Behind the Rescue of Section 936," *Caribbean Business* (August 5, 1993), p. 1.

114. At the end, four drug companies (Pfizer, Merck, American Home Products, and Bristol-Myers Squibb) paid about half a million dollars to a lobbying firm that included former members of Congress. In particular, former Representative Anthony of Arkansas was hired to help persuade his fellow Arkansans, in the White House and in Congress, to compromise. It is impossible to gauge how many millions of dollars were spent in total on the pro-936 campaign. The Puerto Rican government hired a large Washington lobbying firm on a $50,000-a-month retainer, as well as a prominent public-relations firm. New York lawyer Harold Ickes, a friend of the Clintons, was hired by the pharmaceutical firms on a $40,000-a-month retainer. The industry also made many campaign contributions during this period, to candidates in Puerto Rico and on the mainland. Wartzman and Calmes, "Potent Medicine," p. A14.

115. Bradley, known as "the Senate's preeminent tax reformer," had proposed to eliminate 936 completely in his 1986 "Fair Tax" blueprint. Since then, however, he had come to depend on pharmaceutical companies—top employers in New Jersey and top funders of Bradley's campaigns. Bradley had received over $100,000 from the pharmaceutical industry in his close 1990 Senate race, more than any other member of Congress, according to the Center for Responsive Politics. Bradley aides could not defend the 936 incentive on policy grounds, but finally explained that they just couldn't "let go of the income credit. It's important to New Jersey." Ibid.

116. Ibid.

117. Ed Gregory, "Deal to Reopen Boot Plant Set," (Nashville) *Tennessean* (June 10, 1993), p. E1.

118. Sisk said that he had already reached an "outsourcing agreement" with Acme, and he believed he would also receive contracts from Wal-Mart and Endicott Johnson. All of these contracts would necessitate rehiring approximately 240 workers. Sisk, letter to Acme Boot workers, p. 1.

119. "Letter of Intent Signed to Sell Acme Boot Plant," press release (Clarksville, Tenn.: Acme Boot Company, June 9, 1993).

120. Sisk, letter on Acme Boot workers, p. 3. This was not unique to Acme. Once a com-

pany has established its brand name and market niche, it can close its production facilities and market anyone's goods.

121. Ibid., pp. 1–2. Emphasis in original.

122. Greg LeRoy, memo to Mitch Tucker et al., June 29, 1993, p. 1.

123. Ibid., p. 3.

124. As Sisk said, "The Union was able to negotiate wages well above competing facilities, as well as additional payroll burden from health care and paid vacations. Wages in both El Paso and Puerto Rico are $4.50 and $4.25, with [no benefits]." Although Sisk did not say what wages would be, he did say that while Acme's "net labor cost" averaged $14.11 per hour, American Boot's would total only $9.74. Between wages and benefits, the workers' compensation was to be cut by $4.37 an hour. Ibid., p. 7.

125. LeRoy, memo of June 29, 1993, p. 2.

126. Sisk, letter to Acme Boot workers, p. 12. LeRoy called this "an obvious abuse of public monies. Federal JTPA guidelines would prohibit using the funds to train people in jobs they have held for 20 years already. . . . I can hardly believe that the labor movement would support such needless corporate welfare." LeRoy, memo of June 29, 1993, p. 3.

127. Ibid., pp. 1–2.

128. Milt Freudenheim, "Drug Makers Are Already Feeling a Cut in Puerto Rico Tax Breaks," New York Times (August 17, 1993), p. D4.

129. In order to prevent firms from fleeing the island, the tax incentives were phased out slowly, over ten years. Manufacturing companies could continue to enjoy their 936 credits until 2005. California Franchise Tax Board, Water's Edge Manual, November 2001 (http://www.ftb.ca.gov/manuals/audit/water/WEMSec7_1m.htm).

130. Buckner interview.

131. Kellam interview.

132. Luttrell interview.

133. Mittendorf interview.

134. Buckner interview.

135. Mittendorf interview.

136. Luttrell interview.

137. Kellam interview.

138. Ibid.

139. Luttrell interview.

140. Mittendorf interview.

141. Luttrell interview.

142. Buckner interview.

143. Ibid.

144. Kellam interview.

145. Luttrell interview.

146. Buckner interview.

147. Ibid.

148. The union was crucial in providing political leaders with an incentive to respond to workers. After this field research was completed, I notified an Amalgamated Clothing and Textile Workers Union (ACTWU) representative of the situation at Greenbrier. After gathering information about the plant closing and the workers' situation, he contacted Senator Sasser—and Sasser returned his call. Eventually Sasser took up the case and invited Ann Ritter, a Greenbrier worker, to testify in congressional hearings on the WARN Act.

149. Luttrell interview.

150. Mittendorf interview.

151. Charles Schmidt interview.

152. Kellam interview.

153. Buckner interview. The entire Tennessee congressional delegation, except for Senator Sasser, voted for NAFTA, including many House members who had pledged to oppose the treaty for months before. Many made lucrative deals with President Clinton in exchange for their vote.

154. Kellam interview.

155. Mittendorf interview.

156. Kellam interview.

157. Ibid.

158. Mittendorf interview.

159. Charles Schmidt interview.

160. Kellam interview.

161. Buckner interview. The town had floated bonds to help Acme afford its new plant when it moved in. As chapter 2 discusses, bond issues are a common method of raising revenue for "economic development" purposes. Especially in the South, these are often used to benefit essentially private industry, as with Acme.

162. Mittendorf interview.

163. Betty Schmidt interview.

164. Kellam interview.

165. Fran Ansley and Susan Williams, "Southern Women and Southern Borders on the Move: Tennessee Workers Explore the New International Division of Labor," in *Neither Separate Nor Equal: Women, Race, and Class in the South,* ed. Barbara Ellen Smith Philadelphia: Temple University Press, 1999), p. 207.

166. Doreen Hemlock, "Labor Flexes Muscle in 936 Debate," *San Juan Star* (May 17, 1993), p. B6.

167. Richard Leonard, quoted in Hemlock, "Labor Flexes Muscle" p. B6.

168. Because there are so many possible exemptions, including those for small businesses and for financial hardship, only an estimated 2 percent of companies are required to comply with the WARN Act in the first place. Bill Troy, interview with author, Knoxville, Tenn., January 25, 1994.

169. Luttrell interview.

170. As the appendix explains in more detail, the group of workers interviewed were quite similar in terms of demographic characteristics as well as response rates. In both cases the entire leadership group was interviewed.

171. Buckner interview.

172. Kellam interview.

173. Luttrell interview.

174. Buckner interview.

175. Ibid.

176. Luttrell interview.

177. Ibid.

178. The URW's resources were quite limited. During the campaign, the union was forced to make decisions about how to spend scarce resources. For example the workers did not pursue the effort to have the state sponsor a prefeasibility study because it would have required staff time that was better spent elsewhere. The point is that there is a significant difference between a group that possesses close to zero resources and one that has access to some necessities.

179. Local 330 eventually became a member organization of TIRN and payed minimal annual dues to the organization, but that was not a condition of TIRN's involvement and support in the campaign.

180. Greg LeRoy, memo to Mitch Tucker et al., June 29, 1993.

181. Mittendorf interview.

182. Ibid.

CHAPTER 5: SEEDS OF A SOCIAL MOVEMENT

1. Alice Rollins, interview with author, Morristown, Tenn., December 9, 1993.

2. Kathy Muller, interview with author, Morristown, Tenn., December 10, 1993.

3. Ernest Gardiner, interview with author, Morristown, Tenn., January 25, 1994.

4. Shelley Edwards, testimony, Special Joint Legislative Committee to Study Fair Labor Laws, Temporary Services and Contract Labor, Morristown, Tennessee, October 9, 1989, p. 1.

5. Rollins interview.

6. Calvin Brown, testimony, Special Joint Legislative Committee to Study Fair Labor Laws, Temporary Services and Contract Labor, Morristown, Tennessee, October 9, 1989, p. 3.

7. Gardiner interview.

8. Joe Perkinson, interview with author, Morristown, Tenn., December 9, 1993.

9. Calvin Brown, interview with author, Morristown, Tenn., January 25, 1994. To add insult to injury, workers knew that Jack Welch had earned more than nine million dollars in 1993.

10. Rollins interview.

11. Brown interview.

12. Muller interview.

13. Brown interview.

14. Gardiner interview.

15. Linda Yount, testimony, Special Joint Legislative Committee to Study Fair Labor Laws, Temporary Services and Contract Labor, Morristown, Tennessee, October 9, 1989.

16. Yount testimony.

17. Rollins interview.

18. Muller interview.

19. Ibid.

20. Brown interview.

21. Linda Yount and Susan Williams, "Temporary in Tennessee: CATS for Stable Jobs," *Labor Research Review* 15 (1990): 74.

22. Yount testimony.

23. Muller interview.

24. Mary Hutchinson, testimony, Special Joint Legislative Committee to Study Fair Labor Laws, Temporary Services and Contract Labor, Morristown, Tenn., October 9, 1989, p. 1.

25. Yount testimony.

26. Arthur V. Puccini, February 1989 speech, quoted in "Woodmar News" (Parkersburg, W.V.: UE-GE Parkersburg Organizing Committee, March 10–16, 1992), p. 2.

27. Yount and Williams, "Temporary in Tennessee," p. 75.

28. Yount testimony.

29. Ibid.

30. Perkinson interview.

31. Brown interview.

32. Gardiner interview.

33. Mary Hutchinson, testimony, Special Joint Legislative Committee to Study Fair Labor Laws, Temporary Services and Contract Labor, Morristown, Tennessee, October 9, 1989, p. 1.

34. Muller interview.

35. Brown testimony, p. 2. Others concurred: "College people gets their degree and come out here in society and you know where they work? In places like these [fast-food] stores, 'service' personnel, doing things that they're much better qualified to do than that!" Perkinson interview.

36. Rollins interview. Rollins was in particularly dire straits because she had been laid off just prior to her second open-heart surgery and therefore had not been covered by any health insurance. She had tried to get disability insurance, but found that impossible. Although Rollins's doctor had told her she could not work, the government would not classify her as disabled. She had applied three times, but "they say I'm not disabled—I can still move my arms and legs." Rollins was very anxious about paying off many thousands of dollars in hospital bills on a low income. Getting a job that paid a living wage, with health benefits, was absolutely essential.

37. Gardiner interview.

38. More than four years after the plant closing, some of the workers had still not found

jobs. Others had accepted part-time or temporary work, but were still looking for a "real job." Rollins had not found any work. Muller, who was fifty-six years old, had just recently found work at Lowe's home improvement store in Morristown. "It took me four years to get the job I've got . . . I really thought I would *never* get a job. You know, I'm luckier than a lot of people. I looked everywhere. I put applications *everywhere*. And you couldn't even get an interview. Not one." Muller interview.

39. Perkinson interview. Nearly all of the men interviewed who found work had been forced to accept "third shift"—midnight to seven A.M. As Perkinson said, "When do you use security guards? Weekends and holidays." Many had to drive long distances to their new employment, and the very low wages hardly seemed to warrant the effort. Perkinson asked, "What are you going to do with minimum wage? Can you buy a new car or pay for a home?"

40. Rollins interview.

41. Perkinson interview.

42. Rollins interview.

43. Although Muller began as president, the position rotated. Rollins, Simms, Edwards, and others also had turns as president.

44. Rollins interview.

45. Rollins interview.

46. Bill Troy, testimony, Special Joint Legislative Committee to Study Fair Labor Laws, Temporary Services and Contract Labor, Morristown, Tennessee, October 9, 1989, p. 1.

47. Richard Belous, *The Contingent Economy: The Growth of the Temporary, Part-Time and Subcontracted Workforce* (Washington, D.C.: National Planning Association, 1989). Quantitative estimates of contingent work are notoriously controversial. The category includes part-time, seasonal, temp, and short-term employment, and many workers hold more than one such job. Nonetheless many studies in the early 1990s estimated contingent work to be approximately one-third of all jobs. In 1995 approximately 35 percent of the workforce was employed on a contingent basis—about 35 million people. *National Profile of Working Women* (Washington, D.C.: Nine to Five, 1995), p. 1.

48. *National Profile of Working Women,* p. 1.

49. Robert E. Parker, *Flesh Peddlers and Warm Bodies: The Temporary Help Industry and Its Workers* (New Brunswick, N.J.: Rutgers University Press, 1994), p. 27. By 1994, Manpower, Inc.—a temporary-help supply service—was the largest employer in the

United States, with nearly one million employees. Timothy D. Schellhardt, "Manpower's Business Booms as Companies Use More Temps," *Wall Street Journal* (February 3, 1995), p. B6.

50. Troy testimony, p. 2.

51. Yount and Williams, "Temporary in Tennessee," p. 75.

52. Troy testimony, p. 2.

53. Rollins interview.

54. Troy testimony, p. 2.

55. Rollins interview.

56. Troy testimony, p. 2.

57. Shelley Edwards testimony, p. 2.

58. Ibid.

59. Troy testimony, p. 2.

60. Edwards testimony, p. 1.

61. Rollins interview.

62. Troy testimony, p. 3.

63. Rollins interview.

64. Edwards testimony, p. 2. Edwards switched agencies, and the new temporary service offered her a job in Dandridge. The job required a forty-eight-mile commute. Moreover Edwards was to work "two weeks without pay. This was to be a training period." Edwards refused the placement. In 1989 she accepted a job "working for a [temporary services] company that supplies contract labor to several local factories. I am assigned to a factory which pays its [full-time] employees over $11.00 per hour. I am paid $4.00 per hour, with no benefits. I work from 12 midnight to 8:00 A.M., and must work all holidays and weekends."

65. Belous, *The Contingent Economy,* p. 19.

66. Kevin Russell, "An Analysis of Contingent Labor," *Review of Radical Political Economics* 23 (1991): 211.

67. Susan Putz and Nina Gregg, "Organizing Contingent Workers in a Right-to-Work State: Steps Toward an Agenda for Action" (Knoxville, Tenn., 1995), p. 3.

68. "Anne," a laid-off worker, quoted in Putz and Gregg, unpublished report, "Organizing Contingent Workers," p. 1.

69. Hutchinson testimony.

70. Brenda Green, testimony, Special Joint Legislative Committee to Study Fair Labor

Laws, Temporary Services and Contract Labor, Morristown, Tennessee, October 9, 1989.

71. Ibid.
72. Edwards testimony, p. 2.
73. Yount testimony.
74. Green testimony.
75. Gardiner interview.
76. Muller interview.
77. Hutchinson testimony.
78. Ibid.
79. Rollins interview.
80. Ibid.
81. Brown interview.
82. Muller interview.
83. Ibid.
84. Brown interview.
85. Interviews with Perkinson, Brown, Muller.
86. Brown interview.
87. Muller interview.
88. Ibid.
89. Ibid.
90. Rollins interview.
91. Perkinson interview.
92. Gardiner interview.
93. Brown testimony, pp. 1–2.
94. Hutchinson testimony.
95. Troy testimony, p. 1.
96. Ibid., p. 3.
97. Joe Simpson, quoted by Muller in interview with author.
98. Edwards testimony, pp. 2–3.
99. Edwards testimony, p. 2.
100. Anonymous, testimony, Special Joint Legislative Committee to Study Fair Labor Laws, Temporary Services and Contract Labor, Morristown, Tennessee, October 9, 1989.

101. Ibid.

102. Bobbie Hoxit, testimony, Special Joint Legislative Committee to Study Fair Labor Laws, Temporary Services and Contract Labor, Morristown, Tennessee, October 9, 1989, p. 1.

103. Fran Ansley, testimony, Special Joint Legislative Committee to Study Fair Labor Laws, Temporary Services and Contract Labor, Morristown, Tennessee, October 9, 1989, p. 1.

104. Anonymous testimony.

105. Troy testimony, p. 4.

106. Edwards testimony.

107. Gardiner interview. By 1994, GE had begun to take some of these steps. Like other companies, they were moving toward "total quality management," or team management. This style of management, popular in the mid-1990s, was based on exactly Gardiner's insight: the workers know best where the waste is and what improvements can be made.

108. Anonymous testimony.

109. Ibid.

110. Brown testimony, p. 3.

111. Anonymous.

112. Troy testimony, pp. 4–5.

113. Mel Summers, testimony, Special Joint Legislative Committee to Study Fair Labor Laws, Temporary Services and Contract Labor, Morristown, Tennessee, October 9, 1989. GE's actions did not actually constitute an unfair labor practice, but Summers was correct that they had violated the law.

114. Yount testimony.

115. Hutchinson testimony.

116. Brown interview.

117. Muller interview.

118. Michael W. McCann, *Rights at Work: Pay Equity Reform and the Politics of Legal Mobilization* (Chicago: University of Chicago Press, 1994), pp. 307–308.

119. Rollins interview.

120. Brown interview.

121. CATS had lobbied unsuccessfully for this licensing and regulatory activity to be housed in the Department of Labor.

122. Tennessee HB 1777, Public Chapter No. 1026, Sections 49–64, 1990. The temp firms were also required to certify that each employee had received "a written copy of employment benefits, including but not limited to insurance benefits, workers' compensation, unemployment benefits and overtime compensation"—if these were offered by the temporary agencies—and they were obligated to retain records of their employment for two years.

123. "An Act to Amend Tennessee Code Annotated, Title 4–21, Chapter 102 and Chapter 401," (Morristown, Tenn.: Citizens Against Temporary Services, 1990). The CATS/SOCM "bill-writing committee" used the same language as a bill that had been written in Massachusetts the previous year. That bill, which was never even introduced into the legislature, stated, "Any employer who provides benefits to his or her employees may not discriminate against part-time or temporary workers in the terms or conditions of employment and the provision of benefits."

124. Sean McCullough, Letter to SOCM members, May 1, 1990, p. 2.

125. Sean McCullough, "Summary of meeting between SOCM and Jim Neeley," November 20, 1990. Neeley discouraged future legislative action on the issue of contingent work. He argued that the temporary-service agencies and their political associations were even stronger since being galvanized by CATS' 1990 campaign against them. The temporary-service associations were worried about constraints on their freedom, and were willing to go to great lengths to prevent any type of regulation. SOCM staff member Sean McCullough reported that Neeley had argued that the contingent-work lobbyists "would not try anything offensive if we did nothing, but they might well drop in a bill [of their own] if we do." Neeley also argued that "Federal Express would kill us with the Memphis delegation [where FedEx is based], and so would kill the bill." Neeley had considerable experience with the legislature, and believed strongly that they would never support CATS against such powerful lobbies.

126. McCullough, Letter to SOCM members, p. 1.

127. Ibid.

128. Ibid., pp. 1–2.

129. Rollins interview.

130. Ibid.

131. Muller interview.

132. Chapters formed the core of SOCM's grassroots structure. As a chapter, the Hamblen County group would work on the organization's program areas. Since the CATS mo-

bilization, the problem of temporary work had become one of SOCM's statewide issues.

133. Joe Perkinson et al., memo to Legislative and Economics Committees, June 18, 1991, pp. 3–4.

134. SOCM, minutes from meeting, July 23, 1991.

135. Perkinson interview.

136. *Woodmar News* (Parkersburg, West Va.: UE–GE Parkersburg Organizing Committee, March 10–16, 1992), p. 2.

137. GE had announced plans to subcontract even more jobs, included bagging jobs and plant services. These plans were suspended as the UE campaign focused more attention on subcontracting and job cuts. As the UE organizers wrote, "If we hadn't had a Union Organizing Campaign going on here for the past two years, there's no doubt things would be much worse. Our warehouse, and a lot of other jobs, would be subcontracted." *Woodmar News,* p. 2.

138. Muller interview.

139. Ibid.

140. Rollins interview.

141. Gardiner interview.

142. Brown interview.

143. Perkinson interview.

144. Muller interview.

145. Ibid.

146. Brown interview.

147. Muller interview.

148. Mary E. Tong, "Reaching Across the Rio," *Beyond Borders* (Spring 1993), pp. 12–29. See also Susan Williams, "Women Workers from Tennessee and Mexico Learn from Each Other," *FIRR Notes* (Chicago: Federation of Industrial Retention and Renewal, August 1992), p. 3.

149. Jim Benn, "Worker Exchanges: A Powerful Way to Deal with Free Trade Issues," *FIRR Notes* (Chicago: Federation for Industrial Retention and Renewal, August 1992), p. 1.

150. The Mexican workers also learned from the Tennessee delegation. As one example, an observer reported that "Most of the workers in the *maquiladora* plants are young women. . . . The Mexicanas were surprised when they saw how old a woman could

be and still work in a U.S. factory." They were also very interested to meet Americans who came from poor backgrounds and were interested in the Morristown women's workplace conditions and struggles. Ibid., p. 2.

151. Tong, "Reaching Across the Rio," p. 12.

152. Mavis Young, interview with author, Knoxville, Tenn., February 2, 1994.

153. Rollins interview.

154. Muller interview.

155. May Barkin, interview with author, Powell, Tenn., January 24, 1994.

156. Young interview.

157. See, for example: Robert Emil Botsch, *We Shall Not Overcome: Populism and Southern Blue-Collar Workers* (Chapel Hill: University of North Carolina Press, 1980); Katherine S. Newman, *Falling from Grace: The Experience of Mobility in the American Middle Class* (New York: Vintage Books, 1988); David Halle, *America's Working Man: Work, Home, and Politics Among Blue-Collar Property Owners* (Chicago: University of Chicago Press, 1984).

158. Muller interview.

159. Perkinson interview.

160. Muller interview.

161. Brown interview.

162. Muller interview.

163. Doug McAdam, "The Biographical Impact of Activism," in *How Social Movements Matter,* ed. Marco Giugni, Doug McAdam, and Charles Tilly (Minneapolis: University of Minnesota Press, 1999).

164. Muller interview.

165. Rollins interview.

166. Gardiner interview.

167. Brown interview.

168. Perkinson interview.

169. Gardiner interview.

170. Muller interview.

171. Ibid.

172. Rollins interview.

173. Gardiner interview.

174. Rollins interview.

175. Gardiner interview.

176. Muller interview.

177. Yount testimony.

178. Rollins interview.

179. Muller interview.

180. Gardiner interview.

181. Muller interview.

182. Rollins interview.

183. Muller interview.

184. Kathy Muller, testimony, Trade Staff Policy Committee, Office of the U.S. Trade Representative, Hearings on the North American Free Trade Agreement, Atlanta, Georgia, August 29, 1991.

185. Muller interview. After NAFTA passed, Muller said, "You know, we worked hard on NAFTA. And lost it! But if I was still working at GE, I wouldn't have been involved in that. I wouldn't have said anything. I wouldn't have done anything. . . . I became a person that *thought* about what was going on, and looked at a different side of it . . . and I was grateful for that."

186. "Schedule for Issues of the Disposable Contingent Work Force Workshop" (New Market, Tenn.: Highlander Research and Education Center, July 26–28, 1991).

187. Very shortly afterward, Faludi's book *Backlash* was published, and she became busy with its marketing and promotion. She never finished the article(s) on contingent work.

188. Susan Williams, letter to "Friends," February 6, 1992, p. 1.

189. "Report from REJN Contingent Workforce" (Atlanta: Regional Economic Justice Network, September 13–15, 1991), pp. 1–2.

190. Report from REJN Contingent Workforce," p. 1.

191. Susan Williams, letter to "Friends," p. 1.

192. "Summary of Regional Conference on Contingent Work Issues," (Greenville, S.C.: Regional Economic Justice Network, March 27–29, 1992), p. 1.

193. Jean McAllister, "Carolina Temp School Builds Community," *Southern Communities* XIX (March–April 1995): 1–3.

194. The document stated the benefits to a community of a permanent, stable workforce, and the importance of workers' ability to provide for their families. The "rights" enumerated included:

- All workers should have a safe workplace and necessary safety equipment.
- Workers should have a guaranteed livable wage, geared to the prevailing wage for the position and industry.
- All workers should have access to health care.
- Workers should have a fair, systematic grievance procedure to appeal workplace problems.
- All workers in a particular workplace should be treated alike. (This clause explicitly prohibited discrimination between temporary and permanent workers—in terms of benefits eligibility, wages, or treatment—as well as discrimination on the basis of sex, age, race, ethnicity, or sexual preference.)

Susan Williams, "Ideas for a Contingent Workers Bill of Rights," March 1992.

As in the early stages of the civil rights movement, the environmental movement, the gay rights movement, and other movements for social and economic change, the goals of the CATS "movement" had not always been obvious. The group had begun with demands such as "respect as human beings" and "fair and adequate compensation." These were important goals, but hardly conducive to a legislative or direct-action campaign. Through a process of discussion, research, and including more individuals and organizations in evaluating both existing problems and solutions, precise demands were generated. While the eventual list did not encompass every grievance of every worker or group, it did correspond to the most basic concerns of the workers affected by the problem of contingent work. The ability to come together and devise a "bill of rights" highlights the important point that workers were able to articulate clearly not only the outrages of a system that exploited them but also—when given the appropriate time, encouragement, and examples of others—a program for responding to the injustices they faced.

195. "Organizing Contingent Workers," *LRA's Economic Notes* (New York: Labor Research Association, April 1995), p. 8.

196. Glenn Burkins, "Temp Workers May Be Able to Join Unions," *Wall Street Journal* (December 19, 1996), p. A3.

197. See, for example, Robin Alexander and Peter Gilmore, "A Strategic Organizing Alliance Across Borders," and Bruce Nissen, "Cross-Border Alliances in the Era of Globalization," in *The Transformation of U.S. Unions: Voices, Visions, and Strategies from the Grassroots,* ed. Ray M. Tillman and Michael S. Cummings (Boulder, Co. Lynne Rienner Publishers, 1999), pp. 239–254 and 255–66; Hector Figueroa, "International Labor Solidarity in an Era of Global Competition," and Ron Blackwell, "Building a Mem-

ber-Based International Program," in *A New Labor Movement for the New Century*, ed. Gregory Mantsios (New York: Monthly Review Press, 1998), pp. 304–19 and 320–8.

198. Barbara Shailor, "A New Internationalism: Advancing Workers' Rights in the Global Economy," in *Not Your Father's Union Movement*, ed. Jo-Ann Mort (New York: Verso, 1998), pp. 145–55.

199. Ibid., p. 151.

200. Stephanie Luce, "Life Support: Coalition Building and the Living Wage Movement," *New Labor Forum*, Spring–Summer 2002, pp. 81–92.

201. Muller interview.

CHAPTER 6: CONCLUSION

1. Mike Prokosch, "Building Coalitions After Seattle: Seattle, Tennessee, Boston, Washington" *Labor Notes* (April 2000), pp. 8–10.

2. Ibid., p. 8.

3. Ibid., p. 8. Direct Action Network is a participatory grassroots organization including primarily youth and student activists.

4. Louise Lander, ed., *War on Poverty* (New York: Facts on File Inc., 1967), pp. 10–11.

5. Alexis de Tocqueville, quoted in Rufus P. Browning, Dale Rogers Marshall, and David M. Tabb, *Protest Is Not Enough* (Berkeley: University of California Press, 1984), p. 1.

6. Edward C. Banfield and James Q. Wilson, *City Politics* (Cambridge, Mass.: Harvard University Press, 1965), pp. 2–3.

7. Localist theorists of collective action, such as Harry Boyte, have argued that communities tend to struggle over particularist issues, "parochial" concerns, and traditional group identities. Boyte says that "in the course of struggle, people often feel deepened appreciation for their heritage, symbols and institutions close to home," rather than appreciating connections with national and even international groups. The opposite occurred with CATS and Acme Boot. Harry Boyte, *The Backyard Revolution: Understanding the New Citizen Movement* (Philadelphia: Temple University Press, 1980), p. 9; Harry Boyte, Heather Booth, and Steve Max, *Citizen Action and the New American Populism* (Philadelphia: Temple University, 1986).

8. Michael W. McCann, *Rights or Work: Pay Equity Reform and the Politics of Legal Mobilization* (Chicago: University of Chicago Press, 1994), p. 307.

9. Aldon Morris, *The Origins of the Civil Rights Movement: Black Communities Organizing for Change* (New York: Free Press, 1984).

10. Lester Thurow, *The Future of Capitalism* (New York: Basic Books, 1980), pp. 166ff.

11. Paul Krugman, "We Are Not the World," *New York Times* (February 13, 1997), p. A10.

12. Ibid.

13. Ibid.

APPENDIX: RESEARCH METHODOLOGY

1. It is impossible to say whether I succeeded in creating a representative sample. None of the employers involved in the plant closings were willing to talk with me, much less provide me with a list of employees. Since it was impossible to know the underlying population, I could only roughly estimate the demographic makeup of the workforce.

2. There is always the possibility of bias in response. For example, it is possible that the workers who declined to be interviewed were the ones who were disproportionately disaffected, angry, or unhappy with the mobilization efforts or their outcomes. They may have preferred not to think about their experiences or to discuss them with an outsider. This is unlikely, because a good number of the participants who did agree to be interviewed also described their anger and resentment, so this perspective was certainly included in the response group. A few were not available to schedule appointments, or had moved away from the area and were not reachable, and one interview was canceled because of an emergency. Because the response rate is so high, however, these problems do not seriously compromise the research or its conclusions.

3. The workers' names have all been changed, while the public officials' and nonprofit leaders' real names are given.

Acknowledgments

The primary reason for these acknowledgments is to thank the workers and activists whose struggles are documented here. Every person who took the time to talk to me, who re-opened painful topics and shared personal experiences, who patiently explained to me exactly what a sewing-machine operator did in the finishing department, or how to drive from Maynardville to Clinton—they are the backbone of this project. My conversations with workers and activists were the highlight of my years in Tennessee. The Highlander Center and the Tennessee Industrial Renewal Network both were kind enough to open up their doors, meetings, and file cabinets, providing the raw materials I needed to begin the project. Huge thanks to Bill Troy and the TIRN staff, Jim Sessions and the Highlander staff, and especially Susan Williams. My greatest hope is that this book will prove useful to their and others' on-going struggles.

I have been blessed with wonderful friends, readers, and colleagues, all of whom made this project much more interesting and complete than it otherwise would have been. I can only list a few of them here. Rogers Smith and Adolph Reed were both willing to find room for politics in political science, and served as exemplary advisers and teachers. My writing group in New Haven, especially Rachel Roth, Lexi Freeman, and Barbara Blodgett, provided deadlines, structure, and feedback. Others read chapters and commented on earlier drafts, including Kate Dudley, Cathy Cohen, David Plotke, Vicky Hattam, Linda Kerber, Dan Clawson, and George Weinbaum.

Gordon Lafer, Kathy Newman, Rachel Roth, and Corey Robin not only have read my work and helped me figure out what I really thought, they were great comrades in organizing efforts and friends in every sense of the word. I will always be grateful to them.

The groups that taught me the most about politics, power, and mobilization were the unions I have worked with: the Union of Needletrades, Industrial and Textile Employees (UNITE), and the Graduate Employees and Students Organization (GESO), part of the Hotel and Restaurant Employees (HERE) at Yale University. At times it was eerie how closely the research for this book mirrored the events taking place around me. Working with these workers, against powerful forces, taught me more than any number of textbooks and academic conferences ever could.

Financial support for this project was provided by the National Science Foundation, the Social Science Research Council, the Aspen Institute Nonprofit Sector Research Fund, the Yale Program on Agrarian Studies, and the Enders Research Grant.

Finally, love and kisses to my family. Max Page has been an incredible partner in academic and political projects, but especially in life. He is generous, smart, kind, and tolerant even when I am intolerable; I feel lucky to have found him. Our sweet children Jonah and Aviva have made me laugh, think, and work in whole new ways. They have not yet reached kindergarten, but they have already learned a lot about unions, social movements, war and peace, and protests of all varieties. I know they will each move mountains of their own one day.

Index